SECOND EDITION

Curso primero

⋈⫯⋈⫯⋈⫯⋈⫯⋈⫯⋈⫯⋈⫯⋈⫯⋈⫯⋈⫯⋈⫯⋈⫯⋈⫯⋈⫯⋈⫯⋈

Workbook for a First Course in Spanish

MARVIN WASSERMAN

Former Chairman of the Department of Foreign Languages
Susan E. Wagner High School, Staten Island, New York

CAROL WASSERMAN, Ph.D.

Professor of Spanish
Borough of Manhattan Community College of the
City University of New York

AMSCO

AMSCO SCHOOL PUBLICATIONS, INC.,
a division of Perfection Learning®

Books by Marvin Wasserman and Carol Wasserman

Curso primero, 2nd Edition
Curso segundo
Curso tercero
Prosa moderna del mundo hispánico
Susana y Javier en España, 2nd Edition
Susana y Javier en Sudamérica

Please visit our Web sites at: *www.amscopub.com* and *www.perfectionlearning.com*

The photographs in this book have been provided through the
courtesy of the following organizations or individuals:
Image Bank: pp. 44, 52, 196, 206, 235
Image Bank: J. Du Boisberrian, p. 8; Guido A Rossi, pp. 77, 155;
　　　Luis Castaneda, p. 112; Triskel Lozouet, p. 252;
　　　Berard Roussel, p. 258; Andrea Pistoks, p. 268;
　　　Pascal Perret, 271; Angelo Cavalli, 277
Mexican National Tourist Office: pp. 26, 70
Spanish National Tourist Office: pp. 21, 48, 74
The Stock Market: Bill Wassman, p. 4; Robert Freck, p. 66
Marvin Wasserman: pp. 34, 185

Cover and Text Design by MERRILL HABER

Text Illustrations by Monotype Composition Company, Inc.

When ordering this book, please specify:
either **13497**
or CURSO PRIMERO/WORKBOOK, SECOND EDITION

ISBN 978-1-56765-476-9

Preface

Curso primero, Second Edition, while retaining many of the features that made the First Edition so successful, has brought the workbook up-to-date by reflecting the communicative approach to language learning. In doing so, we have not abandoned what we believe to be sound, solid and time-tested approaches to learning a foreign language. We are certain that most foreign-language teachers—if not all—want their students to acquire a firm foundation of the language at the very beginning of their instruction. And we believe that this can be done through effective drill material, starting with the simplest elements and gradually proceeding to the more complex ones. An examination of the material will reveal a variety of exercises adapted to all levels of ability among the student body.

Some of the newer aspects of this workbook include exercises containing pictures which provide visual association of the topics being studied—real-life situations reflecting the students' own experiences, but not neglecting those of their older and younger friends, family members and other members of our society with whom they may or may not come in contact. Numerous cultural blurbs, many of which are accompanied by photographs, reflect various aspects of the Hispanic world which we hope will encourage our young readers to learn more about their Spanish-speaking counterparts. The vocabulary has been updated and includes words like *computadora, disco compacto, tienda de informática,* etc. Many sentences in the exercises have been modified to reflect the diversity in our world today. Several selections in the section on Reading Practice have been substituted by more interesting and relevant passages and include applications for jobs of interest to the students.

An additional unit has been added to the section on Optional Chapters, namely the Imperfect Tense. Many teachers of first-year Spanish classes, including the authors, have often introduced the Imperfect Tense as a prelude to the second year of study. So we only thought it fitting to include it, in simplified form, in this new edition. The first two chapters dealing with the Spanish-speaking world have also been updated.

We have retained the original format of the text in that the chapters are not arranged in a cumulative sequence, as in a basal text. Therefore, the mastery of a topic does not require mastery of the topics preceding it, thus giving the teacher the opportunity to assign these chapters in any order he or she chooses.

The authors hope that their faithful followers throughout the years will find this Second Edition even more invaluable to both them and their students.

The Authors

Contents

El Mundo Hispánico

Part 1
The Spanish-Speaking World

⋈⋈⋈⋈⋈⋈⋈⋈⋈⋈⋈⋈⋈⋈⋈⋈⋈⋈⋈⋈

1
The Hispanic World

▰ The Difference Between "Hispanic" and "Spanish"

Although people often use Hispanic and Spanish as synonyms, a distinction should be pointed out. The word Hispanic refers to any person whose native language is Spanish or to anything that is characteristic of the people or culture of the Spanish-speaking world. The word Spanish on the other hand refers only to the people and culture of Spain. Of course, the word Spanish also refers to the Spanish language. A useful word that may be used to refer to Spanish-speaking person is *hispanohablante* or *hispanoparlante*, which means *Spanish-speaking*.

▰ El Mundo Hispano

The Hispanic world consists of Spain (which includes its island province of the Balearic Islands in the Mediterranean Sea to the east of the mainland; two provinces of the Canary Islands in the Atlantic Ocean to the west of Morocco, Africa; and Ceuta and Melilla, two small Spanish enclaves on the Mediterranean coast of Morocco) and the 19 Spanish-speaking countries of the Western Hemisphere. The population of these Spanish-speaking countries is approximately 357 million people. Spanish is the native language of about 22 million Americans. (See next chapter.) So, we can see that the Hispanic population of the world is approximately 380 million people.

▰ La América Española

The countries of Spanish America can be grouped as follows:

A. México

B. Centroamérica. The republics of Central America are:

Guatemala	*Nicaragua*	*Costa Rica*
Honduras	*El Salvador*	*Panamá*

1

C. Las Antillas (the islands of the Caribbean). The Hispanic countries in this group are:

Puerto Rico (a self-governing commonwealth of the United States)

Cuba

la República Dominicana (the Dominican Republic). This republic shares the island of Hispaniola with the republic of Haiti. (Since the language of Haiti is French, it is not part of the Hispanic world.)

D. Sudamérica. The Spanish-speaking countries of South America are:

Venezuela	*el Perú*	*la Argentina*
Colombia	*Chile*	*el Uruguay*
el Ecuador	*Bolivia*	*el Paraguay*

Although these countries differ from one another in some important ways, they have a common language and many cultural similarities that reflect their common Spanish heritage.

Some Aspects of Hispanic Civilization

1. **The Spanish Language**. The English language as spoken in the United States differs slightly from the language spoken in Britain: a truck is a *lorry* in England, where gasoline is called *petrol*, an elevator a *lift*, and all Americans are *Yanks*.

Like English, the Spanish language also has its varieties. Spoken Spanish differs slightly from one Hispanic country to another. There are, for instance, differences in pronunciation. Most Spaniards (but not those of southern Spain) pronounce *cinco* as "theenko" and *zapato* as "thapato"; they also pronounce the **J** in *José* more harshly than do their Spanish-American cousins. The Argentineans (and other Hispanic Americans) pronounce *ll* and *y* like the sound of *s* in the English word "pleasure"; if we use *zh* to represent that sound, then *yo me llamo Pepilla* sounds like " zho me zhamo Pepizha." Many people in southern Spain and Spanish America do not pronounce the final *s* or *d*, the *s* preceding a consonant, or the *d* in the endings *-ado* and *-ido*. For example, *los mismos estados* becomes "lo mi'mo e'ta-o." Despite such variations in pronunciation, Hispanics of different countries generally have no difficulty in understanding one another.

There are also differences in vocabulary. The word for potato is *patata* in Spain but *papa* in most of Spanish America. The word for orange is *naranja* everywhere but in Puerto Rico, where that fruit is called a *china*. The Spanish word for bus is *autobús* in most of the Hispanic world, but not in Cuba, Puerto Rico, and the Canary Islands, where a bus is a *guagua*.

Words that mean one thing in one country may mean something else in another country. In Chile, *guagua* is a baby; in Mexico, the word for bus is *camión*, which means "truck" in the rest of the Hispanic World. A *bodega* is a wine cellar or a winery in Spain but a grocery store in many parts of Spanish America.

And, as we shall learn: in most of Spain the plural of tú is *vosotros*, whereas most Spanish Americans use *ustedes* as the plural of both *tú* and *usted*.

2. **Nombres y Apellidos** (names). Many Hispanics are named after saints—Pedro, José, Juan, María, Teresa, etc., and they generally celebrate their saint's day rather than their birthday. You may have noticed that Hispanic people have more than one last name, or *apellido*; for example, Ramón **López Rodríguez**. Ramón has taken his mother's maiden name (Rodríguez) and added it to his father's name (López).

Another example: María **Rodríguez Molina** marries Pedro **Vargas Vélez**. She now calls herself María **Rodríguez de Vargas**. Of course she may carry her name further if she wishes: María **Rodríguez Molina de Vargas Vélez**. But this could become confusing. Suppose that María and Pedro have a daughter named Carmen. Her complete named would be Carmen **Vargas Rodríguez**—the father's name followed by the mother's. She would be formally addressed as "Señorita Vargas," for short.

3. **Los Deportes** (sports). **El fútbol**, the Spanish word for soccer, should not be confused with football, the American game. Soccer is very popular throughout the Hispanic world. Each country takes its national matches very seriously and the great event is the **Copa Mundial** (World Cup), which is played every four years.

   La corrida de toros, or bullfight, has been the most popular sport in Spain and in a few Spanish-American countries for the last two centuries. In recent years, however, its popularity has been declining in favor of soccer. During the season of **corridas**, the bullfight takes place on Sunday at about five o'clock in the afternoon. On special occasions, bullfights may be held on other days of the week.

   Jai alai, a sport similar to our handball, originated in the Basque Provinces of Spain. It is played on a court called a **frontón**. The game is played at great speed and requires much skill.

   El béisbol (baseball) is very popular in Puerto Rico, Cuba, the Dominican Republic, Mexico, and Venezuela.

4. **La Siesta**. In the early hours of the afternoon, when the intense heat of the sun discourages physical activity, people take a rest period, **la siesta**. Business people shut their doors at about one o'clock and go home, returning to work at about four o'clock. During this period, they eat their midday meal, generally the heaviest of the day, and take a nap or rest.

   In the past few years, however, the custom of taking a siesta has been disappearing in many Hispanic cities. Nowadays, many shops remain open for business during the siesta period. One often finds the streets and cafés as crowded during that period as at any other time of day.

5. **Las Comidas** (meals). In Hispanic countries, the meals of the day are generally as follows: Breakfast (**el desayuno**) usually consists of a cup of coffee and small roll or sweet cake. The coffee is much stronger than American coffee and is often taken with a great deal of boiled milk.

   El almuerzo (lunch) is a second breakfast in some countries, where it is eaten at about 10 o'clock. In other countries, it corresponds more closely to an American lunch and is eaten at about 1:30—that is, just before the siesta begins. Also called **la comida** in many places, it is usually a heavy meal consisting of several courses.

   La merienda, an afternoon snack, is taken at the end of the siesta and may consist of coffee, hot chocolate, rolls or cakes, and perhaps an **aperitivo**, which may be an alcoholic beverage.

   La cena (dinner) is often a light meal eaten fairly late in the evening, sometimes as late as 11 o'clock.

6. **Las Fiestas Patronales**. Every Hispanic country, town, and city is dedicated to a patron saint who has been adopted as its *protector*. For example, the patron saint of Madrid is San Isidro (Saint Isidore) and that of San Juan, Puerto Rico, is, of course, San Juan (Saint John).

   In honor of their patron saint, people hold annual **fiestas patronales**. These are festivals that may last as long as a week. Fireworks and parades, food and drink, merry-go-rounds and various games all contribute to the festive atmosphere.

7. **Los Días de Fiesta** (holidays). **La Navidad** (Christmas), **Pascua de Resurrección** (Easter) and **el Día de la Raza** also known as **el Día de la Hispanidad** (which celebrates Columbus's discovery of America) are celebrated in all Hispanic countries.

   Until recently, although it still happens in Spain, it was the custom for Hispanic boys and girls to receive gifts on January 6, the day the three kings (called **los Reyes Magos** in Spanish) brought gifts to the infant Jesus. In recent years, however, there has been a growing tendency (especially in Spanish America) to distribute gifts at Christmas time, as in the United States.

   Every Hispanic country has its own holiday commemorating its discovery or its independence from Spain. For example, Puerto Rico celebrates its discovery by Columbus on November 19. Mexican Independence Day is September 16.

8. **El Mercado**. The marketplace in Spain and Spanish-American countries is a lively and colorful place. Many towns and villages have outdoor markets that are assembled once a week, each town having its own market day. The numerous stands and booths sell every kind of merchandise: food and drink, clothing, souvenirs, etc. The customer is often expected to reject the first price that is asked and to haggle (*regatear*) with the vendor until he or she reduces the price.

   All towns have at least one market situated inside a building. This market is generally open every day but Sunday. Here, too, everything is sold, including groceries. The housewife can often be seen going from stand to stand, comparing prices. Since many homes in small towns do not have adequate refrigeration, shopping each morning for the day's meals is a common practice.

Barcelona. Barcelona, situated on the Mediterranean coast of Spain, is an active seaport and the commercial and financial center of Spain. It is in the province of Cataluña, the most prosperous region of the country. The people of Cataluña speak catalán (a Romance language also spoken by many French people north of the Pyrenees Mountains) as their principal language, and Spanish (castellano) as their secondary language. One of the most attractive parts of Barcelona is an area called Las Ramblas, wide avenues on which the lanes of traffic are separated by a wide walk for pedestrians (*peatones*).

Along these Ramblas there are numerous outdoor book shops, cafés and flower stands. On the top of Monte Tibidabo, which overlooks Barcelona, there is a shrine and a very popular amusement park. At the other end of Barcelona, on the top of a hill, is el Castillo de Montjuïch (pronounced "monjweek," in which the "J" sounds like the *s* in pleasure). This castle was fortified in 1640. Near this castle is an amusement park which is illuminated at night, and can be seen throughout the city.

EXERCISES

A.   Complete the sentences

1. "Hispanic" and "Spanish" should not be used as synonyms; for example, people from Costa Rica, Mexico, and Spain are all _countries_, but only citizens of Spain are _Spanish_.

2. Argentina and Chile are countries of _South America_

3. The Dominican Republic and Cuba are countries of the _Las Antillas_.

4. Most Spaniards pronounce the "z" of **azul** as we pronounce _sh_ in English.

5. *Guagua* means _bus_ in Puerto Rico.

6. The pronoun **vosotros** and its corresponding verb forms are used only in _Spain_.

7. The maiden name of Ana Molina de Vega is _Molina_.

8. _Jai alai_ is played on a *frontón*.

9. The last meal of the day in Hispanic countries is called _cena_ in Spanish.

10. The bullfight is very popular in _Spain_.

11. The patron saint of Madrid is _San Isidro_.

12. Columbus Day in Spanish is called _el Día de la Hispanidad_

13. Puerto Rico was discovered by _Columbus_.

14. *El Día de los Reyes Magos* falls on _6 January_.

15. Many Hispanic people take a _siesta_ during the afternoon.

B.   If the statement is true, write true in the blank at the right. If it is false, cross out the capitalized words and write the correct words in the blank.

1. In New York, many members of the SPANISH community are Cubans.
    1. _false / Puerto Rican_

2. Haiti is one of the SPANISH-speaking republics of the Caribbean.
    2. _false / French_

3. The Spanish word CHINA means "orange" in Puerto Rico.
    3. _true_

4. In the name Luis Meléndez Fernández, MELÉNDEZ is the family name of Luis's father.
    4. _false / Fernández_

5. LA CORRIDA DE TOROS is the most popular sport in Hispanic countries.
    5. _false / El fútbol_

6. In most Hispanic countries, the heaviest meal of the day is called EL DESAYUNO.

7. The *aperitivo* is popular around the time of the MERIENDA.

8. Melilla is a city in MEXICO.

9. SPANISH and HISPANIC are synonyms.

10. SPAIN celebrates its independence on September 16.

6. false / el almuerzo

7. true

8. false / Melilla es una país

9. false

10. false / Mexico

2
Hispanic Influences in the United States

If we glance at a map of the United States, we can see many signs of Spain's impact on the development of our country. The names of the states of Colorado, Nevada, Florida, and Montana are Spanish, and the entire Southwest is studded with Spanish names for cities, towns, parks, rivers, and other geographic features. Some of these names are especially prominent: Los Angeles, San Diego, San Francisco, Sacramento, and the San Joaquín Valley in California; the Mesa Verde National Park and the Sangre de Cristo mountain range in Colorado; Las Vegas in Nevada; Santa Fe and Los Alamos in New Mexico; El Paso, San Antonio, and the Río Grande in Texas; and many others.

Other signs of Hispanic influence can be found in our language. Popular films and stories about the "Wild West" have made us all familiar with many cowboy expressions that are of Spanish origin: lasso (from *lazo*), lariat (*la reata*), "vamoos!" (¡*vamos!*), hoosegow (*juzgado*), sierra, mesa, rodeo, etc.

Explorations in the New World

Names on a map, a few words of cowboy-talk: these are only the barest clues to the important role played by Spain and Mexico in American history. This role is part of a long and interesting story that can be summarized as follows:

After Columbus discovered the New World in 1492, he was followed by many Spanish explorers and *conquistadores* (conquerors). In April 1513, Juan Ponce de León arrived at the mouth of a river near the present site of Jacksonville, Florida, and took possession of the entire peninsula, which he mistook for an island. He named it La Florida because of its abundance of pretty flowers (*florida* means "flowery") and because he had discovered it during the Easter season (la Pascua Florida).

In 1519, Hernán Cortés and some 550 soldiers landed on the gulf of Mexico near present-day Veracruz. In two and a half years of intermittent warfare, he subdued the Aztecs, killed their ruler, Montezuma, and captured their capital city, Tenochtitlán (the site of Mexico City today). After this victory, the Spaniards gradually conquered all of Mexico. The vast area of this conquest included most of the American Southwest, which had been an integral part of Mexico until the Mexican War (1846–48).

In the year 1528, an expeditionary force commanded by Álvar Núñez **Cabeza de Vaca** started out from Tampa Bay, Florida, and sailed up the coast of the peninsula. On reaching the mouth of the Mississippi river, the ship was blown by a violent storm all the way to Galveston Island, off the coast of Texas. Crossing to the mainland, Cabeza de Vaca and three other survivors trudged hundreds of miles through Texas till they reached San Miguel de Culiacán in what is now Sinaloa, México. During this expedition into México, Cabeza de Vaca was captured by the Sioux Indians and lived among them for a time, serving as their medicine man.

In 1539, Hernando **de Soto**, governor of Cuba, journeyed to Florida and the Carolinas, turned westward and discovered the Mississippi River. In Mexico, Francisco **Vázquez de Coronado**, a conquistador, led an expedition northward in search of the fabled cities of Cíbola. These "seven cities of gold" were supposed to lie somewhere in the region now called New Mexico. Coronado never found those legendary cities, but his expedition discovered the Grand Canyon instead.

Two other Spanish conquerors should be mentioned here, although the story of their exploits falls outside the scope of this chapter: Vasco Núñez de **Balboa,** who discovered the Pacific Ocean on the shores of Panama, and Francisco **Pizarro,** Conqueror of Peru.

When California was part of the Spanish Empire, missions were founded there to convert the Indians to Christianity. This task was assigned to the Franciscan missionaries of Mexico, who were led by Father Junípero **Serra.** Between 1769 and 1823, the missionaries built 21 missions along the *Camino Real* ("the King's Highway"), which extended from San Diego to San Francisco.

In 1824, Mexico achieved its independence from Spain, an event that opened a new chapter in the history of the Southwest.

Hispanic Communities in the United States

Spanish-speaking Americans can be found in all parts of our country, but most Hispanics live in the following areas:

1. **The Southwest.** Most Hispanic residents of California, Texas, and other southwestern states are descendants of the Spanish settlers who had lived in those areas when they were still part of Mexico. To their number must be added the many thousands of Mexicans who have been traveling back and forth across our southern border since the turn of the century. In search of jobs, these migrants came to the US as *braceros*, or farm workers. Many of them eventually settled permanently in California and other states.

Market in Guatemala.

2. **Florida.** After the Cuban Revolution of 1959, many Cubans who did not wish to live under a Communist government sought refuge in the United States. About 500,000 Cubans settled in the vicinity of Miami, Florida. Most of these refugees were high school or college graduates who had been business people or professionals before leaving Cuba. Although they had to start their lives over again in Florida, many eventually established new businesses or resumed their former careers. Today the Cuban *colonia* in Miami is one of the most prosperous Hispanic communities in the United States.

3. **New York City.** Spanish-speaking New Yorkers come from all parts of the Hispanic world. Many of them are from the island of Puerto Rico. There are about 2.7 million people of Puerto Rican origin in the United States.

   Puerto Ricans have been coming to the mainland ever since the United States took possession of the island in 1898, at the end of the Spanish-American War. They have been able to enter the country in large numbers because, as citizens of the United States, they are not subject to immigration quotas.

   The greatest influx of Puerto Ricans occurred in 1945 and 1951. Most of them settled in New York, where they had friends and relatives. New York also offered a wide variety of employment opportunities, especially to unskilled and semiskilled workers.

4. **Other Hispanic Groups.** As we have seen, many Hispanics in the United States are of Mexican, Cuban or Puerto Rican origin. But there are also large numbers of immigrants from Spain, the Dominican Republic and the countries of Central and South America. Like all other immigrants, whatever their nationality, these people have come to our shores for the same basic reasons: to escape from hopeless poverty or from political oppression, to improve the quality of their lives, and to secure a better future for their children.

▲ EXERCISES ▲

A. Next to each item in column *A*, write the letter of the item in column *B* that best describes it.

Column A	Column B
___ **1.** rodeo	a. founded missions in California
___ **2.** Ponce de León	b. section of Miami in which Cuban-Americans live
___ **3.** de Soto	c. end of Spanish-American war
___ **4.** Tenochtitlán	d. fabled cities of gold
___ **5.** Padre Junípero Serra	e. discovered the Mississippi River
___ **6.** bracero	f. conquered Peru
___ **7.** colonia	g. a Spanish word used in English
___ **8.** 1898	h. Mexican farm laborer
___ **9.** Cíbola	i. discovered Florida
___ **10.** Pizarro	j. old name of Mexico City

B.   Complete the sentences.

1. ___Hispanics___ are persons in the U.S. or any other part of the world whose native language is Spanish.

2. The cowboy expression "___hoosegow___" comes from the Spanish word *juzgado,* meaning "courtroom."

3. ___Cabeza de Vaca___ led an expedition from Florida to Mexico.

4. The Spaniards built a highway from San Diego to San Francisco called ___Camino Real___.

5. ___Cortes___ conquered the Aztecs.

6. An expedition led by ___Coronado___ discovered the Grand Canyon.

7. Mexico lost much of its territory to the United States as a result of its defeat in the ___Mexican War___.

8. ___Balboa___ discovered the Pacific Ocean.

9. Many Cubans have settled in the state of ___Florida___.

10. Many people of ___Puerto Rican___ origin settled in New York City.

Part 2
The Present Tense

3
-AR Verbs in the Present Tense

comprar el libro, to buy the book

Singular

yo compro el libro	I buy (am buying) the book
tú compras	you buy (are buying)
usted (Ud.) compra	you buy (are buying)
él compra	he buys (is buying)
ella compra	she buys (is buying)

Plural

nosotros (-as) compramos el libro	we buy (are buying) the book
vosotros (-as) compráis	you buy (are buying)
ustedes (Uds.) compran	you buy (are buying)
ellos compran	they (m.) buy (are buying)
ellas compran	they (f.) buy (are buying)

1. *You* is expressed in four ways. In the singular, **usted** (often abbreviated **Ud.**) is the formal mode of address; **tú** is informal or familiar. **Tú** is used when speaking to members of your family, classmates, close friends, children, and animals.

   The plural of **usted** is **ustedes (Uds.)** The plural of **tú** is **vosotros** in Spain, **ustedes** in Spanish America.

2. The form **comprar** is called an *infinitive*. A Spanish infinitive can often be translated by an English infinitive, which usually begins with "to": *to buy, to run, to take,* etc.

Some Common -AR Verbs

bailar, to dance
    Yo **bailo** con María.   I dance (am dancing) with Mary.

cantar, to sing
    Tú **cantas** siempre.   You always sing (are always singing).

enseñar, to teach
    Ud. **enseña** muy bien.   You teach (are teaching) very well.

estudiar, to study
    Él **estudia** español.   He studies (is studying) Spanish.

hablar, to speak
    Ella **habla** inglés.   She speaks (is speaking) English.

mirar, to look (at)
    Nosotros **miramos** la pizarra.   We look (are looking) at the blackboard.

pagar, to pay
    Vosotros **pagáis** mucho.   You pay (are paying) a lot.

tomar, to take; to have drink or food
    Uds. **toman** el tren.   You take (are taking) the train.
    Uds. **toman** el almuerzo.   You have (are having) lunch.

trabajar, to work
    Ellos **trabajan** en Barcelona.   They work (are working) in Barcelona.

visitar, to visit
    Ellas **visitan** la ciudad.   They visit (are visiting) the city.

3. Every conjugated verb in the present tense can be translated in two ways.

    Practice A: Show your Spanish-speaking friend how English has two ways of expressing his/her statements.

    EXAMPLE: Yo trabajo mucho.   I work a lot or I'm working a lot.

1. Yo hablo italiano.

    _____

2. Tú bailas muy bien.

    _____

3. Nosotros estudiamos en casa.

    _____

4. Ellos trabajan en una tienda.

    _____

5. Ella canta muy mal.

    _____

4. The six present-tense forms of an -AR verb can be derived from the infinitive form by dropping the -AR of the infinitive and adding the following endings. Notice that these endings are used with certain pronouns:

yo	............**o**	nosotros(-as)	............**amos**
tú	............**as**	vosotros(-as)	............**áis**
usted	............**a**	ustedes	............**an**
él	............**a**	ellos	............**an**
ella	............**a**	ellas	............**an**

(él y ella = ellos)

The Present Tense

Practice B: Here are other common -AR verbs. Show how each person performs each action.

EXAMPLE: *contestar*, **to answer** Yo _____contesto_____ en inglés.

1. *escuchar*, to listen (to)   Nosotros _____ la música.

2. *explicar*, to explain   Ud. _____ la lección muy bien.

3. *llegar*, to arrive   Tú _____ tarde.

4. *preguntar*, to ask   Ella _____ mucho.

5. *preparar*, to prepare   Él _____ la comida.

6. *saludar*, to greet   Uds. _____ al profesor.

7. *terminar*, to finish, to end   Vosotros _____ la tarea.

8. *viajar*, to travel   Ellas _____ por España.

9. *patinar*, to skate   Yo _____ en el lago.

10. *lavar*, to wash   Ellos _____ el coche.

5. The subject pronoun is often omitted, especially if the verb ending clearly indicates who the subject is. For that reason, the pronouns **yo**, **tú**, **nosotros**, and **vosotros** are rarely expressed, except for emphasis. (Example: from the **-o** ending in **saludo**, we know that the subject pronoun is **yo**, or *I*.)

Practice C: Repeat what each person says adding the pronoun that was omitted, then give the English equivalent.

EXAMPLE: **Cantas bien**   Tú cantas bien.   You sing well.

1. Hablo español.

_____

2. Contestas muy bien.

_____

3. Terminamos el trabajo.

_____

4. Viajáis mucho.

_____

5. Patinan sobre el hielo.

_____

6. If a verb ends in **-a**, its subject may be **usted**, **él**, or **ella**. If it ends in **-an**, its subject may be **ustedes**, **ellos**, or **ellas**. For example, the sentence "Escucha la música" may have the following possible meanings:

> You listen (are listening) to the music.
> He listens (is listening) to the music.
> She listens (is listening) to the music.

Practice D: Without changing the verb form, clarify each verb with three different subject pronouns.

EXAMPLE: **Termina la lección.**
        Él termina la lección.   *Ella* termina la lección.   *Ud.* termina la lección.

1. Miran el reloj.

_____   _____   _____

2. Baila el tango.

_____   _____   _____

Practice E: On page 11, we learned that both *usted* and *tú* mean *you*, but *usted* is formal or "polite," *tú* is informal or familiar. Rewrite each sentence, replacing *Ud.* by *tú* or vice versa.

EXAMPLE: **Tú tomas café.**   Ud. toma café.

1. Ud. habla muy bien.

_____

2. Tú compras los libros.

_____

3. Ud. mira la película.

_____

4.   Tú contestas muy bien.

_____

5.   Ud. baila en la fiesta.

_____

7.   **Él**, **ella**, **ellos**, and **ellas** may replace a noun or the name of a person. For example:

> El muchacho (or Él) habla inglés.
> María y Elena (or Ellas) compran libros.
> Juan y Ana (or Ellos) trabajan en la ciudad.

In this last sentence, note that **ellos** represents a mixed group of male and female persons.

Practice F: Rewrite each sentence, changing the pronoun in italics to an equivalent noun subject, to be chosen from the following:

La profesora   El padre   La madre y el padre   La tía y la abuela   José

1.   _Él_ trabaja en la computadora.

_____

2.   _Ella_ enseña en Madrid.

_____

3.   _Ellos_ miran la comedia.

_____

4.   _Ellas_ cocinan muy bien.

_____

5.   _Él_ trabaja en Bogotá.

_____

LA TUNA

La Tuna is a music group of university students formed of guitarists and singers. Each member of the group is called a **tuno**. They wear long black capes adorned with lively colored ribbons. It is not uncommon at any time of the day or night to see this group of strolling singers in the street providing free entertainment to the passerby. Some **tunas** have recorded their music on CDs and tapes. Several tunas have performed in the United States, often in universities.

8.   Note that a subject consisting of **yo** + another person is equivalent to **nosotros**:

> **Gilberto y yo** compramos ropa.   **María y yo** (f.) somos hermanas
>
> **Nosotros**   **Nosotras**

◄ EXERCISES ►

A. José is teaching his little sister Lola to speak correct Spanish. When José makes a statement, he changes the subject, and Lola has to restate the sentence.

    EXAMPLE: *La chica* baila en la fiesta.   Yo también _____*bailo en la fiesta*_____ .

  1. *Nosotros* tomamos café.   Ellos también _____ .

  2. *Vicente y Alberto* hablan italiano.   Tú también _____ .

  3. *Uds.* contestan en inglés.   Ud. también _____ .

  4. *Yo* estudio por la noche.   Mi amigo y yo también _____ .

  5. *La profesora* enseña la regla.   Ella también _____ .

  6. *Los profesores* explican la lección. El alumno también _____ .

  7. *Nosotros* escuchamos la música.   Yo también _____ .

  8. *Jorge y María* miran la televisión.   Mi amigo también _____ .

  9. *La señora Rivera* compra pan.   Los niños también _____ .

10. *Yo* trabajo en un banco.   Vosotros también _____ .

B. How inventive are you? Rewrite each sentence, supplying a noun subject wherever possible, and a subject pronoun in other cases. Also, add some words to make the sentence longer.

    EXAMPLES: **Tomo una naranjada.**   Yo tomo una naranjada con mi almuerzo.
                  Llega temprano.   José llega temprano a la escuela.

  1. Trabajamos en una tienda.   _____ .

  2. Visitan el parque.   _____ .

  3. Hablas muy bien.   _____ .

  4. Baila con Antonio.   _____ .

  5. Compro un disco compacto.   _____ .

C. Here are some activities and facts about the López Family. Complete each sentence by writing the verb in parentheses in its proper form.

    EXAMPLE: **(hablar)**   Pepe baila con Francisca y luego _____habla_____ con Ricardo.

  1. (estudiar)   Juan y Ana miran la televisión y _____ en la sala.

  2. (contestar)   Nosotros escuchamos al abuelo y luego _____ rápidamente.

3. (pagar)   Mi papá compra la carne y _____ al carnicero.

4. (terminar)   Los muchachos escuchan la música y después _____
                   las tareas.

5. (visitar)   Mi tío trabaja en España pero _____ a nuestra familia
                   con frecuencia.

D. Nacho is playing a game with his little nephew Rogelio. Each time Nacho says something, Rogelio has to say a new sentence adding new subjects. What does Rogelio have to say each time? Follow the example.

   EXAMPLE: **Juan habla español.** **(y yo)**   Juan y yo hablamos español.

   1. Elena baila rápidamente.   (y Luis)

   _____

   2. Felipe prepara la comida.   (y yo)

   _____

   3. Mi mamá trabaja en el centro.   (y mi hermano)

   _____

   4. José visita a Bárbara.   (y yo)

   _____

   5. Él contesta mal.   (y Luisa)

   _____

E. Nacho and Rogelio are playing a similar game. This time Rogelio has to omit a subject, as in the example.

   EXAMPLE: **Carlos *y yo* estudiamos en casa.**   Carlos estudia en casa.

   1. Pablo *y Lola* toman el autobús.

   _____

   2. Ud. *y Ana* viajan por México.

   _____

   3. Mi amigo *y yo* cantamos en español.

   _____

   4. El profesor *y los alumnos* visitan el museo.

   _____

   5. Tú *y Gerardo* compráis zapatos.

   _____

F. Complete each sentence which tells what different members of the Pérez Family are doing at different times.

1. I am finishing my lessons.

   _____ mis lecciones.

2. We work at the computer.

   _____ en la computadora.

3. The boys and girls are having soda.

   Los muchachos _____ gaseosas.

4. Paul and I are practicing our Spanish.

   Pablo y yo _____ nuestro español.

5. You (*Tú*) are watching T.V.

   _____ la televisión.

6. John and Philip are having lunch

   Juan y Felipe _____ el almuerzo.

7. You (*Vosotras*) are spending a lot of money.

   _____ mucho dinero.

8. Aunt Jennie (*La tía Jennie*) is always traveling in Mexico.

   _____ siempre por México.

9. I'm wearing my new shirt.

   _____ mi camisa nueva.

10. They are buying tapes.

    _____ cintas.

4
-ER and -IR Verbs in the Present Tense

aprender español, to learn Spanish

Singular	Plural
yo aprend*o* español	nosotros (-as) aprend*emos* español
tú aprend*es*	vosotros aprend*éis*
Ud. aprend*e*	Uds. aprend*en*
él aprend*e*	ellos aprend*en*
ella aprend*e*	ellas aprend*en*

escribir la carta, to write the letter

yo escrib*o* la carta	nosotros (-as) escrib*imos* la carta
tú escrib*es*	vosotros (-as) *escribís*
Ud. escrib*e*	Uds. escrib*en*
él escrib*e*	ellos escrib*en*
ella escrib*e*	ellas escrib*en*

◼ Some Common -*ER* and -*IR* Verbs

beber, to drink
Bebemos agua mineral en casa.

We drink (are drinking) mineral water at home.

comer, to eat
Ellos **comen** temprano.

They eat (are eating) early.

comprender, to understand
Yo **comprendo** la lección.

I understand (am understanding) the lesson.

correr, to run
Juan **corre** por la calle.

John runs (is running) through the street.

leer, to read
    Tú **lees** el periódico.   You read (are reading) the newspaper.

responder, to answer
    Uds. **responden** bien.   You answer (are answering) well.

vender, to sell
    Mi padre **vende** la casa.   My father sells (is selling) the house.

abrir, to open
    Yo **abro** la puerta.   I open (am opening) the door.

cubrir, to cover
    Mi hermano **cubre** la mesa.   My brother covers (is covering) the table.

describir, to describe
    Los alumnos **describen** la sala de clase.   The pupils describe (are describing) the classroom.

dividir, to divide
    Dividimos la pizza en ocho partes.   We divide (are dividing) the pizza into eight parts.

partir, to leave, to depart
    El tren **parte** a las ocho.   The train leaves (is leaving) at 8:00.

recibir, to receive
    Tú **recibes** mucho dinero.   You receive (are receiving) a lot of money.

vivir, to live
    Ellos **viven** en una casa grande.   They live (are living) in a large house.

1. Like **-AR** verbs, **-ER** and **-IR** verbs have their own sets of personal endings. These replace the **-ER** or **-IR** ending of the infinitive.

	-ER Verbs	*-IR* Verbs
yo	**-o**	**-o**
tú	**-es**	**-es**
Ud.	**-e**	**-e**
él	**-e**	**-e**
ella	**-e**	**-e**
nosotros	***-emos***	***-imos***
vosotros	***-éis***	***-ís***
Uds.	**-en**	**-en**
ellos	**-en**	**-en**
ellas	**-en**	**-en**

2. Note that the endings of **-ER** and **-IR** verbs are identical except for the *nosotros* (*-as*) and *vosotros* (*-as*) forms.

Seville. An April festival in Seville, Spain.

▲ EXERCISES ▲

A. Here is a lesson José is teaching Lola. Play Lola's role by following the example.

    EXAMPLE: *El muchacho* **aprende la lección.** Nosotros <u> aprendemos la lección </u> .

    1. *Ana* comprende el programa.

        José y yo _____ .

    2. *María y yo* leemos la novela.

        Ellos _____ .

    3. *El profesor* abre la ventana.

        Los alumnos _____ .

    4. *Tú* vives en el campo.

        Yo _____ .

    5. *Mi* familia come a las seis.

        Uds. _____ .

    6. *Yo* escribo la tarea.

        Ella _____ .

    7. *Papá y yo* cubrimos la mesa.

        Elena _____ .

8. *La clase* aprende la gramática.

    Las clases _____.

9. *Ud.* bebe mucha agua.

    Vosotros _____.

10. *Los niños* reciben muchos regalos.

    José _____.

B. Nacho and Rogelio are at it again. Follow the example.

>   **EXAMPLE: Alberto y Tomás reciben las cartas.**   Alberto recibe las cartas.

1. Mi abuelo y *yo* leemos la revista.

    _____

2. Mi tío y *mi* abuelo viven en San Juan.

    _____

3. María y *Fernando* corren por el parque.

    _____

4. Tú y *Juana* dividís el pastel.

    _____

5. José y *yo* escribimos el ejercicio.

    _____

===== **LAS ESCUELAS** =====

Education in Hispanic countries generally begins in **la escuela primaria** or **la escuela elemental**, which the children attend for six years. The next level is a secondary school, which has various names, depending on the country (**el instituto, el liceo, el colegio**). The children attend these schools for five or six years, and on graduating they receive a diploma called **el bachillerato** (not to be confused with the American Bachelor's degree). The next level is **la universidad**. The Spanish word **colegio**, a type of private high school, should not be confused with the American *college*, which is *universidad* in Spanish. In Hispanic countries, the school day is generally longer than the American school day, since the boys and girls study more subjects a semester.

C. With a partner, play the game of "Add-a-Subject." One partner reads the sentence and gives the new subject. The other partner states the new sentence.

>   **EXAMPLE: Eugenio lee la frase (y yo)**   Eugenio y yo leemos la frase.

1. El tren parte a las siete. (y el autobús)

    _____

2. Tú vives en México. (y yo)

    _____

   3. Mi padre bebe la limonada. (y mi abuelo)

   4. Ella lee el periódico. (y yo)

   5. Ud. recibe mucho dinero. (y Juan)

D. Rewrite each sentence replacing the verb in italics with the verb in parentheses.

   EXAMPLE: **El hombre *compra* la casa. (vender)** El hombre vende la casa.

   1. *Tomamos* agua. (beber)

   2. *Visitan* la ciudad. (describir)

   3. Pablo *estudia* delante de la televisión. (leer)

   4. Tú *cantas* en español. (responder)

   5. Mi padre *trabaja* en Sudamérica. (vivir)

   6. Mi amigo y yo *leemos* la novela. (recibir)

   7. Ellos *dividen* la pizza. (pagar)

   8. *Escucho* la música. (comprender)

   9. Vosotros cantáis muy rápidamente. (correr)

   10. Los chicos comen hamburguesas. (comprar)

E. Complete the Spanish sentences to describe the following activities. Choose from the list of verbs.

beber   abrir   vivir   correr   escribir
vender   leer   comer   recibir   partir

   1. Mi familia y yo _____ en un apartamento.

   2. Nosotros _____ las revistas.

3. El niño _____ la leche.

4. El avión _____ a las ocho y media.

5. Yo _____ una hamburguesa.

6. Los niños _____ rápidamente.

7. Uds. _____ los regalos.

8. Ella _____ una carta.

9. Mi amigo y yo _____ los libros.

10. Jorge y Enrique _____ las ventanas.

5
Forming Negative and Interrogative Sentences

Forming Negative Sentences

Luis habla español.	Louis speaks (is speaking) Spanish.
Luis **no** habla español.	Louis does not speak (is not speaking) Spanish.
Nosotros vivimos en Costa Rica.	We live (are living) in Costa Rica.
Nosotros **no** vivimos en Costa Rica.	We do not live (are not living) in Costa Rica.
Como temprano.	I eat (am eating) early.
No como temprano.	I do not eat (am not eating) early.

1. To make a sentence negative, place the word **no** directly before the verb.

   Practice A: Make each sentence negative.

   1. Juanito toma agua. _____

   2. Escribimos la regla. _____

   3. Yo respondo en inglés. _____

   4. Venden la bicicleta. _____

   5. Ella compra pan. _____

Forming Questions

Juana lee el libro.	Joan reads (is reading) the book.
¿**Lee Juana** el libro?	Does Joan read (Is Joan reading) the book?
Ellos escriben las palabras.	They write (are writing) the words.
¿**Escriben ellos** las palabras?	Do they write (Are they writing) the words?
Hablan inglés.	They speak (are speaking) English.
¿Hablan inglés?	Do they speak (Are they speaking) English?

2. To change a statement to a question, place the subject after the verb. If the subject is not expressed, only the tone of voice indicates that the speaker is asking a question. In writing, this is shown by the two question marks (¿...?).

3. The "helping" verbs *do*, *does*, *am*, *are* and *is* ("do you take?" "they are writing") are not expressed in Spanish.

4. Sometimes the subject is placed at the end of the sentence if the question is short. This is often done if the short question has a comparatively "long" subject consisting of several words or syllables:

Luis y Ana leen el libro.   ¿Leen el libro **Luis y Ana**?

Practice B: Rewrite each statement as a question.

1. Jorge vive en Nueva York.   _____

2. Los muchachos cantan en inglés.   _____

3. Partimos para España mañana.   _____

4. El padre y el hijo escuchan la música. _____

5. Trabajan en la computadora.   _____

The central library, University of Mexico. The library is part of the National University, which is situated on the outskirts of Mexico City. The mural was painted by Juan O'Gorman, one of Mexico's outstanding artists. This face of the mural contains images representing the Spanish colonial period of Mexico's history.

Forming Negative Questions

Ella aprende español.	She learns (is learning) Spanish.
¿**No aprende** ella español?	Doesn't she learn (Isn't she learning) Spanish?
Juan vive en Madrid.	John lives (is living) in Madrid.
¿**No vive** Juan en Madrid?	Doesn't John lives (Isn't John living) in Madrid?
Pedro y su amigo corren por el parque.	Peter and his friend run (are running) through the park.
¿**No corren** por el parque Pedro y su amigo?	Don't Peter and his friend run (Aren't Peter and his friend running) through the park.

5. A question is made negative in the same way as any other kind of sentence: by placing the word **no** directly before the verb.

   Practice C: Rewrite each statement as a negative question.

   1. Yo miro el reloj.   _____

   2. Los tíos visitan a la familia.   _____

   3. Recibimos mucho dinero.   _____

   4. Mi abuelo bebe café.   _____

   5. Vive en San Juan.   _____

Replying to Questions

¿Vive **Ud.** aquí?
  Sí, **yo** vivo aquí.
  No, **yo** no vivo aquí.

¿Hablas **tú** con María?
  Sí, **yo** hablo con María.
  No, **yo** no hablo con María.

¿Aprenden **Uds.** a usar el Internet?
  Sí, **nosotros** aprendemos a usar el Internet.
  No, **nosotros** no aprendemos a usar el Internet.

¿Coméis **vosotros** frutas.
  Sí, **nosotros** comemos frutas.
  No, **nosotros** no comemos frutas.

¿Trabaja Juan en la ciudad?
  Sí, Juan trabaja en la ciudad.
  No, Juan no trabaja en la ciudad.

6. In replying to questions, be careful to notice whether you are being addressed as "you" singular or "you" plural. A question directed to **usted** or **tú** is answered by **yo** ("I"); a question directed to **ustedes** or **vosotros** is answered by **nosotros** ("we").

   Also keep in mind that **nosotros** and **vosotros** have the feminine forms **nosotras** and **vosotras**. Thus, if you and the students in your class are all girls and you express the Spanish word for "we" in your reply to a question, the form to use is **nosotras**. If you address a group of girls or women in the familiar plural, use **vosotras**.

7. An affirmative answer generally begins with "**Sí,** … ," a negative answer with "**No,** . . . ."

¿Quién?—¿Quiénes?

| ¿Quién contesta al profesor? | Roberto contesta al profesor. |
| ¿Quiénes contestan al profesor? | Los alumnos contestan al profesor. |

8. **¿Quién?** takes the third person singular form of the verb; **¿Quiénes?** takes the third person plural.

¿Qué?, ¿Por qué?, ¿Cómo?, ¿Cuándo?

¿Qué toma Ud. ahora?	Yo tomo el libro ahora.
¿Por qué lees tú el libro?	Leo el libro porque es interesante.
¿Por qué trabajan Uds.?	Trabajamos para ganar dinero.

9. Interrogative words like **¿qué?**, **¿cómo?**, **¿cuándo?**, **¿dónde?**, **¿cuánto, -a?**, **¿cuántos, -as?**, and **¿por qué?** directly precede the verb in a question.

10. The answer to **¿por qué?** generally contains the word **porque** + a conjugated verb or **para** + an infinitive.

Translating the Present Tense

Vicente escribe una carta.	{ Vincent writes a letter. { Vincent is writing a letter.
Vicente no escribe una carta.	{ Vincent does not write a letter. { Vincent is not writing a letter.
¿Escribe Vicente una carta?	{ Does Vincent write a letter? { Is Vincent writing a letter?
¿No escribe Vicente una carta?	{ Doesn't Vincent write a letter? { Isn't Vincent writing a letter?

11. Statements and questions in the present tense can generally be translated in two ways.

12. Spanish does not use "helping" verbs as English does; the words *do, does, am, are,* and *is* are expressed in Spanish only if they are used as a single verb form. For example:

| He does the work. | Él **hace** el trabajo. |
| I am here. | Yo **estoy** aquí. |

Compare:

She is writing.	Ella escribe.
She is my friend.	Ella es mi amiga.
She is here.	Está aquí. (See **estar**.)
They do the exercise.	Hacen el ejercicio.
They do not speak Spanish.	No hablan español.

In the sentence "She is writing," the word *is* is merely a "helping" verb. In the sentence "They do not speak Spanish," the word *do* is used to form the negative.

Practice D: Express each sentence in English in two ways.

1. Yo visito la catedral.

_____

2. Mi padre no trabaja aquí.

_____

3. ¿Venden Uds. la casa?

_____

4. ¿No parte el tren a las seis?

_____

5. ¿Por qué no escucha Ud. la música?

_____

◣ EXERCISES ◢

A. You and a friend are having a feud. Whatever you say in the negative, he/she restates in the affirmative. Tell what your friend says each time to contradict you.

EXAMPLE: Yo no hablo español.   Yo hablo español.

1. Nosotros no contestamos en inglés.   _____

2. La profesora no pregunta en español.   _____

3. Los niños no corren por el campo.   _____

4. Alberto y yo no bebemos naranjada.   _____

5. No llegáis tarde a la clase.   _____

B. In this case we have the opposite of the previous exercise. Your friend restates what you've said, but in the negative.

 EXAMPLE: **Los niños escriben la lección.**   Los niños no escriben la lección.

1. Yo uso la computadora. _____

2. Lola aprende francés. _____

3. Vivimos en California. _____

4. Enseñan en mi escuela. _____

5. Los padres compran los artículos. _____

C. Rewrite each question as a statement.

 EXAMPLE: **¿Comprende Ud. la música?**   Ud. comprende la música.

1. ¿Tomas la comida? _____

2. ¿Leen ellos los cuentos? _____

3. ¿Vende los lápices? _____

4. ¿Bailan el tango Rosa y Felipe? _____

5. ¿Cantamos nosotros esta noche? _____

D. Rewrite each statement as a question.

 EXAMPLE: **Mis amigos visitan el planetario.**   ¿Visitan mis amigos el planetario?

1. Pepe abre la ventana. _____

2. Comprendo las reglas. _____

3. Los alumnos leen las revistas. _____

4. Miran la pizarra. _____

5. Pepe y Julio terminan la tarea. _____

E. Change the question by adding the word in parentheses.

 EXAMPLE: **(por qué) ¿Lees tú despacio?**   ¿Por qué lees tú despacio?

1. (qué) ¿Escriben los alumnos? _____

2. (cuándo) ¿Viajan Uds.? _____

3. (cuánto) ¿Paga José? _____

4. (cómo) ¿Canto yo? _____

5. (dónde) ¿Enseña el señor Gómez? _____

F. Answer each question affirmatively or negatively as indicated.

    EXAMPLES: **¿Hablan Uds. francés?** No, _____nosotros no hablabamos francés_____ .

            ¿Estudia Ud. en casa? Sí, _____yo estudio en casa._____ .

1. ¿Vende Ud. la casa mañana? No, _____.

2. ¿Toman Uds. té en casa? Sí, _____.

3. ¿Escribe Ud. cartas? Sí, _____.

4. ¿Trabaja su padre hoy? No, mi padre _____.

5. ¿Canta Elena en la escuela? No, _____.

6. ¿Vivís vosotros(-as) en el campo? Sí, _____.

7. ¿Bebes tú leche por la mañana? Sí, _____.

8. ¿Recibe Ud. el dinero? No, _____.

9. ¿Explica la lección el profesor? Sí, _____.

10. ¿Viajan ellas por México? No, _____.

G. Answer each question as indicated in parentheses.

    EXAMPLE: **¿Qué lenguas hablan Uds. en la clase? (inglés y español)**
            Nosotros hablamos inglés y español en la clase.

1. ¿Dónde estudia Ud. las lecciones? (en la biblioteca)

    _____

2. ¿Cuándo visita Ud. a sus amigos? (los domingos)

    _____ a mis amigos _____.

3. ¿Cuántas horas mira su hermano/hermana la televisión? (cinco)

    Mi hermano/hermana _____.

4. ¿Qué escribe la profesora en la pizarra? (la tarea para mañana)

    _____

5. ¿Cómo contesta la muchacha al profesor? (muy bien)

    _____

6. ¿Dónde come su familia? (en el comedor)

   Mi familia _____

7. ¿Quién no comprende la lección? (Alberto)

   _____

8. ¿Quiénes reciben las cartas? (los abuelos)

   _____

9. ¿Cuántas revistas leen Uds. en una semana? (dos)

   _____

10. ¿Qué miras ahora? (la luna)

   _____

H. Complete the Spanish sentences. (Remember: the "helping" verbs *do*, *does*, *am*, *are*, and *is* are not expressed in Spanish.)

1. Do you spend a lot of money?

   ¿_____ mucho dinero?

2. They aren't selling the bicycle.

   _____ la bicicleta.

3. She does not drink tea.

   _____ té.

4. Don't you (**Uds.**) take the bus?

   ¿_____ el autobús?

5. John is not reading the story.

   Juan _____ el cuento.

6. Does the teacher teach well?

   ¿_____ bien _____?

7. Don't the students learn in class?

   ¿_____ en la clase?

8. Why doesn't she answer in English?

   ¿_____ en inglés?

9. Who is cooking the dinner?

   ¿_____ la cena?

10. What are the children buying in the store?

   ¿_____ en la tienda?

6
Irregular Verbs in the Present Tense—Part 1

Verbs That Are Irregular Only in the First Person Singular

Group A: the YO Form Ends in -GO

	yo	tú	Ud. él ella	nosotros(-as)	vosotros(-as)	Uds. ellos ellas
caer, to fall	**caigo**	caes	cae	caemos	caéis	caen
hacer, to do, make	**hago**	haces	hace	hacemos	hacéis	hacen
poner, to put	**pongo**	pones	pone	ponemos	ponéis	ponen
salir, to leave	**salgo**	sales	sale	salimos	salís	salen
traer, to bring	**traigo**	traes	trae	traemos	traéis	traen

Practice A: Change the subject and verb to the first person singular.

1. ella pone _____

2. nosotros hacemos _____

3. ellos salen _____

4. caemos _____

5. traen _____

Group B: Other Irregular YO Forms

	yo	tú	Ud. él ella	nosotros(-as)	vosotros(-as)	Uds. ellos ellas
conocer, to know	**conozco**	conoces	conoce	conocemos	conocéis	conocen
dar, to give	**doy**	das	da	damos	dais	dan
saber, to know	**sé**	sabes	sabe	sabemos	sabéis	saben
traducir, to translate	**traduzco**	traduces	traduce	traducimos	traducís	traducen
ver, to see	**veo**	ves	ve	vemos	veis	ven

33

A gate in the walls of Ávila. Ávila, an ancient city in Castile, is one of the most picturesque towns in Spain. It is surrounded by a granite wall typical of fortified towns during the Middle Ages.

1. The forms **dais** and **veis** do not have an accent mark.

    Practice B: You are a "do-it-all" and "know it all." Answer each question in the first person singular.

    EXAMPLE: **¿Quién ve la película?**   Yo veo la película.

    1. ¿Quién sabe la repuesta?   _____

    2 ¿Quién da el dinero a los pobres?   _____

    3. ¿Quién traduce la frase?   _____

    4. ¿Quién conoce al señor Rodríguez? _____

    5. ¿Quién trae las cintas?   _____

Saber—Conocer

María **sabe** el nombre del nuevo maestro.	Mary knows the new teacher's name.
Juan **sabe** que mañana no hay clases.	John knows there's no school tomorrow.
Ana **sabe** conducir.	Anne knows how to drive.
María **conoce** al nuevo maestro.	Mary knows the new teacher.
Juan **conoce** bien el país.	John knows the country well.

2. *To know* is expressed by two verbs in Spanish:

Saber is used in the sense of to know a fact or to have information about something or someone. It also means to know how to do something when followed by an infinitive.

Conocer is used in the sense of to be acquainted with people or places.

Practice C: Underline the correct verb in each sentence.

1. Yo no (sé-conozco) la lección de hoy.

2. Los niños (saben-conocen) los verbos muy bien.

3. ¿(Sabe-Conoce) usted a mi hermano?

4. (Sabemos-Conocemos) bien esta ciudad.

5. (Sé-Conozco) que la clase es importante.

6. ¿(Sabes-Conoces) hacer la tarea para mañana?

7. (Sabéis-Conocéis) al señor Mendoza, ¿verdad?

◆ EXERCISES ◆

A. Choose the verb in parentheses that correctly completes the sentence, and write it in the blank.

1. (traduzco-veo)   No _____ la pizarra muy bien.

2. (traigo-caigo)   Ahora _____ los libros a casa.

3. (hago-doy)   Yo no _____ el trabajo muy bien.

4. (Sé-Salgo)   _____ de la escuela a las tres.

5. (conozco-pongo)   No _____ bien a José.

6. (caigo-traigo)   Siempre _____ en la alfombra.

7. (Conozco-Sé)   _____ que Ud. es muy rico.

8. (Doy-Veo)   _____ el disco compacto a mi amigo.

9. (Pongo-Traduzco)   _____ el plato en la mesa.

10. (Traduzco-traigo)   _____ la palabra al inglés.

B. María is playing a question-and-answer game with her little brother Manolo. Write Manolo's answers as shown in the examples.

EXAMPLES: **¿Ves el libro?**   **¿Sabes la palabra?**
            Sí, ___veo el libro___   No, ___no sé la palabra___ .

1. ¿Traes el azúcar a la mesa?   No, _____.

2. ¿Sabes la verdad?   Sí, _____.

3. ¿Sales de casa temprano?   No, _____.

4. ¿Conoces tú al señor González?   Sí, _____.

5. ¿Das la cinta a José?   No, _____.

C. Answer each question as indicated.

EXAMPLE: **¿Quién ve a mi tío?** Juan ___ve a mi tío___ .

1. ¿Quiénes dan la información? Nosotros _____.

2. ¿Quién hace la comida?   Mamá _____.

3. ¿Quiénes traen las notas?   Los muchachos _____.

4. ¿Quién sabe la respuesta?   Yo _____.

5. ¿Quién ve el televisor?   Ana _____.

D. After studying the irregular verbs in this lesson, how fast can you complete the following sentences in Spanish without referring to the charts? Check your work when you're done.

1. Are you (**tú**) bringing the flowers?

   ¿_____ las flores?

2. I don't know how to drive.

   _____ conducir.

3. When are you (**vosotros**) leaving for Spain?

   ¿Cuándo _____ para España?

4. They don't see the map.

   _____ el mapa.

5. I'm translating the exercise.

   _____ el ejercicio.

6. Why isn't she doing the homework?

¿ Por qué _____ la tarea?

7. I know the city very well.

_____ muy bien la ciudad.

8. I'm not leaving school now.

_____ de la escuela ahora.

9. Is the snow still falling?

_____ la nieve todavía?

10. I'm putting the drinks on the table.

_____ las bebidas en la mesa.

7
Irregular Verbs in the Present Tense—Part 2

	yo	tú	Ud. él ella	nosotros(-as)	vosotros(-as)	Uds. ellos ellas
decir, to say, to tell	**digo**	**dices**	**dice**	decimos	decís	**dicen**
estar, to be	estoy	estás	está	estamos	estáis	están
tener, to have	tengo	tienes	tiene	tenemos	tenéis	tienen
venir, to come	vengo	vienes	viene	venimos	venís	vienen
ir, to go	voy	vas	va	vamos	vais	van
oír, to hear	oigo	oyes	oye	oímos	oís	oyen
poder, to be able, can	puedo	puedes	puede	podemos	podéis	pueden
querer, to want	quiero	quieres	quiere	queremos	queréis	quieren
ser, to be	soy	eres	es	somos	sois	son

1. All forms of **ir** and **ser** are irregular.

2. The forms **vais** and **sois** do not have accent marks. Note the accent mark on the form **oímos**.

3. The other verbs in the list are irregular in all forms except those for **nosotros(-as)** and **vosotros(-as)**.

4. **Poder** and **querer** are regular in the present tense except for the changes in the stem vowel. (For other stem-changing verbs, see Chapters 8 and 9.)

    When a form of **poder** or **querer** is followed by another verb, the second verb is in the infinitive form:

No puedo salir.	I cannot leave (I am not able to leave.)
¿Quién quiere hablar?	Who wants to speak?

5. Both **ser** and **estar** mean *to be*, but they cannot be used interchangeably. For the special uses of **ser** and **estar**, see Chapter 14.

Practice A: Rewrite each sentence, replacing the infinitive in italics with the infinitive in parentheses.

1. (estudiar)   No podemos *leer* hoy.   _____

2. (ver)   Quieren *visitar* a Luis.   _____

3. (vender)   Mi padre quiere *comprar* una casa.   _____

4. (ir)   ¿Puedes *venir* a casa?   _____

5. (escribir)   Voy a *leer* la carta.   _____

▲ EXERCISES ▲

A. You and a friend are studying Spanish together and decide to play the game of **cierto** or **falso**. Your friend asks you the first five questions and you answer "cierto" or "falso." Then you switch roles for sentences 6–10.

1. En casa oímos música en la radio.   _____

2. Voy a la escuela los sábados y los domingos.   _____

3. El presidente de los Estados Unidos viene a mi casa todos los días.   _____

4. Mi perro siempre dice buenas palabras.   _____

5. En la escuela podemos aprender muchas cosas.   _____

6. España está en Europa.   _____

7. Todas las personas tienen gatos.   _____

8. No quiero ser millonario.   _____

9. Mi padre es un hombre y mi madre es una mujer.   _____

10. Vamos a México todos los días.   _____

B. Complete each sentence with the new subject. Change the verb form accordingly.

   EXAMPLE: José va a casa ahora.   Yo ____voy a casa ahora____ .

1. Mis abuelos vienen hoy.   Mi abuela _____.

2. Nosotros estamos en casa esta noche.   Yo _____.

3. ¿Quién tiene un resfriado?   ¿Quiénes _____.

4. Luis no dice la verdad.   Tú _____.

5. ¿Oyen ustedes el ruido?   ¿ _____ ellos _____?

6. Yo quiero ir al cine esta noche.   Jorge y yo _____.

7. Ella es una persona importante.   Yo _____.

8. ¿No puedes ver el cuadro?   ¿ _____ ellos _____?

9. Mi hermano y yo somos felices.   Juan y María _____.

10. ¿Dónde están ustedes?   ¿ _____ tú?

C. An exchange student from Nicaragua is staying at your house. He wants to know many things about you. Answer his questions.

1. ¿Cuándo estás muy ocupado(a)?

_____

2. ¿Cuántos amigos tienes?

_____

3. ¿Adónde van tus amigos y tú los domingos?

_____

4. ¿Cuándo pueden jugar al béisbol tus amigos y tú?

_____

5. ¿Quién viene a tu casa esta noche?

_____

6. ¿En qué calle está tu casa?

_____

7. ¿Quién es tu profesor(a) de español?

_____

8. ¿Qué quieres ser algún día?

_____

9. ¿Oyen ustedes música en la clase de español?

_____

10. ¿Dice tu profesor(a) cosas interesantes sobre Nicaragua?

_____

D. Rewrite the sentences, changing the subjects and verbs in italics from the singular to the plural or vice versa. Use the following table as a guide.

Singular		Plural
yo	....	nosotros
tú	....	vosotros(-as) or ustedes
él	....	ellos
Ud.	....	Uds.
ella	....	ellas
		él y ella = ellos

1. ¿Dónde *están ellos* ahora? _____

2. *Ella* no *va* a la escuela hoy. _____

3. ¿Qué *tienes tú?* _____

4. No *somos* de Francia. _____

5. *Él* no *oye* la música. _____

6. ¿*Pueden ellos* venir a las ocho? _____

7. *Quiero* hablar con Pedro. _____

8. *Estoy* en mi cuarto. _____

9. ¿Adónde *van ustedes* esta tarde? _____

10. *Nosotros decimos* muchas cosas. _____

E. Speed test. Without consulting the list of verbs at the beginning of this chapter, complete each sentence. If you are doing this exercise with a partner either at home or in class, have a race to see who finishes first. The race is invalid if either of you makes any errors.

1. Do you (**Ud.**) want to go to the movies?

   ¿_____ ir al cine?

2. John is not at home today. (Use **estar.**)

   Juan _____ en casa hoy.

3. Who is coming tonight?

   ¿Quién _____ esta noche?

4. What are they saying now?

   ¿Qué _____ ahora?

5. I can't go to school today.

    _____ ir a la escuela hoy.

6. Aren't you my friend? (Use **ser**.)

    _____

7. Who hears the noise?

    ¿Quién _____ el ruido?

8. How many books does she have?

    ¿Cuántos libros _____?

9. We want to read the novel.

    _____ la novela.

10. Where are Vincent and Nilda?

    ¿Dónde _____ Vicente y Nilda?

═══════════════════════ **CHAPULTEPEC** ═══════════════════════

On a hill in Chapultepec Park (el Bosque de Chapultepec), the largest park of Mexico City, is Chapultepec Castle (el Castillo de Chapultepec). This castle was the residence of the presidents of Mexico until 1940. Today it is a museum of colonial history. In 1945 it was the scene of an Inter-American conference that passed the Act of Chapultepec to ensure assistance and solidarity in the Western hemisphere.

8
Stem-Changing Verbs in the Present Tense: O to UE

recordar, to remember

yo	rec**ue**rdo	nosotros(-as)	recordamos
tú	rec**ue**rdas	vosotros(-as)	recordáis
Ud.		Uds.	
él	rec**ue**rda	ellos	rec**ue**rdan
ella		ellas	

volver, to return

yo	v**ue**lvo	nosotros(-as)	volvemos
tú	v**ue**lves	vosotros(-as)	volvéis
Ud.		Uds.	
él	v**ue**lve	ellos	v**ue**lven
ella		ellas	

dormir, to sleep

yo	d**ue**rmo	nosotros(-as)	dormimos
tú	d**ue**rmes	vosotros(-as)	dormís
Ud.		Uds.	
él	d**ue**rme	ellos	d**ue**rmen
ella		ellas	

1. To obtain the stem of a verb, drop the **-ar, -er,** or **-ir** ending of the infinitive. The stem vowel is the last vowel of the stem: record-, encontr-, etc.

2. In the present tense, the stem vowels of verbs like **recordar, volver,** and **dormir** change from **o** to **ue** in the four forms. No stem change occurs in the **nosotros** and **vosotros** forms of the verbs.

   These verbs are often called *boot* or *shoe* verbs. Look at the pattern of each verb to see why.

Common Stem-Changing Verbs: O→UE

almorzar, to have lunch

contar, to count, to tell

costar (3rd sing. and pl. only), to cost

encontrar, to find

llover (3rd sing. only), to rain

morir, to die

mostrar, to show

poder, to be able, can (See page 38, note 4.)

Practice A: Complete each sentence saying what you are doing.

1. almorzar   yo _____ a la una.

2. jugar   yo _____ en el parque.

3. encontrar   yo no _____ mi libro.

4. morir   yo _____ de hambre.

5. poder   yo no _____ ver la televisión.

A view of the Cathedral of Mexico City. This beautiful old cathedral, which dominates the Zócalo—the city's central plaza—was built on the site of an ancient Aztec temple.

▲ EXERCISES ▲

A. Test your skills by rewriting each sentence, substituting the new subject for the subject in italics. Change the verb form according to the new subject, if necessary.

>   **EXAMPLE:**   *Mi padre* **vuelve tarde esta noche.**   <u>Nosotros volvemos</u> tarde esta noche.

1. ¿Recuerdas *tú* mi nombre?   ¿_____ Uds. mi nombre?

2. *El niño* duerme toda la noche.   Nosotros _____ toda la
                                         noche.

3. *Yo* no encuentro el reloj.   Ellos _____ el reloj.

4. ¿A qué hora almuerzan *ustedes*?   ¿A qué hora _____ tú?

5. *Los niños* mueren de risa.   El viejo _____ de risa.

6. *Nosotros* mostramos el vestido a Juana.   Yo _____ el vestido a
                                               Juana.

7. *El comerciante* cuenta su dinero.   La madre _____ su
                                         dinero.

8. ¿Dónde juegan *los niños*?   ¿Dónde _____ vosotras?

9. *Mi amigo y yo* volvemos a casa.   Juana _____ a casa.

10. *Los esquíes* cuestan mucho.   La revista _____ mucho.

B. Answer affirmatively or negatively as indicated.

1. ¿Cuenta usted su dinero todas las noches?

    Sí, _____

2. ¿Duermen ustedes diez horas cada noche?

    No, _____

3. ¿Vuelves a casa tarde los sábados?

    Sí, _____

4. ¿Encuentran ustedes regalos en la clase?

    No, _____

5. ¿Recuerda usted todos los verbos?

    No, _____

C. Answer each question that your pen pal asks you.

> EXAMPLE: **¿Dónde almuerzas en la escuela?   (en la cafetería)**
> Yo almuerzo en la cafetería.

1. ¿A qué hora vuelve tu padre a casa?   (a las seis)

   _____

2. ¿Quién cuenta historias en tu clase?   (el profesor)

   _____

3. ¿Dónde duermes tú?   (en el dormitorio)

   _____

4. ¿Cuándo almuerzan ustedes los domingos?   (a las dos)

   _____

5. ¿Qué muestra la profesora a los alumnos?   (las revistas)

   _____

6. ¿Cuándo pueden Uds. ir al cine?   (los sábados)

   _____

7. ¿Cuánto cuesta una buena comida en un restaurante?   (seis dólares)

   _____

8. ¿Dónde juegas con tus amigos?   (en el parque)

   _____

9. ¿Llueve mucho en agosto en tu ciudad?   (no)

   _____

10. ¿Dónde encuentran Uds. árboles?   (en el parque)

    _____

D. Complete the following Spanish sentences.

1. I cannot remember the movie.

   _____ la película.

2. You are returning late tonight, aren't you?

   Tú _____ tarde esta noche, ¿verdad?

3. My cats sleep ten hours every night.

   Mis gatos _____ diez horas cada noche.

4. Do you have lunch at home?

   ¿ _____ vosotros en casa?

5. Where are the girls playing today?

   ¿Dónde _____ las chicas hoy?

6. My father is telling the news.

   Mi padre _____ las noticias.

7. We do not sleep well the night before a test.

_____ la noche antes de un examen.

8. Is it raining now?

¿ _____ ahora?

9. How much do the tapes cost?

¿Cuánto _____ las cintas?

10. I am showing the photographs to my friends.

_____ las fotos a mis amigos.

9
Stem-Changing Verbs in the Present Tense: E to IE and E to I

■■■ *E→IE*

empezar, to begin

yo	emp*ie*zo	nosotros(-as)	emp*e*zamos
tú	emp*ie*zas	vosotros(-as)	emp*e*záis
Ud.		Uds.	
él }	emp*ie*za	ellos }	emp*ie*zan
ella		ellas	

entender, to understand

yo	ent*ie*ndo	nosotros(-as)	entendemos
tú	ent*ie*ndes	vosotros(-as)	entendéis
Ud.		Uds.	
él }	ent*ie*nde	ellos }	ent*ie*nden
ella		ellas	

sentir, to be sorry

yo	s*ie*nto	nosotros(-as)	sentimos
tú	s*ie*ntes	vosotros(-as)	sentís
Ud.		Uds.	
él }	s*ie*nte	ellos }	s*ie*nten
ella		ellas	

1. In verbs of this group, the stem vowel changes from **e** to **ie**. No stem change occurs in the **nosotros** and **vosotros** forms. Note that these verbs follow the same pattern as the verbs in Chapter 8.

2. Remember that the stem vowel is the last vowel of the stem: emp**e**z-, entend-, pref**e**r-, etc.

▆▛ Common Stem-Changing Verbs: E→IE

cerrar, to close   **perder**, to lose

comenzar, to begin   **preferir**, to prefer

nevar (3rd sing. only), to snow   **querer**, to want, to wish
                                        (see page 38, note 4.)
pensar, to think, to intend (+ inf.)

3.   Since the **qu-** in **querer** serves as a consonant, the stem vowel of **querer** is **e**.

Practice A: Complete each sentence in the first person singular.

1.   cerrar   Yo _____ la puerta.

2.   pensar   Yo _____ en mis vacaciones.

3.   perder   Yo _____ mi dinero.

4.   preferir   Yo _____ ir al cine.

5.   querer   Yo _____ jugar con mis amigos.

▆▛ E→I

repetir, to repeat

yo	rep*i*to	nosotros(-as)	repetimos
tú	rep*i*tes	vosotros(-as)	repetís
Ud.		Uds.	
él	rep*i*te	ellos	rep*i*ten
ella		ellas	

4.   Verbs in this group change their stem vowel from **e** to **i**, except, of course, for the **nosotros** and **vosotros** forms.

▆▛ Common Stem-Changing Verbs: E→I

pedir, to ask for, to request   **servir**, to serve

Practice B: Write the two verbs in the indicated forms.

1.   (pedir) Yo _____ papas fritas; ¿_____ Uds. Coca Cola?

2.   (servir) Nosotros _____ café; ¿_____ tú la comida?

 EXERCISES

A. Complete the following story by writing one of the following verb forms in each blank.

comenzamos repetir entendemos empieza pide
cierra queremos entiende repetimos quieres

El profesor entra y pregunta: "José, ¿ _____ cerrar la puerta?" José contesta:

1

"Sí, señor," y _____ la puerta. Ahora la clase _____ . El

2 3

profesor _____ atención y nosotros _____ a escribir. El

4 5

profesor dice que debemos _____ sus frases si _____

6 7

aprender a hablar bien el español. Así nosotros _____ cada frase. El profesor

8

pregunta si todos nosotros _____ la lección. José _____ muy

9 10

poco porque él no escucha.

B. Rewrite each sentence, forming a new subject by omitting the words in italics.

   EXAMPLE: **Lola *y Eugenio* piensan ir al cine.**
   Lola piensa ir al cine.

   1. El *alumno y* la alumna no entienden la lección.

   _____

   2. *Julio y* yo preferimos el béisbol.

   _____

   3. *Roberto y* María cierran la puerta.

   _____

   4. Mis amigos *y yo* queremos visitar el museo.

   _____

   5. Mi *familia y* yo pensamos ir a España.

   _____

C. Rewrite each sentence, forming a new subject by adding the words in parentheses.

> **EXAMPLE:** **Mi abuela sirve la comida. (y yo)**
> Mi abuela y yo servimos la comida.

1. Mi tío pierde mucho dinero.   (y mi madre)

_____

2. Ramón prefiere jugar al fútbol.   (y Ana)

_____

3. ¿Qué pide él?   (y ella)

_____

4. Juanita lo siente mucho.   (y yo)

_____

5. Juan empieza la tarea ahora.   (y su amigo)

_____

D. You are going to a birthday party this weekend and your friend wants some details about it. Answer his/her questions according to the cues.

1. ¿Qué prefieres hacer el sábado?   (tener una fiesta)

_____

2. ¿A qué hora comienza la fiesta?   (a las ocho)

_____

3. ¿Qué sirve Luisa en la fiesta?   (pasteles deliciosos)

_____

4. ¿Dónde piensas poner los refrescos?   (en la mesa)

_____

5 ¿Qué hacen tus amigos si nieva?   (llevan botas)

_____

6. ¿Qué pierde siempre Alberto?   (su cartera)

_____

7. ¿Quiénes repiten las canciones?   (Nilda y Josefina)

_____

8. ¿Entienden Uds. las reglas de sus padres?   (no)

_____

9. ¿Cuándo empiezan a abrir los regalos?   (a las diez)

_____

10. ¿Prefieren Uds. servir frutas o dulces?   (frutas)

_____

Cuzco. Cuzco was the ancient capital of the Incas of Peru. It is situated in the Andes Mountains more than 11,000 feet above sea level. Because of the high altitude of Cuzco, which may cause a dizzying discomfort called *el soroche*, tourists arriving at the city are advised to rest a while before attempting to visit any sites. On the outskirts of Cuzco, there are several interesting places including an outdoor market where articles made by the natives can be bought, an Inca fortress, and a ritual bath used by the Incas. About 50 miles from Cuzco are the ruins of Machu Picchu, the lost city of the Incas, which was discovered in 1911. Among its important sites are the ruins of a fortress and an Inca temple. The photograph shows a market near Cuzco.

E.   Complete the Spanish sentences.

    1.   I'm very sorry. (I regret it very much.)

        Lo _____ mucho.

    2.   Who serves dinner at your house?

        ¿Quién _____ la comida en su casa?

    3.   Our class begins at 9:20.

        Nuestra clase _____ a las nueve y veinte.

    4.   We prefer to eat early.

        _____ comer temprano.

    5.   What are you asking for?

        ¿Qué _____ tú?

    6.   Don't you understand the sentence?

        ¿_____ vosotros la frase?

    7.   He always loses his keys.

        Él siempre _____ sus llaves.

    8.   Does the teacher repeat his questions?

        ¿_____ el profesor sus preguntas?

9. She intends to go to the country.

   Ella _____ ir al campo.

10. Is it snowing a lot today?

   ¿_____ mucho hoy?

REVIEW EXERCISES: CHAPTERS 3-9

A. In each of the following sentences, replace the verb in italics with the proper form of the verb in parentheses. Write your answer in the blank on the right.

    EXAMPLE: **(encontrar)** **El niño** *pierre* **su libro.** _____encuentra_____

1.	(vender)	Mi madre *compra* el automóvil.	_____
2.	(cerrar)	¿Quién *abre* la puerta?	_____
3.	(vivir)	¿Dónde *trabajan* José y Ana?	_____
4.	(ver)	No *oigo* la televisión.	_____
5.	(explicar)	El profesor *repite* su pregunta.	_____
6.	(empezar)	La película *termina* a las dos.	_____
7.	(recibir)	Yo no *doy* el dinero.	_____
8.	(volver)	¿A qué hora *parte* el tren?	_____
9.	(entender)	¿Quiénes *comprenden* la cinta?	_____
10.	(beber)	En la fiesta *cantamos* mucho.	_____
11.	(comprar)	Los hombres *muestran* muchos artículos.	_____
12.	(venir)	*¿Duerme* Juan ahora?	_____
13.	(escuchar)	¿*Oyes* el disco compacto?	_____
14.	(preferir)	¿Quién *conoce* la ciudad?	_____
15.	(estar)	¿Dónde *trabajan* ahora?	_____

B. Complete the following stories by filling each blank with one of the verb forms given in parentheses.

    1. (trae, viene, ir, llueve, están, quieren, deben, jugar)

Hoy _____ mucho y los niños _____
              1   2

_____ en la casa. Juanito _____ y
              3   4

_____ sus juguetes. Todos _____ muy
              5   6

contentos porque no _____ _____ a la escuela.
                                    7   8

    2. (vamos, comienza, termina, da, dice, explica, es)

Nuestra clase de español _____ a las nueve y media y
                                              1

_____ a las diez y cuarto. El profesor _____
              2   3

muy bueno porque no _____ muchas tareas. Él
                                        4

_____ las lecciones muy bien, y _____ que
              5   6

mañana _____ a un museo.
                    7

C.   **1.** Rewrite the following sentence, changing each verb to the *yo* form.

En la clase traducimos frases, aprendemos cuentos, escribimos palabras, repetimos reglas y hacemos cosas interesantes.

_____

_____

_____

    2. Rewrite the following paragraph, replacing " Los hermanos García" with "Mi amigo" and changing the verbs accordingly.

Los hermanos García piden libros en la biblioteca y leen los libros allí. Luego salen de la biblioteca con los libros, van a casa, muestran los libros a su madre y finalmente recuerdan que deben hacer su tarea.

_____

_____

_____

D. Your teacher will read aloud ten statements in Spanish. If the statement is true, write *Sí*; if it is false, write *No*.

1. _____   3. _____   5. _____   7. _____   9. _____

2. _____   4. _____   6. _____   8. _____   10. _____

E. In the following items 1 to 5, read the description of each situation and the first line of dialogue, then choose the most likely response that the second speaker would make. Circle the letter of your choice.

Before you begin, review the following words and expressions:

todas las tardes, every afternoon	**la sección de anuncios**, want-ad section
todos los días, every day	**no me gusta**, I do not like
mismo, -a, -os, -as, same	**ninguno**, any, none
todo el día, all day, the whole day	**el miembro**, member
el pastel, pie, pastry	**él**, him
ya, already	**hacer preguntas**, to ask questions
deber, must, should, ought to	**acerca de**, about
el empleo, job	**todo el mundo**, everybody

1. El padre de Antonio trabaja en la ciudad y vuelve a casa todas las tardes a las seis. El padre habla con Antonio.

EL PADRE PREGUNTA:

Antonio, ¿qué hacen ustedes en la escuela todos los días?

ANTONIO CONTESTA:

    a. Tomamos el almuerzo todo el día.
    b. Escuchamos a nuestros profesores.
    c. Los profesores sirven café con pasteles durante las clases.

2. Pepe mira un programa de televisión con su hermana Isabel. Ya son las diez de la noche.

PEPE DICE:

Creo que este programa es muy interesante.

ISABEL CONTESTA:

    a. Yo duermo ahora.
    b. Llueve mucho en casa.
    c. Es verdad, pero es tarde y debemos ir a la cama ahora.

3. Usted y su amiga almuerzan en la cafetería de la escuela. Ustedes creen que la comida es muy mala.

SU AMIGA DICE:

No puedo comer este sandwich. Es horrible.

USTED CONTESTA:

   a. Sí, él baila muy bien en las fiestas.
   b. Mi madre prepara buenos sandwiches. Voy a traer uno mañana.
   c. Yo conozco muy bien a María. Ella canta muy mal.

4. Francisca, una muchacha de quince años, quiere trabajar durante el verano. Busca empleo en la sección de anuncios del periódico. Ella habla con su madre.

LA MADRE PREGUNTA:

¿Puedes encontrar un buen empleo?

FRANCISCA CONTESTA:

   a. Hay muchos empleos pero no me gusta ninguno.
   b. Sí, pienso ser profesora en una escuela secundaria.
   c. Sí, me gusta uno para una señora de treinta años.

5. En la clase de español hay un muchacho cubano que se llama Santiago. Los miembros de la clase le hacen preguntas acerca de su país.

UN ALUMNO PREGUNTA:

¿Entiendes bien el inglés?

SANTIAGO CONTESTA:

   a. Sí, todo el mundo habla inglés en Cuba.
   b. No, pero quiero aprender la lengua rápidamente.
   c. No, porque en mi país hablan solamente francés.

Part 3
Nouns, Articles, Adjectives, "To Be"

✂✂✂✂✂✂✂✂✂✂✂✂✂✂✂✂✂✂✂✂

10
Gender; Nouns and Articles in the Singular

◼ **Some Nouns Used in the Classroom**

Masculine Nouns	Feminine Nouns
el asiento, the seat	**la puerta**, the door
el cuadro, the picture	**la ventana**, the window
el pupitre, the (pupil's) desk	**la pluma**, the fountain pen
el cuaderno, the notebook	**la pizarra**, the chalkboard
el papel, the paper	**la pared**, the wall
el libro, the book	**la luz**, the light
el lápiz, the pencil	**la lección**, the lesson
el bolígrafo (el lapicero), the pen	**la computadora**, the computer

1. Nouns in Spanish have gender; that is, they are either masculine or feminine.

2. The definite article (the) has two Spanish forms in the singular:

   Masculine nouns take the article **el**.

   Feminine nouns take the article **la**.

3. Many masculine nouns end in **-o**.

Many feminine nouns end in **-a**, **-d**, or **-ión**.

Some exceptions: **el avión**, the airplane
                          el camión, the truck

4. If a noun does not end in **-o**, **-a**, **-d**, or **-ión**, its gender must be learned individually.

Practice A: Indicate the gender of the noun by writing **el** in the blank if it is masculine, **la** if it is feminine.

1. _____ tiempo   **4.** _____ amigo   **7.** _____ tarea

2. _____ semana   **5.** _____ ciudad   **8.** _____ dictado

3. _____ lección   **6.** _____ atención   **9.** _____ bondad

Male and Female, Masculine and Feminine

el hombre, the man   **la mujer**, the woman

el muchacho, the boy   **la muchacha**, the girl

el señor, the gentleman   **la madre**, the mother

5. A noun that denotes a male person is masculine; a noun that denotes a female person is feminine.

Practice B: Write the definite article in the blank.

1. _____ padre   **6.** _____ joven (= young woman)

2. _____ hermana   **7.** _____ joven (= young man)

3. _____ profesor   **8.** _____ estudiante (= male student)

4. _____ profesora   **9.** _____ estudiante (= female student)

5. _____ tío   **10.** _____ tía

Some Exceptions

Masculine Nouns That End in -a   Feminine Nouns That End in -o

    el día, the day   **la mano**, the hand

    el mapa, the map   **la radio**, the radio

    el programa, the program

    el clima, the climate

    el idioma, the language

    el problema, the problem

6. **El agua**, the water, and **el hambre**, the hunger, are feminine nouns although they take the article **el**. This article is used instead of **la** because the words begin with the stressed sound of **a** (**a**-gua, **ham**-bre). The use of **la** before a stressed **a** sound would make it difficult to pronounce the article and the noun as two distinct words.

The Indefinite Article

el libro, the book	**un** libro, a (one) book
la frase, the sentence	**una** frase, a (one) sentence

7. **El** and **la** are the definite articles and mean *the*. **Un** and **Una** are the indefinite articles and mean *a*, *an*, or *one*.

Practice C: Rewrite each noun with its indefinite article.

1. la escuela _____
2. el papel _____
3. el tío _____
4. la camisa _____
5. la noche _____

6. el plato _____
7. la computadora _____
8. el mapa _____
9. el día _____
10. la mano _____

Country dancers are one of the attractions at a *charreada*, or Mexican rodeo.

 **EXERCISES**

A. Rewrite each sentence, changing **el** to **un**, **la** to **una**, or vice versa.

   EXAMPLE: **Quiero comprar *un* abrigo.**   Quiero comprar el abrigo.

   1. *La* mujer viene esta noche.

   _____

   2. *Una* cama está en *el* dormitorio.

   _____

   3. *El* hospital y *la* iglesia están en *una* calle.

   _____

   4. Escucho *un* programa musical.

   _____

   5. Vivimos en *la* ciudad.

   _____

   6. Quiero cantar *una* canción y bailar *el* tango.

   _____

   7. No podemos comprar *el* reloj en *la* farmacia.

   _____

   8. *Un* hombre habla con *la* mujer.

   _____

   9. *La* alumna lee *una* frase.

   _____

   10. *El* alumno aprende *un* verbo.

   _____

B. Supply the Spanish word for the English word in parentheses. If you are not sure of the gender of the noun, check the Vocabulary at the end of this book.

   1. (a)   Hay _____ parque cerca de mi casa.

   2. (the)   Siempre leemos _____ periódico.

   3. (a)   María es _____ joven muy hermosa.

   4. (a)   Escuchamos _____ programa de deportes.

   5. (an)   El caballo es _____ animal.

6. (The) _____ flor es muy bonita.

7. (a) Hoy hace frío y llevo _____ abrigo.

8. (The) _____ mano es una parte del cuerpo.

9. (The) _____ lección de hoy es interesante.

10. (the) Dormimos en _____ dormitorio.

11. (a) El español es _____ lengua.

12. (a) Necesito _____ lápiz.

13. (an) Papá quiere comprar _____ automóvil.

14. (the) Prefiero viajar en _____ tren.

15. (the) Hablo con _____ profesor.

16. (The) _____ hermana de Isabel se llama Ana.

17. (a) Ella tiene _____ perro simpático.

18. (The) _____ profesor enseña muy bien.

19. (the) ¿Dónde está _____ cine?

20. (a) ¿Tienes _____ mapa de España?

C. Supply **el, la, un,** or **una** to complete the meaning of the sentence. In some cases either definite or indefinite article may be used.

1. Por la noche yo siempre miro _____ televisión y como _____ postre en _____ sala.

2. En _____ clase aprendemos _____ lección muy interesante.

3. _____ padre y _____ madre van a _____ ciudad para comprar _____ computadora en _____ tienda.

4. Abrimos _____ puerta con _____ llave.

5. Lavo _____ perro en _____ cuarto de baño.

6. _____ tigre es _____ animal.

7. _____ jirafa es también _____ animal.

8. ¿Haces tú _____ tarea en casa?

9. En _____ pared hay _____ cuadro interesante.

10. Hoy _____ sol brilla y hace mucho calor.

D.   Complete each sentence by supplying the missing Spanish words.

1.   The school is near a house and a large building.

_____ está cerca de _____ y

_____ grande.

2.   I have a pencil, a pen, a notebook, and a book.

Tengo _____, _____, _____ y

_____.

3.   Are you reading the magazine or the newspaper?

¿Lees tú _____ o _____?

4.   She is at the movies and is seeing a good film.

Ella está en _____ y ve _____ buena película.

5.   The teacher writes the sentence on the board.

_____ escribe _____ en _____.

6.   Is there a light in the room?

¿Hay _____ en _____?

7.   Do you see a picture on the wall?

¿Ves tú _____ en _____?

8.   Why don't they drink the water?

¿Por qué no beben _____?

9.   Johnny lives with a grandfather and an aunt.

Juanito vive con _____ y _____.

10.   The tree is in the garden.

_____ está en _____.

11.   The father and the mother have a son and a daughter.

_____ y _____ tienen _____

y _____.

12.   Where is the map of Spain?

¿Dónde está _____ de España?

13.   I'm watching a program on (the) television.

Veo _____ en _____.

14.   Do they live in the city or in the country?

¿Viven _____ o en _____?

15. French is a beautiful language.

El francés es _____ hermosa.

16. The hand, the foot, the head, and the arm are parts of the body.

_____, _____, _____ y

_____ son partes del cuerpo.

17. Sunday is a day of the week.

El domingo es _____ de _____.

18. The lesson is not very difficult today.

_____ no es muy difícil hoy.

19. In the bedroom there are a bed, a chair, a mirror, a desk, a rug, and a chest of drawers.

En _____ hay _____, _____,

_____, _____, _____ y

_____.

20. To get to the school, I can take the bus or the train.

Para llegar a _____, puedo tomar _____ o

_____.

11
Nouns and Articles in the Plural

Nouns That Add -s

Singular	Plural
el hombre, the man	**los** hombres, the men
la mesa, the table	**las** mesas, the tables

1. The plural of **el** is **los**; the plural of **la** is **las**.

2. Nouns that end in a vowel add **-s** for the plural.

Nouns That Add -es

el animal, the animal	**los** animales, the animals
la pared, the wall	**las** paredes, the walls

3. Nouns that end in a consonant add **-es** for the plural.

Nouns in Which z Becomes c Before Adding -es.

el lápiz, the pencil	**los** lápices, the pencils
la luz, the light	**las** luces, the lights

4. Nouns that end in **-z** change **z** to **c** before adding **-es** for the plural.

Nouns That Lose an Accent Mark

el jardín, the garden	los jardines, the gardens
la lección, the lesson	las lecciones, the lessons

5. Nouns that have an accent mark on the last syllable in the singular lose the accent mark in the plural.

Practice: Rewrite each article and noun in the plural.

1.	la flor	_____	5.	la vez	_____
2.	el libro	_____	6.	el guante	_____
3.	el sillón	_____	7.	el hospital	_____
4.	la madre	_____	8.	la ventana	_____

Plural Forms of the Indefinite Article

un edificio, a building   **unos** edificios, some buildings

una escuela, a school   **unas** escuelas, some schools

6. The plural forms **unos** and **unas** mean *some*.

▲ EXERCISES ▲

A.   If the word in italics means *the*, replace it by writing the Spanish word for *some* in the blank below it, or vice versa.

EXAMPLE: *Los* niños están en el jardín con *unas* niñas.
                    Unos   las

1.   *Unos* alumnos están en *las* clases ahora.

     _____   _____

2.   ¿Escriben Uds. *las* frases y *los* verbos?

                    _____   _____

3.   Queremos comprar *los* lápices en *las* tiendas.

                    _____   _____

4.   *Unos* profesores y *unas* profesoras enseñan el español.

     _____   _____

5.   Vamos a *unos* mercados para comprar *las* verduras.

          _____   _____

B.   Rewrite each sentence, changing the italicized word to the plural.

EXAMPLE: **¿Qué hay en *el plato*?**   ¿Qué hay en los platos?

1.   No quieren comer en *el restaurante*.   _____

2.   No podemos ver sin *la luz*.   _____

3.   En *la sala* de clase hay *una pizarra*.   _____

4.   ¿Vas a comprar *un lápiz* o *una pluma*?   _____

5.   ¿Qué *lección* aprendemos hoy?   _____

6.   En *la pared* hay *un cuadro* de Goya.   _____

7.   En *la familia* hay *la tía*, *el nieto* y *la sobrina*.   _____

8.   Tomamos *la comida* en *el comedor*.   _____

9. ¿Tienes *un borrador* y *un mapa*?   _____

10. Paca canta *la canción* ahora.   _____

C.   Rewrite each phrase in the singular.

   Example: los hombres y las mujeres   el hombre y la mujer

   1. los dedos y las piernas   _____

   2. unos jardines y unas flores   _____

   3. unas violetas y unos claveles   _____

   4. los abogados y las profesoras   _____

   5. las noches y los días   _____

   6. unas luces y unas lámparas   _____

   7. las lecciones y los ejercicios   _____

   8. unos borradores y unos lápices   _____

   9. los calcetines y las corbatas   _____

   10. los comedores y las salas   _____

Las Líneas de Nazca.   The Nazca civilization of southern Peru flourished between 200 and 600 A.D. They were noted for their unique textiles and ceramics. The Nazca region is famous for the Nazca Lines, which are lines on the ground that extend thirty miles from north to south and are visible only from the air. These lines form rectangles, squares, circles, and animal, bird, and human figures. Some of the figures date back to civilizations prior to the Nazcas. One theory of the lines is that they were drawn by extraterrestrial beings. Another theory states that the Indians drew the lines in the earth, guided by others who flew above them in balloons full of smoke. It is believed that these geometric drawings are a symbolic type of writing in which the same words have been written in gigantic letters, others in small letters. All the drawings are different and there are no two alike. One figure depicts a monkey the size of a soccer field and his left hand is almost forty feet long. Another figure is that of a killer whale, a symbol of a tribe of head hunters. A careful look will reveal a human head hanging from the body of the whale. The photo on the right shows the giant scorpion.

D.   In the blank, write the Spanish word for the word in parentheses.

1.   (The) _____ hoteles de la ciudad están el la calle principal.

2.   (some)   ¿Tienes _____ mapas?

3.   (some)   En la ciudad hay _____ edificios grandes.

4.   (the)   ¿Dónde están _____ bicicletas?

5.   (the)   ¿Cuáles son _____ estaciones?

6.   (some)   ¿Ven ellos _____ carteras en la tienda?

7.   (some)   Hay _____ animales interesantes en el zoo.

8.   (the)   ¿Dónde están _____ niños?

9.   (The) _____ abuelos de Felipe vienen hoy.

10.   (The) _____ padres de Francisco van al campo.

E.   Complete the Spanish sentences.

1.   Where are the boys and the girls?

¿Dónde están _____ y _____?

2.   Do you have some watches to sell?

¿Tiene usted _____ para vender?

3.   The streets are empty tonight.

_____ están vacías esta noche.

4.   There are some pictures on the walls.

Hay _____ en _____.

5.   What are the lessons that we are learning this week?

¿Cuáles son _____ que aprendemos esta semana?

6.   We are watching the programs on television.

Vemos _____ en la televisión.

7.   The men and the women are at the dance.

_____ y _____ están en el baile.

8.   Where can we buy the shoes?

¿Dónde podemos comprar _____?

9.   The trains leave at nine o'clock.

_____ parten a las nueve.

10. I need some pencils, some pens, and some rulers.

Necesito _____, _____ y

_____ .

11. The spoons, the forks, the dishes, and the glasses are on the tables.

_____ , _____ , _____

y _____ están en _____ .

12. Today the prices are very high in the markets.

Hoy _____ son muy altos en _____ .

13. We are going to buy some vegetables and some eggs.

Vamos a comprar _____ y _____ .

14. The mother and (the) father are looking for the children.

_____ y _____ buscan a

_____ .

15. There are some armchairs in the living room near the windows.

Hay _____ en _____ cerca de

_____ .

12
A and DE; Contractions AL and DEL; Using DE to Express Possession

A + Definite Article = "to the," "at the"

Hoy vamos **a la** ciudad.	Today we are going to the city.
Viajo **al** campo mañana	Tomorrow I am traveling to the country.
Me gusta ir **a las** montañas.	I like going to the mountains.
Quiero viajar **a los** países de Sudamérica.	I want to travel to the South American countries

1. The preposition **a** combines with **el** to become **al**. It does not combine with any other article.

Practice A: Supply *a* + definite article.

1. Mañana vamos _____ cine con José.

2. No quiero ir _____ escuela hoy.

3. ¿Traes tus libros _____ clases?

4. Mañana vamos _____ partido de fútbol.

5. ¿Vas _____ mercados esta tarde?

De + Definite Article = "of the," "from the"

Hablamos	**de la** película.	We speak of the movie.
	del hombre.	of the man.
	de las películas.	of the movies.
	de los hombres.	of the men.
Venimos	**de la** tienda.	We're coming from the store.
	del edificio.	from the building.
	de las tiendas.	from the stores.
	de los partidos.	from the games.

2. The preposition **de** combines with **el** to become **del**. It does not combine with any other article.

> *Practice B*: Supply *de* + a definite article.
>
> **1.** ¿Hablan ustedes _____ muchachos?
>
> **2.** No hablamos _____ profesoras.
>
> **3.** Mi madre viene _____ mercado.
>
> **4.** Mi padre llega _____ ciudad.
>
> **5.** La familia sale _____ comedor.

Using *DE* to Express Possession

El libro de Felipe es interesante.	Philip's book is interesting.
El tío de la muchacha es rico.	The girl's uncle is rich.
María es **la prima del chico**.	Mary is the boy's cousin.
Los tíos de las muchachas son ricos.	The girls' uncles are rich.
María es **la prima de los chicos**.	Mary is the boys' cousin.

3. **De** is used in Spanish to express possession. Note that "the teacher's house" becomes "the house of the teacher" (**la casa del profesor**), "Mary's books" becomes "the books of Mary" (**los libros de María**), etc.

4. To express possession in Spanish, use **de** before a person's name, **de la** before a feminine singular noun, **del** before a masculine singular noun, **de las** before a feminine plural noun, and **de los** before a masculine plural noun.

5. Remember that the position of the apostrophe in English indicates whether the possessor is singular or plural:

> the girl's friend = the friend of the girl
> the girls' friend = the friend of the girls

> *Practice C*: Write in Spanish.
>
> **1.** Robert's school   _____
>
> **2.** the father's watch   _____
>
> **3.** the mother's dress   _____
>
> **4.** the girls' teacher   _____
>
> **5.** the boys' friends   _____

▲ EXERCISES ▲

A. Change the words in italics from the singular to the plural or vice versa.

EXAMPLES: **Necesito el libro *del profesor*.**   **Damos los sombreros *a las chicas*.**
                   de los profesores   a la chica

1. ¿Haces tú el trabajo *de la clase*?

   _____

2. No leemos los libros *de los profesores*.

   _____

3. ¿Vas *al teatro* con frecuencia?

   _____

4. Quiero ir *a la montaña*.

   _____

5. ¿Tienes el regalo *del abuelo*?

   _____

6. No vamos *a las clases* hoy.

   _____

7. Las muchachas escriben *a los muchachos*.

   _____

8. ¿Salen *de las clases*?

   _____

9. Mis padres siempre vuelven tarde *del concierto*.

   _____

10. ¿Van ellos *a los mercados* hoy?

    _____

B. Supply one of the following to complete the meaning: *a, al, a la, a los, a las*; *de, del, de la, de los, de las*.

1. Hablo por teléfono _____ médico.

2. Tengo el sombrero _____ José.

3. Siempre hablamos _____ tiempo.

4. ¿Qué sección _____ revista prefieres leer?

5. Los habitantes _____ ciudades _____ México son simpáticos.

6. ¿Qué das tú _____ amigos _____ Roberto?

7. Ahora vamos _____ casa _____ Manuel.

8. Pasamos _____ comedor para almozar.

9. ¿Qué sabes _____ países de Sudamérica?

10. ¿Quién sale _____ cuarto?

C. A visitor to your Spanish class from La Paz, Bolivia, wishes to find out how much Spanish
    you have learned. How would you answer her questions? If your teacher wishes, you may
    practice with a partner.

1. ¿Va usted a la escuela los domingos?

    _____

2. ¿Cuál es la capital de los Estados Unidos?

    _____

3. ¿En qué habitación de la casa duerme usted?

    _____

4. ¿Cuándo van ustedes al cine?

    _____

5. ¿Va su madre al mercado para comprar un automóvil?

    _____

A bullfight in Spain. The *corrida de toros* has been popular in Spain for centuries. It also draws large crowds in Mexico, Peru, Venezuela, and Colombia. The bulls are bred for their ferocity. The bullfight is a test of courage and daring in which the *torero* must show grace and skill in dodging the deadly horns.

6. ¿Cuándo vamos a la playa?

_____

7. ¿Recibe usted dinero del amigo de su padre?

_____

8. ¿Dan ustedes regalos al profesor de español?

_____

9. ¿Es enero un mes del verano?

_____

10. ¿Quién es el director de su escuela?

_____

D. Complete the sentences in Spanish.

1. Do you have the teacher's (*m*) book?

   ¿Tienes _____?

2. No, but I have Albert's pen.

   No, pero tengo _____.

3. At what time are you going to the party?

   ¿A qué hora vas _____?

4. We are not talking to the neighbors.

   No hablamos _____.

5. They are returning from the country tonight.

   Vuelven _____ esta noche.

6. We always go to the museums on Sundays.

   Siempre vamos _____ los domingos.

7. She is the boys' (*note apostrophe*) grandmother.

   Ella es _____.

8. The heat of the sun is strong.

   El calor _____ es fuerte.

9. She gets to the train at 6:00.

   Llega _____ a las seis.

10. Manuel always talks to the girls of the class.

    Manuel siempre habla _____.

13
Adjectives

Agreement of Adjectives

El hombre es **alto**.   The man is tall.
La mujer es **alta**.   The woman is tall.

Los hombres son **altos**. The men are tall.
Las mujeres son **altas**. The women are tall.

El hombre y la mujer son **altos**. The man and the woman are tall.

1. An adjective that ends in **-o** in the masculine singular has four possible forms, depending on whether the noun or pronoun it describes is masculine or feminine, singular or plural.

2. An adjective agrees in form with the noun or pronoun it describes. Thus:

 a. *Singular*: If the noun or pronoun is masculine, the adjective ends in **-o**; if it is feminine, the adjective ends in **-a**.

 b. *Plural*: If the noun or pronoun is masculine, the adjective ends in **-os**; if it is feminine, the adjective ends in **-as**. If the same adjective describes two or more nouns of different genders, the masculine plural form is used.

Practice A: Complete each sentence with the correct form of the adjective in parentheses.

 1. (largo, larga, largos, largas) La calle es _____.

 2. (ancho, ancha, anchos, anchas) Las avenidas son _____.

 3. (gordo, gorda, gordos, gordas) El niño no es _____.

 4. (viejo, vieja, viejos, viejas) Los abuelos son _____.

 5. (simpático, etc.)   María y Juan son _____.

Adjectives That Have Only Two Forms

El árbol es **grande**. The tree is large.
La casa es **grande**.   The house is large.

Los árboles son **grandes**. The trees are large.
Las casas son **grandes**. The houses are large.

3. An adjective that does not end in **-o** in the masculine singular generally has two forms: singular or plural. The masculine and feminine forms are the same.

    Practice B: Complete each sentence with the correct form of the adjective in parentheses.

    1. (difícil, difíciles)   La lección no es muy _____.

    2. (verde, verdes)   Las hojas son _____.

    3. (popular, populares)   José es muy _____.

    4. (pobre, pobres)   Mis amigos son _____.

    5. (amable, amables)   La niña y su padre son _____.

Adjectives of Nationality

El chico es **español**.	The boy is Spanish.
La chica es **española**.	The girl is Spanish.
Los chicos son **españoles**.	The boys are Spanish.
Las chicas son **españolas**.	The girls are Spanish.

4. Adjectives of nationality that end in a consonant in the masculine singular add **-a** for the feminine singular, **-es** for the masculine plural, and **-as** for the feminine plural.

5. If the masculine singular form has an accent mark on the last vowel, the accent mark disappears in the other forms:

    francés,   francesa,   franceses,   francesas

    Practice C: Complete each sentence with the correct form of the adjective in parentheses.

    1. (alemán, alemana, alemanes, alemanas)   Mi tío es _____.

    2. (francés, francesa, franceses, francesas)   Las señoras son _____.

    3. (portugués, portuguesa, portugueses, portuguesas)   ¿Son ellos _____?

    4. (inglés, inglesa, ingleses, inglesas)   Roberto y Juan son _____.

    5. (español, española, españoles, españolas)   María no es _____.

6. Statements like those given above are generally changed to a question as follows:

La chica es española.	The girl is Spanish.
¿Es española la chica?	Is the girl Spanish?
Las casas son grandes.	The houses are large.
¿Son grandes las casas?	Are the houses large?

If we were to say, for example, **¿Es la chica española?** it could be translated as: *Is she the Spanish girl?* (See next section.)

Practice D   Change each statement to a question.

EXAMPLE: El profesor es inteligente.   ¿Es inteligente el profesor?

1. La mujer es simpática.   _____

2. Sus amigos son ricos.   _____

3. El hombre es viejo.   _____

4. André es francés.   _____

5. Las calles son anchas.   _____

Adjectives That Follow the Noun

Juanito es un niño **inteligente**.   Johnny is an intelligent child.
Raquel es una niña **simpática**.   Rachel is a nice (likable) child.

Los alumnos **aplicados** trabajan mucho.   The studious pupils work a lot.
Los platos **italianos** son deliciosos.   The Italian dishes are delicious.

7. In Spanish, an adjective of description or nationality generally follows its noun, whereas it generally precedes its noun in English:

an *interesting* lesson = una lección **interesante**

Adjectives That Generally Precede the Noun

Tengo **muchos** libros.   I have many books.
Ana tiene **poco** dinero.   Ann has little money.
Hay **varias** personas en casa.   There are several people at home.
Tenemos **cinco** clases.   We have five classes.

8. Adjectives of quantity, number, and amount generally precede their nouns in Spanish, as in English.

Practice E: Place the adjective before or after its noun, depending on whether it is descriptive or denotes quantity or number.

EXAMPLES: (bonita)   María es una _____ muchacha _____*bonita*_____ .

(pocas)   Hay _____*pocas*_____ alumnas _____ en la clase.

1. (cuatro)   Tenemos _____ plumas _____.

2. (mucho)   ¿Tienes _____ dinero _____ en el banco?

3. (pequeño)   El gato es un _____ animal _____.

4. (populares) Rosa y Ana son _____ muchachas _____.

5. (algunas)   Hay _____ tiendas _____ en esta calle.

6. (rica)   Mi tía es una _____ mujer _____.

7. (americanas) Las _____ escuelas _____ son buenas.

8. (diez)   Quiero comprar _____ discos _____.

9. (grandes)   Hay _____ árboles _____ en este parque.

10. (unos)   Veo _____ aviones _____ en el cielo.

Las Islas Galápagos.   In the Pacific Ocean, 600 miles to the west of Ecuador, are the Galápagos Islands. These islands take their name from the enormous tortoises (galápagos) that were found there. Unfortunately these tortoises are practically extinct, victims of pirates, whalers, and oilmen who killed them for food. It is believed that these islands originated more than three million years ago due to volcanic eruptions, and that the tortoises and iguanas are descendants of prehistoric animals.

EXERCISES

A. Rewrite the following sentences changing the words in italics from the singular to the plural or vice versa.

> EXAMPLES: **Estudio *las lecciones difíciles.***   **¿Tienes *el libro verde?***
> Estudio la lección difícil.   ¿Tienes los libros verdes?

1. Escribo con *la pluma roja.*

   _____

2. Quiero hablar con *los hombres franceses.*

   _____

3. Aquí vemos *las casas grandes.*

   _____

4. El niño siempre juega con *unos muchachos españoles.*

   _____

5. ¿Puedes traer *el cuaderno pequeño?*

   _____

6. Felipe quiere comprar *los perros blancos.*

   _____

7. No comprendemos *la frase difícil.*

   _____

8. Vivimos cerca de *unas familias francesas.*

   _____

9. No puedo escribir con *el lápiz azul.*

   _____

10. Fotografiamos *unos campos verdes.*

    _____

B. Mario's little sister Laura likes to contradict him once in a while just to tease him. Write what Laura says following the example given.

> EXAMPLE: *Las casas* **son blancas.** **(el edificio)**   El edificio es blanco.

1. *Juanito* es muy simpático.   (la profesora)

   _____

2. *Mis abuelos* son viejos.   (mi tía)

   _____

3. *La pluma* es verde.   (los lápices)

_____

4. *Los caballeros* son alemanes.   (la señora)

_____

5. *María* no es perezosa.   (Luis)

_____

6. *Mi padre* es muy fuerte.   (mi madre)

_____

7. *El actor* es español.   (los profesores)

_____

8. *Rosa y Vicente* son rubios.   (Rosa)

_____

9. *La lección* no es fácil.   (los ejercicios)

_____

10. *Los alumnos* son muy inteligentes.   (las alumnas)

_____

C. Answer each question according to the picture.

1. ¿De qué color es el cielo?

_____

2. ¿Es simpático(-a) el profesor (la profesora) de español?

_____

3. ¿Son difíciles las lecciones de español?

_____

4. ¿Es grande o pequeña su escuela?

_____

5. ¿Hay gatos negros en la casa?

_____

6. ¿Hay árboles altos en el jardín?

_____

7. ¿Hacen ustedes muchas tareas en casa?

_____

8. ¿Quién es perezoso(-a)?

_____

9. ¿Quiénes son fuertes?

_____

10. ¿Dónde hay muchas personas francesas?

_____

D. Complete each sentence with words chosen from the list given in parentheses. (Each word must be used in the same form as in the list.)

1. (bonita, italianos, mucho, muchos, italiano, populares, popular)

Mi amigo _____ tiene _____ discos _____,

y siempre escuchamos la música _____ en su casa.

2. (poco, gorda, poca, demasiados, muchas, gordo)

Rosita es muy _____ porque come _____ dulces y _____ carne.

3. (grandes, muchos, muchas, grande, viejos, vieja)

Mis abuelos son _____; vienen a visitarnos y traen _____

regalos de las tiendas _____ de su ciudad.

4. (bueno, buena, interesantes, muchas)

En nuestra clase siempre aprendemos _____ cosas _____.

5. (perezosa, español, fácil, perezosos, española, difícil, aplicados, fáciles)

La lengua _____ no es _____ para los alumnos

_____.

E. Pedro Méndez, a Mexican teenager, is describing his family, friends and surroundings to his pen pal, Billy. You are given part of each of his statements. Complete the sentences in Spanish.

1. We live in a white house.

Vivimos en _____.

2. Our house is on a narrow street.

Nuestra casa está en _____.

3. My sister Lola has many friends.

Mi hermana Lola tiene _____.

4. Our family reads interesting books.

Nuestra familia lee _____.

5. My other sisters, Charlotte and Helen, are popular girls.

Mis otras hermanas, Carlota y Elena, son _____.

6. The children never have enough money.

Los niños nunca tienen _____.

7. My parents prefer to shop in the small stores.

Mis padres prefieren hacer sus compras en _____.

8. My friend Albert is French and his cousin Rachel is English.

Mi amigo Alberto es _____ y su prima Raquel es _____.

9. We do not have old grandparents.

No tenemos _____.

10. We have two lazy cats and one big dog.

Tenemos dos _____ y un _____.

14
SER and ESTAR;
Using TENER and HACER
to Express "To Be"

	ser	estar	
yo	**soy**	**estoy**	I am
tú	**eres**	**estás**	you are
usted			you are
él	**es**	**está**	he is
ella			she is
nosotros (-as)	**somos**	**estamos**	we are
vosotros (-as)	**sois**	**estáis**	you (*pl.*) are
ustedes			you (*pl. formal*) are
ellos	**son**	**están**	they (*m.*) are
ellas			they (*f.*) are

How *SER* Is Used

1. Alberto **es** mi amigo.   Albert is my friend.

2. Él **es** ingeniero.   He is an engineer.

3. Él **es** mexicano.   He is Mexican.

4. Él **es** católico.   He is Catholic.

5. Él **es** alto y delgado.   He is tall and thin.

6. Él **es** inteligente.   He is intelligent.

7. Él **es** de México.   He is from Mexico.

1. The seven sentences above either *identify* or *describe* Alberto; that is,

sentence   1 tells *who* he is   5 tells his *physical makeup*

2 tells his *profession*   6 tells his *mental ability*

3 tells his *nationality*   7 tells *where he comes from*

4 tells his *religion*

How *ESTAR* Is Used

1. — ¿Dónde **está** Rosa?   Where is Rose?
— Ella **está** en la escuela.   She is at school.

2. — ¿Cómo **están** ustedes?   How are you?
— Yo **estoy** muy bien, pero Elena está   I am very well, but Helen is sick today.
enferma hoy.

3. Juan **está** cansado.   John is tired.

4. Juan **está** triste porque tiene un   John is sad because he has a test today.
examen hoy.

5. — ¿**Está** caliente el café?   Is the coffee hot?
— No, **está** frío.   No, it is cold.

6. La maestra **está** sentada a su escritorio.   The teacher is seated (sitting) at her desk.
María **está** de pie cerca del estante.   Mary is standing near the bookshelf.

The six sets of examples above illustrate the most common uses of **estar**.

Jai alai, traditional sport of the Basques, in northern Spain. The game is also popular in Mexico, Cuba, and Florida. It resembles handball but is played off three walls, on a court called a *frontón*. The jai alai player (*el pelotari*) uses a curved wicker basket (*la cesta*) attached to his wrist. He catches the ball (*la pelota*) in the basket and hurls it against the wall with great force.

2. Both **ser** and **estar** mean *to be*, but **estar** is generally used in two cases:

   a.   Location: **Estar** answers the question Where? (Example 1.)

   b.   A reversible condition that often alternates with its opposite: well and sick, sad and happy, hot and cold, seated and standing, etc. (Examples 2-6.)

Practice A: Underline the correct verb.

1.   Mi hermana (es—está) en casa ahora.

2.   Yo (soy—estoy) el hermano de José.

3.   Nosotros (somos—estamos) españoles.

4.   La leche no (es—está) fría.

5.   Ellos (son—están) muy tímidos.

6.   ¿(Eres—Estás) triste hoy?

7.   El profesor (es—está) de España.

8.   Los muchachos (son—están) sentados en el banco.

9.   Luisa (es—está) una muchacha bonita.

10.   (Somos—Estamos) cansados.

La Casa *ES* . . .

1.   La casa **es** un edificio.   The house is a building.

2.   **Es** grande.   It is big.

3.   **Es** roja.   It is red.

4.   **Es** vieja.   It is old.

5.   **Es** de madera.   It is (made) of wood. (It is wooden.)

6.   **Es** de Juan.   It is John's.

3.   In sentences 1 to 6 above, we are describing a house with respect to

1. what it is.	3. its color.	5. what it is made of.
2. how big it is (size).	4. its age.	6. to whom it belongs.

The verb **ser** is used in all such sentences.

La Casa *ESTÁ* . . .

1.   La casa **está** en la ciudad.   The house is in the city.

2.   **Está** bien construida.   It is well constructed.

3.   **Está** cerrada ahora.   It is closed now.

4. The above sentences indicate

   1. where the house is

   2. its physical state or condition

   3. a reversible state, that is, one that is easily changed to its opposite (open—closed).

The verb **estar** is used in such sentences.

   Practice B: Underline the correct verb.

1. ¿Dónde (es—está) su escuela?

2. Mi libro (es—está) azul.

3. Las paredes (son—están) verdes.

4. La ventana (es—está) abierta.

5. El niño (es—está) muy pequeño.

Summary of Differences Between *SER* and *ESTAR*

Uses of *SER*

1. Identity

   Ser tells *who* or *what* someone or something is:

      Soy médico.   **Es** una escuela.   Ellos **son** mis amigos.

2. *Personal trait or physical characteristic*

      María **es** inteligente.   Juan **es** fuerte.   El libro **es** grande.

3. *Nationality or place of origin*

      Son cubanos.   **Soy** de Chicago.   **Somos** de México.

4. *Telling time, the day of the week, the date, etc.*

   (See Chapters 19 and 20.)

Uses of *ESTAR*

1. Location

      Estar tells *where* someone or something is:

         Madrid **está** en España.   **Estamos** en la escuela.

2. A reversible state that often alternates with its opposite: sick and well, sad and happy, hot and cold, open and closed, seated and standing, etc.

         Está enfermo.   La comida **está** fría.
         María no **está** contenta.   La ventana **está** cerrada.

Observe:

a. Both **ser** and **estar** may be followed by an adjective (**son simpáticos, están contentos**), but only **ser** may be followed by a noun (**somos amigos**).

b. **Ser** is generally used with the adjectives **rico** (rich), **pobre** (poor), **viejo** (old) and **joven** (young): **Mi abuela es vieja. Juanito es joven.**

c. An adjective that follows **ser** or **estar** must agree in gender and number with the noun or pronoun it modifies (see Chapter 13):

La chica es **rica**.   **Mis amigos** esán **contentos**.

Señorita Brown, ¿es Ud. **inglesa**? **Nosotras** estamos **enfermas**.

▰▰ Using **TENER** and **HACER** to Express "To Be"

tener

tener . . . años to be . . . years old

 ¿Cuántos años tiene Ud.? How old are you?

 Tengo doce **años**.   I am twelve years old.

tener calor to be warm (hot); **tener frío**, to be cold

 Tenemos mucho **calor**.   We are very warm. (We are hot.)

 ¿Tiene ella **frío**?   Is she cold?

tener hambre to be hungry; **tener sed** to be thirsty

 ¿Tiene Ud. (mucha) **hambre**? Are you (very) hungry?

 Ellos **tienen** (mucha) **sed**. They are (very) thirsty.

tener sueño to be sleepy

 ¿Tienes (mucho) **sueño**? Are you (very) sleepy?

5. In some cases, the verb **tener** is used to translate *to be*. Such cases are called *idioms*. An idiom is an expression that cannot be translated word for word into another language.

Practice C: Write in Spanish.

 1. She is ten years old. _____

 2. We are very hungry. _____

 3. I am very sleepy. _____

 4. Are you thirsty? _____

 5. She is very cold. _____

hacer (Used in Weather Expressions)

¿Qué tiempo hace hoy?	How is the weather today?
Hace buen tiempo ahora.	The weather is good (pleasant) now.
Hace mal tiempo en el invierno.	The weather is bad in winter.
Hace mucho calor en el verano.	It is very warm (It is hot) in summer.
Hace (mucho) frío en enero.	It is (very) cold in January.
Hoy **hace (mucho) fresco.**	Today it is (very) cool.
No **hace (mucho) viento.**	It is not (very) windy.
¿Hace (mucho) sol?	Is it (very) sunny?

1. Statements about the weather can be changed to questions simply by changing the tone of voice or by adding ¿ . . . ? when written.

¿Hace frío?	Is it cold?
¿Hace sol?	Is it sunny?

2. In the present tense, only the form **hace** is used in weather expressions.

Four Ways of Translating "To Be"

1.	Mi padre **es** médico.	My father is a doctor.
2.	Mi padre **está** en el hospital.	My father is in the hospital.
3.	Hoy **hace** frío.	Today it is cold.
4.	Mi padre **tiene** sueño.	My father is sleepy.

6. **Hacer** and **tener** are sometimes translated by using the verb *to be*, although *to be* is normally expressed by **ser** or **estar**.

   Practice D: Underline the word that completes the sentence correctly—that is, choose the Spanish word that corresponds to *is* or *are*.

   1. ¿Quién no (es—está—tiene) aquí?

   2. (Tengo—Soy—Estoy) mucha hambre ahora.

   3. Ellos (tienen—son—están) amigos.

   4. ¿(Tienes—Eres—Estás) cansado ahora?

   5. En el invierno (tenemos—somos—hacemos) frío.

   6. Madrid (hace—es—está) la capital de España.

   7. Paco (tiene—es—está) enfermo hoy.

   8. Hoy (hace—está—es) mucho calor.

   9. Mi primo (tiene—es—está) diez años.

   10. Lola no (es—está—tiene) sed.

▲ EXERCISES ▲

A. In each sentence, write the correct form of **ser** or **estar** in the present tense.

1. ¿ _____ ustedes norteamericanos?

2. Mi madre _____ enferma hoy.

3. ¿Quién _____ ese hombre?

4. ¿Qué _____ estas cosas?

5. Mi tío _____ de Guatemala.

6. La sopa _____ caliente.

7. Roberto y yo _____ amigos.

8. ¿Por qué _____ tú triste?

9. Estos hombres _____ abogados.

10. Nuestra escuela _____ muy vieja.

11. Su prima _____ rica.

12. Yo _____ en mi cuarto.

13. ¿Dónde _____ sus compañeros?

14. ¿Cómo _____ su hermano hoy?

15. Esas personas _____ francesas.

16. Mi reloj _____ de plata.

17. Nosotros no _____ bien hoy.

18. Yo _____ de los Estados Unidos.

19. Las puertas no _____ abiertas.

20. El señor González no _____ pobre.

B. Complete each sentence, using the new subject. (Be sure to change the form of the adjective.)

EXAMPLE: **Mi primo es inglés.** Nosotros _____ somos ingleses _____.

1. Mis padres son viejos.   Mi madre _____.

2. ¿Es Ud. español?   ¿_____ Uds. _____?

3. Nosotros estamos contentos.   Ella _____.

4. ¿Estás tú enfermo?   ¿_____ ellos _____?

5. Yo soy rico.   Mis amigas _____.

C. Answer each question with a complete sentence in Spanish according to the pictures.

1. ¿Dónde están los muchachos ahora?

_____

2. ¿Quién es esta mujer?

_____

3. ¿Es médico su padre?

_____

4. ¿Dónde está su escuela?

_____

5. ¿Qué tiempo hace?

_____

6. ¿Cuántos años tiene Marta?

_____

7. ¿Está abierta o cerrada la puerta de la sala de clase?

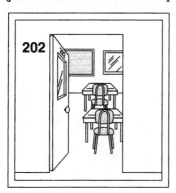

_____

8. ¿Qué tiene Carlitos?

_____

9. ¿Cómo está Benjamín hoy?

_____

10. ¿Es Manolo alto o bajo?

_____

D. In the following paragraph, fill each blank with a form of **ser**, **estar**, **tener**, or **hacer** in the present tense.

La familia López

La familia López _____ de Venezuela pero ahora _____ en Nueva

    1   2

York. La familia _____ muy grande. Los miembros de la familia

                    3

_____ el padre, la madre, los hijos José, Luis y Roberto, las hijas Rosa y María,

    4

el abuelo, la abuela y el tío Manuel. El padre _____ mecánico y _____

                                                5   6

40 años. El tío Manuel _____ profesor. Todos _____ sentados en la

                          7   8

sala ahora, excepto Luis. Las ventanas de la sala _____ cerradas porque

                                                      9

_____ frío. Hoy Luis no _____ bien y _____ mucho

    10   11   12

sueño. La madre prepara una sopa para Luis. Pero Luis no puede comer porque no

_____ hambre. Luis no _____ contento. Cuando sus amigos visitan

    13   14

a Luis, él dice: — No puedo salir hoy porque _____ enfermo.

                                                15

E. In items 1 to 5 below, read the description of each situation and the first line of the dialogue, then choose the most likely response that the second speaker would make. Circle the letter of your choice.

    1. Jorge no está en la escuela hoy porque está enfermo. El profesor llama por teléfono y habla con la madre de Jorge.

        EL PROFESOR: ¿Por qué no está Jorge en la escuela hoy?

        LA MADRE: a. Jorge está bien.
                      b. Hace buen tiempo.
                      c. Está enfermo.

    2. Felipe y Bárbara son hermanos. Por la noche miran la televisión.

        FELIPE: Este programa es muy interesante.

        BÁRBARA: a. Sí, y los actores son muy buenos.
                      b. María tiene sed.
                      c. Estamos en la calle.

    3. El padre de Luis es abogado. Un día Luis habla con su amigo Paco.

        LUIS: Mi padre es abogado. ¿Qué es tu padre?

        PACO: a. Somos abogados también.
                      b. Tiene 50 años.
                      c. Es arquitecto.

    4. Francisco está en la ciudad con su tío. Quieren comprar ropa para Francisco.

        EL TÍO: Vamos a entrar en esta tienda.

        FRANCISCO: a. Tienen calor.
                      b. La ropa aquí es muy elegante.
                      c. Estamos en casa ahora.

    5. Los alumnos están en el baile. Alfredo quiere bailar con Elena.

        ALFREDO: ¿Quieres bailar, Elena?

        ELENA: a. Gracias, pero no estoy muy bien ahora.
                      b. Sí, soy mexicana.
                      c. Sí, hace mucho viento.

F. Write the Spanish equivalent of the following.

    1. Who is thirsty?   _____

    2. Where are the tapes?   _____

    3. Henry and Philip are not tall.   _____

    4. The family is happy today.   _____

5. It is warm today. _____

6. She is my aunt. _____

7. Are you (*tú*) from Puerto Rico? _____

8. We are not French. _____

9. I am very cold. _____

10. He is an architect. (Omit *un*) _____

11. Are they sick today? _____

12. The girl is very nice (*likeable*) _____

13. They are not at home. _____

14. The dish is hot (caliente). _____

15. Are you (*tú*) 20 years old? _____

REVIEW EXERCISES: CHAPTERS 10-14

A. Rewrite each of the following paragraphs, changing its subject to the person indicated. Be careful to change articles, nouns, and adjectives when necessary.

1. Mi amigo Roberto

   Mi amigo Roberto es un muchacho bueno. Él es alto, delgado y muy inteligente. Es un alumno aplicado. Ahora él está cansado porque estudia mucho.

   Change to: Mi amiga Juana

   _____
   _____
   _____

2. Susana

   Susana es una chica española. Es rica. No es pobre. Hoy ella no está contenta porque está enferma.

   Change to: Felipe

   _____
   _____
   _____

3. Mis padres

Mis padres son jóvenes y simpáticos. Son muy inteligentes. Hoy ellos están tristes porque están muy cansados. Ellos están sentados en la sala.

Change to: Mi madre

_____

_____

_____

4. Mi casa

Vivo en una casa pequeña. La casa es roja y azul. Es vieja y muy hermosa. Está situada cerca del parque.

Change to: Mi edificio

_____

_____

_____

B. Change each of the following phrases to a sentence by inserting a form of **ser** or **estar**, as shown in the following examples.

EXAMPLE: **la puerta cerrada**   **el profesor alto**

La puerta *está* cerrada.   El profesor *es* alto.

1. los discos baratos   _____

2. las mujeres ricas   _____

3. la ventana cerrada   _____

4. el niño contento   _____

5. la muchacha rubia   _____

6. los hombres simpáticos _____

7. el alumno triste   _____

8. las puertas abiertas   _____

9. el trabajo fácil   _____

10. la noticia importante _____

C. With each group of words, form three sentences by using **ser** or **estar** to combine the given subject with expressions a, b, and c.

> **EXAMPLE:** **La escuela:**   a. grande   b. en la ciudad   c. famosa
>
> a. La escuela es grande.
> b. La escuela está en la ciudad.
> c. La escuela es famosa.

1. Mis abuelos: a. pobres   b. en el campo   c. simpáticos

a. _____

b. _____

c. _____

2. María: a. triste   b. rubia   c. joven

a. _____

b. _____

c. _____

3. Las chicas: a. enfermas   b. malas   c. gordas

a. _____

b. _____

c. _____

4. El profesor: a. inglés   b. bajo   c. contento

a. _____

b. _____

c. _____

5. Los libros: a. aquí   b. abiertos   c. interesantes

a. _____

b. _____

c. _____

D. Form a sentence stating that the article on the left belongs to the person on the right.

> **EXAMPLE:** **la pluma: el hombre**   La pluma es del hombre.

1. los libros: la profesora   _____

2. el paquete: Juanito   _____

3. las flores: las mujeres   _____

4. el mapa: el profesor   _____

5. la casa: los vecinos   _____

E. Form a sentence stating that you are giving the article on the left to the person on the right.

EXAMPLE: **el lápiz: el niño** Doy el lápiz al niño.

1. las cartas: el abogado _____

2. el dinero: los hombres _____

3. los artículos: la profesora _____

4. el periódico: Rosa _____

5. la comida: el niño _____

F. **Jumbled sentences.** The publisher's computer has gone haywire. Rearrange the following groups of words to form logical sentences.

EXAMPLE: **nueva la del es hombre casa**
La casa del hombre es nueva. Or: La casa nueva es del hombre.

1. del los interesantes son profesor libros

_____

2. coche tío mi azul es el de

_____

3. de contentas muchas están las niñas

_____

4. primos las escribimos los largas a cartas

_____

5. el doy al cuaderno profesor verde

_____

G. Read each paragraph and answer the questions that follow.

Before you begin, review the following expressions:

el deporte	the sport	**trabajador**	industrious
el jugador	the player	**casarse**	to get married
de habla española	Spanish-speaking	**el apellido**	the family name

1. El fútbol es un deporte muy popular en España y en Hispanoamérica. Es diferente al «football» de los Estados Unidos, pero hay también mucho contacto físico entre los jugadores.

In the blank, write *Sí* if the statement is true, *No* if it is false:

a. La gente juega al fútbol solamente en España. _____

b. El fútbol no es como el «football» de los Estados Unidos. _____

2. En España y en muchos otros países de habla española, la siesta es una parte importante de la vida de la gente. Generalmente las personas cierran las tiendas por tres horas y todo el mundo va a casa para comer y dormir. Después de la siesta la gente vuelve al trabajo.

Answer in Spanish.

a. ¿Dónde observan la siesta? _____

b. ¿Qué cierran durante la siesta? _____

c. ¿Para qué van todos a casa? _____

d. ¿Qué hacen las personas después de la siesta? _____

_____

3. Antonio, mi amigo español, vive en España. Su familia tiene un coche nuevo. Es un SEAT—el nombre de una marca (make) que se fabrica (is manufactured) en España—. Es un coche pequeño y es muy hermoso. No es grande como muchos coches norteamericanos.

Underline the correct answer:

a. Antonio es (1) norteamericano.   (2) español.   (3) un SEAT.

b. El SEAT es un (1) automóvil.   (2) tren   (3) niño.

c. Los coches norteamericanos son (1) pequeños.   (2) grandes.   (3) españoles.

4. María Gómez es una chica muy bonita. Juan Pérez es un chico muy trabajador. El domingo María y Juan se casan. Después, ella va a llamarse María Gómez de Pérez.

Answer in Spanish.

a. ¿Quién es María Gómez? _____

b. ¿Cómo es Juan Pérez? _____

c. ¿Qué pasa el domingo? _____

d. ¿Quién es María Gómez de Pérez? _____

5. Enrique es un chico mexicano que visita a su amigo Mike en Los Ángeles. Mike presenta a Enrique a sus amigos y dice: —Éste es mi amigo Enrique García López.

Los amigos de Mike quieren saber por qué Enrique tiene dos apellidos. Enrique explica que en su país cada persona tiene dos apellidos: el apellido de su padre y el apellido de su madre. García es el apellido del padre de Enrique; López es el apellido de su madre.

Answer in Spanish.

a. ¿De dónde es Enrique? _____

b. ¿Quién vive en Los Ángeles? _____

c. ¿Qué dice Mike a sus amigos? _____

d. ¿Cuántos apellidos tiene Enrique? _____

e. ¿Cuál es el apellido de la madre de Enrique? _____

H. Your teacher will read aloud a question in Spanish. Circle the letter of the correct answer.

1. a. enfermo
    b. en la escuela

2. a. inteligente y bonita
    b. alto y hermoso

3. a. quince
    b. hambre

4. a. mi amiga
    b. mi hijo

5. a. del gato
    b. de mi padre

6. a. en julio
    b. en febrero

7. a. muy bien
    b. en el cine

8. a. negras y azules
    b. amarilla y verde

9. a. Tengo sed.
    b. Estoy triste.

10. a. mi tío
    b. nuestros padres

Part 4
Other Adjectives, Numbers, Time

⋈⋈⋈⋈⋈⋈⋈⋈⋈⋈⋈⋈⋈⋈⋈⋈⋈⋈⋈⋈⋈⋈⋈⋈⋈⋈⋈⋈⋈⋈

15
Shortened Forms of Some Adjectives

◼◼ Adjectives That Precede the Noun

uno:	Tengo **un** libro, **una** pluma, **unos** papeles y **unas** flores.	I have a book, a pen, some papers, and some flowers.
alguno:	Tengo **algún** dinero en el banco.	I have some money in the bank.
	Tengo **algunos** amigos en Argentina.	I have some friends in Argentina.
	Tengo **alguna** idea de eso.	I have some idea of that.
	Tengo **algunas** ideas.	I have some ideas.
ninguno:	**Ningún** alumno sabe la respuesta.	No pupil knows the answer.
	Ninguna profesora está aquí.	No teacher is here.

1. The forms of **uno**, **alguno**, and **ninguno** generally precede the noun.

2. Before a masculine singular noun, **uno**, **alguno**, and **ninguno** drop the final **-o**.

3. **Ningún** and **ninguna** have the plural forms **ningunos** and **ningunas**, but these plurals are not required in any of the exercises of this book.

4. *Some* in the plural may be expressed in Spanish by either **unos**, **unas**, or **algunos**, **algunas**.

Practice A: Rewrite each phrase, replacing the word in italics with the word in parentheses.

100

EXAMPLE: una *historia*   (cuento)   _____un cuento_____

1. ninguna *alumna*   (chico)   _____
2. algunas *casas*   (edificio)   _____
3. un *libro*   (chicas)   _____
4. alguna *mesa*   (niño)   _____
5. unos *amigos*   (amiga)   _____

Adjectives That May Precede or Follow the Noun

bueno   good

Roberto es un **buen chico**.
Roberto es un **chico bueno**.   } Robert is a *good boy.*

Ellos son **buenos alumnos**.
Ellos son **alumnos buenos**.   } They are *good pupils.*

Ana es una **buena esquiadora**.
Ana es una **esquiadora buena**.   } Ann is a *good skier.*

Ellas son **buenas esquiadoras**.
Ellas son **esquiadoras buenas**.   } They are *good skiers.*

5. The forms of **bueno** may either precede or follow the noun.

6. Before a masculine singular noun, **bueno** drops the final -o.

Other Adjectives Like **bueno**

malo bad   **un mal hijo** or **un hijo malo**
primero first   **el primer capítulo** or **el capítulo primero**
tercero third   **el tercer libro** or **el libro tercero**

Practice B: Underline the proper form of the adjective.

1. Luis y José son niños (mal—malos—mala—malas).
2. Yo escribo el (tercero—tercer—tercera—terceros) ejercicio.
3. Ana y Luisa son (buenas—buen—bueno—buena) muchachas.
4. Los capítulos (primer—primero—primeros—primera) son interesantes.
5. ¿Es José un (buen—bueno—buena—buenos) chico?

grande and **gran**

Washington fue un **gran** hombre.   Washington was a *great* man.

La reina Isabel fue una **gran** mujer.   Queen Isabel was a *great* woman.

Los dos fueron **grandes** personas.   Both were *great* people.

But: Una ciudad **grande** tiene escuelas **grandes**.   A *large* city has *large* schools.

7. **Gran** before a singular noun, masculine or feminine, means *great*.

8. The plural of **gran** is **grandes**.

9. **Grande** and **grandes** used after a noun mean *large* or *big*.

▲ EXERCISES ▲

A. Little Pedro loves to correct his father every time he makes a statement or asks a question. Rewrite each statement or question according to Pedro's corrections.

EXAMPLE: **José tiene una buena *profesora.*** (profesor)
José tiene un *buen profesor.*

1. ¿Quieren ustedes algunos *lápices?* (flores)

   _____

2. Es un buen *muchacho.* (niña)

   _____

3. Vivimos en la tercera *casa.* (piso)

   _____

4. Son malos *chicos.* (chicas)

   _____

5. Ninguna *novela* es interesante. (libro)

   _____

B. This time Pedro wants to show up his father by restating what he says in another way.

EXAMPLE: **Pedro es un mal chico.** Pedro es un chico malo.

1. Luis es un aviador bueno.   _____

2. ¿Tomas tú un tercer postre?   _____

3. Ellos tienen un mal amigo.   _____

4. Las primeras frases son interesantes.   _____

5. Raúl y Felipe son amigos buenos.   _____

C. Write the correct form of the adjective in parentheses.

EXAMPLE: **(alguno)**   ¿Tienes tú ____algunos____ pañuelos?

1. (ninguno)   _____ libro es interesante.

2. (tercero)   Leemos la lección _____.

3. (bueno)   Mi tío es un _____ actor.

4. (grande)   Nueva York es una ciudad _____ .

5. (primero)   ¿Vives en el _____ piso?

6. (grande)   El presidente es un _____ hombre.

7. (alguno)   _____ familias son famosas.

8. (malo)   No tocamos los _____ discos.

9. (uno)   _____ hombre y _____ mujer van a visitar la escuela.

10. (bueno)   Cantamos una canción _____ .

D. Write the word that has the opposite meaning of the italicized word.

1. En nuestra escuela tenemos una biblioteca *pequeña*.   _____

2. José es un *buen* chico.   _____

3. *Ningún* alumno estudia hoy.   _____

4. Voy a comer el *último* dulce.   _____

5. Ana y Luisa son chicas *malas*.   _____

E. A friend of your Spanish teacher who comes from Guatemala is visiting your class. In order for her to find out how much Spanish you have learned, she asks the following questions. Answer each question with a complete Spanish sentence.

1. ¿Recibe usted buenas notas en su clase de español?

Sí, _____

2. ¿Quién fue (was) el primer presidente de los Estados Unidos?

_____

3. ¿Es una gran persona el profesor (la profesora) de español?

Sí, _____

4. ¿Viven ustedes en una ciudad grande?

No, _____

5. ¿Cuál es el tercer mes del año?

_____

6. ¿Cuándo hace mal tiempo en su ciudad (pueblo)?

_____

7. ¿Mira usted un programa de televisión a las nueve de la noche?

No, _____

8. ¿Tiene usted algún dinero?

Sí, _____

9. ¿Lee su padre alguna revista por la noche?

Sí, _____

10. ¿Pasan ustedes un buen día en la escuela?

No, _____

F. Complete each sentence in Spanish.

1. Some boys are not playing today.

_____ no juegan hoy.

2. Today is not a bad day. (Say it in two ways.)

a. Hoy no es _____.

b. Hoy no es _____.

3. Toledo is a great city but not a large city.

Toledo es _____ pero no _____.

4. Are you writing the third exercise? (Say it in two ways.)

a. ¿Escribes tú _____?

b. ¿Escribes tú _____?

5. No student knows the answer.

_____ sabe la respuesta.

6. No house is small on this street.

_____ es pequeña en esta calle.

7. Are you eating in a good restaurant? (Say it in two ways.)

a. ¿Comen ustedes en _____.

b. ¿Comen ustedes en _____.

8. We live in the first building of the first street. (Say it in two ways.)

a. Vivimos en _____ de _____.

b. Vivimos en _____ de _____.

9. I have some Mexican coins.

Yo tengo _____ monedas mejicanas.

10. For the trip we need one coat and one jacket.

Para el viaje necesitamos _____ y _____.

16
Demonstrative Adjectives: "This" and "These," "That" and "Those"

▰ Este(-a), Estos(-as)

Leo **este** libro y **esta** revista.   I am reading *this* book and *this* magazine.

Leemos **estos** libros y **estas** revistas.   We are reading *these* books and *these* magazines.

1. *This* is expressed in Spanish by **este** before a masculine noun, **esta** before a feminine noun.

2. *These* is expressed in Spanish by **estos** before a masculine noun, **estas** before a feminine noun.

Practice A: Write the correct Spanish form for *this* or *these* before each noun.

1. _____ casa   4. _____ mano

2. _____ hombres   5. _____ ciudades

3. _____ día   6. _____ señor

▰ Ese(-a), Esos(-as)

¿Ve usted **ese** papel y **esa** pluma?   Do you see *that* paper and *that* pen?

¿Ven ustedes **esos** papeles y **esas** plumas?   Do you see *those* papers and *those* pens?

3. *That* is expressed in Spanish by **ese** before a masculine noun, **esa** before a feminine noun.

4. *Those* is expressed in Spanish by **esos** before a masculine noun, **esas** before a feminine noun.

Practice B: Write the correct Spanish form for *that* or *those* before each noun.

1. _____ manos   4. _____ sillas

2. _____ días   5. _____ chico

3. _____ profesor   6. _____ mujer

Aquel(-la), Aquellos(-as)

¿Ven Uds. **aquel** edificio y **aquella** iglesia?

Do you see *that* building (over there) and *that* church (over there)?

¿Ven Uds. **aquellos** edificios y **aquellas** iglesias?

Do you see *those* buildings (over there) and *those* churches (over there)?

5. Both **ese(-a)** and **aquel(-la)** mean *that*; both **esos(-as)** and **aquellos(-as)** mean *those*. **Ese** and **esos** point out nearby objects or persons, whereas **aquel** and **aquellos** point out objects or persons that are at some distance from the speaker and the person spoken to.

Practice C: Write the correct Spanish form for *that* or *those* (over there) before each noun.

1. _____ toro
4. _____ muchacho

2. _____ señora
5. _____ papeles

3. _____ revistas
6. _____ árboles

◄ EXERCISES ►

A. Change the italicized words from the singular to the plural, or vice versa.

EXAMPLES: **¿Tiene Ud.** *ese papel?*   ¿Tiene Ud. esos papeles?
No veo *aquella casa.*   No veo aquellas casas.

1. ¿Estudian ellos *esas lenguas?*   _____

2. Ponemos *este plato* en la mesa.   _____

3. Vivimos en *esa casa.*   _____

4. ¿Quién hace *ese trabajo?*   _____

5. En la distancia vemos *aquellas montañas.*   _____

6. Mis amigos trabajan en *estas tiendas.*   _____

7. Tenemos que tomar *esos trenes.*   _____

8. Queremos comprar *estos automóviles.*   _____

9. Siempre jugamos en *aquel parque.*   _____

10. No comprendo *esta regla.*   _____

B. Pedro is at it again. When Ana makes a statement or asks a question, Pedro likes to substitute his own noun for hers. Play the role of Pedro as in the model.

EXAMPLE: **Quiero *ese libro*. (revista)**   esa revista

1. ¿Vives en *ese barrio*? (avenida) _____

2. *Aquella tienda* es grande. (edificio) _____

3. *Esta película* es interesante. (cuento) _____

4. Hoy visitamos *aquellos museos*. (iglesias) _____

5. Quiero comer *este postre*. (ensalada) _____

6. *Esas camas* son cómodas. (sillones) _____

7. ¿Sabe Ud. *esas lenguas*? (verbos) _____

8. ¿Hablas tú con *estos hombres*? (mujeres) _____

9. Siempre compramos en *aquel supermercado*. (bodega) _____

10. No podemos hacer *esos ejercicios*. (tareas) _____

C. You are in a restaurant. Each time the waiter/waitress asks you a question, you answer using the opposite demonstrative adjective. Do not use the forms of **aquel**.

EXAMPLE: **¿Quiere Ud. este pastel?**   No, quiero ese pastel.

1. ¿Toma Ud. este plato? _____

2. ¿Come Ud. esas frutas? _____

3. ¿Desea Ud. ese postre? _____

4. ¿Bebe Ud. esta naranjada? _____

5. ¿Lleva Ud. a casa estos panecillos? _____

D. Complete the sentences in Spanish. Use a form of **aquel** when *over there* appears in parentheses.

1. We are going to eat that meat, those potatoes, these vegetables, and this dessert.

   Vamos a comer _____, _____,

   _____ y _____.

2. I want to buy those flowers (over there), this newspaper, these magazines, and that wallet.

   Quiero comprar _____, _____,

   _____ y _____.

3. I am going to speak with this man, that girl, these women, and that boy.

Voy a hablar con _____, _____,

_____ y _____.

4. During the lesson we use that chalk board (over there), these books, this notebook, and those pencils.

Durante la lección usamos _____, _____

, _____ y _____.

5. When it rains I wear those shoes, this hat, these pants, and that raincoat (over there). I also use that umbrella.

Cuando llueve llevo _____, _____,

_____ y _____. También uso

_____.

17
Possessive Adjectives: "My," "Your," "His," "Her," "Our," "Their"

MY

Yo tengo **mi** abrigo.	I have my coat.
mi corbata.	my tie.
mis abrigos.	my coats.
mis corbatas.	my ties.

YOUR, familiar singular

Tú hablas con **tu** hermano.	You speak with your brother.
tu tía.	your aunt.
tus hermanos.	your brothers.
tus tías.	your aunts.

YOUR, formal singular

Ud. vende **su** libro.	You sell your book.
su casa.	your house.
sus libros.	your books.
sus casas.	your houses.

HIS

Él tiene **su** lápiz.	He has his pencil.
su pluma.	his pen.
sus lápices.	his pencils.
sus plumas.	his pens.

HER

Ella estudia **su** ejercicio.	She studies her exercise.
su lección.	her lesson.
sus ejercicios.	her exercises.
sus lecciones.	her lessons.

OUR

Nosotros visitamos **nuestro** pueblo.	We visit our town.
nuestra ciudad.	our city.
nuestros pueblos.	our towns.
nuestras ciudades.	our cities.

YOUR, familiar plural

Vosotros vais a **vuestro** banco.	You go to your bank.
vuestra iglesia.	your church.
vuestros bancos.	your banks.
vuestras iglesias.	your churches.

YOUR, formal plural

Uds. leen **su** periódico.	You read your newspaper.
su revista.	your magazine.
sus periódicos.	your newspapers.
sus revistas.	your magazines.

THEIR, masculine

Ellos comen en **su** restaurante favorito.	They eat at their favorite restaurant.
su cafetería favorita.	their favorite cafeteria.
sus restaurantes favoritos.	their favorite restaurants.
sus cafeterías favoritas.	their favorite cafeterias.

THEIR, feminine

Ellas juegan en **su** cuarto.	They play in their room.
su escuela.	their school.
sus cuartos.	their rooms.
sus escuelas.	their schools.

1. The only possessive adjectives that have *four* forms (masculine singular, feminine singular, masculine plural, and feminine plural) are **nuestro** and **vuestro**. The other possessive adjectives have only a singular and a plural form. That is, no distinction is made between masculine and feminine.

2. The possessive adjective must have the same gender (masculine or feminine) and number (singular or plural) as the noun that immediately follows it:

Juan lee su̱s libro̱s.	John reads his books.
Contamos nuestro̱ dinero̱.	We count our money.

3. **Su** and **sus** can mean *his, her, its, your,* or *their,* depending on the subject:

Ella habla con **sus** amigos.	*She* speaks with *her* friends.
Él habla con **sus** amigos.	*He* speaks with *his* friends.
Ellos hablan con **su** amigo.	*They* speak with *their* friend.

▲ EXERCISES ▲

A. Change the words in italics by using the plural form of the noun.

    EXAMPLE: **¿Tiene usted su *pluma?***   sus plumas

    1. ¿Le escribes tú a *tu tío?*   _____

    2. Yo no quiero estudiar *mi lección.*   _____

    3. José vende *su coche.*   _____

    4. Hablamos con *nuestra amiga.*   _____

    5. ¿Habláis con *vuestro profesor?*   _____

B. Change the words in italics by using the singular form of the noun.

    1. No tengo *mis cuadernos.*   _____

    2. Queremos vender *nuestras bicicletas.*   _____

    3. Ella compra *sus libros* en la Librería López.   _____

    4. ¿Tienes *tus llaves?*   _____

    5. Quiero usar *sus ideas.*   _____

C. Write the Spanish form of the possessive adjective in parentheses.

    1. (our)   ¿Dónde está _____ profesora?

    2. (her)   Ella no tiene _____ blusas.

    3. (their)   ¿Tienen ellos _____ automóvil?

    4. (my)   _____ amigos son muy simpáticos.

    5. (your)   ¿Hablas tú con _____ abuelos?

    6. (his)   _____ escuela es grande.

    7. (your)   ¿Quieren Uds. _____ periódico?

    8. (our)   ¿Cuándo vienen _____ primos?

    9. (my)   Voy a la escuela con _____ hermana.

    10. (her)   _____ padre es arquitecto.

La Isla de Pascua. La Isla de Pascua (Easter Island) is located about 2300 miles west of the coast of Chile. It is so named because it was discovered on Easter Sunday, 1722, by the Dutch discoverer Jacob Roggeveen. The most interesting aspect of the island are the *Moai*, some 600 stone statues that are found along the coast. They are erected on pedestals called *ahus*. When the Norwegian anthropologist Thor Heyerdahl arrived at the island in 1947, he found all the statues overturned and he restored them to their *ahus*. According to legend, the *moai* walked by themselves to be placed on their *ahus*. According to archaeologists, the *moai* were transported on boards of wood pulled by ropes made of tree fibers.

D. Change the word in italics to the possessive adjective that corresponds to the new subject.

EXAMPLE: **Yo tengo *mis* discos en casa.**   Ella tiene ____sus____ discos en casa.

1. ¿Escribe Ud. a *sus* abuelos?   ¿Escribes tú a _____ abuelos?

2. ¿Dónde ponen ellos *su* ropa?   ¿Dónde ponemos _____ ropa?

3. Escribo a *mis* amigos en España.   Escriben a _____ amigo en España.

4. Nosotros vamos a *nuestra* escuela.   Ellos van a _____ escuela.

5. Anita va en *su* coche.   Yo voy en _____ coche.

6. ¿Reciben Uds. *su* dinero?   ¿Recibís vosotros _____ dinero?

7. Mi amigo viene con *su* hermano.   Tú vienes con _____ hermano.

8. Tú tocas *tus* discos todo el día.   Yo toco _____ discos todo el día.

9. ¿Traen ellas *sus* guitarras?   ¿Trae él _____ guitarras?

10. Esta noche estamos en *nuestra* casa.   Esta noche Isabel está en _____ casa.

E.   Answer each question as indicated in parentheses.

   EXAMPLE: **¿Tienes tu libro?**   (sí)   Sí, tengo mi libro.

   1.   ¿Escribe usted a su profesor en el verano?   (no)

   _____

   2.   ¿Cuándo toca usted sus cintas?   (por la noche)

   _____

   3.   ¿Es grande nuestra escuela?   (sí)

   _____

   4.   Dónde prepara su padre las comidas?   (en la cocina)

   _____

   5.   ¿Qué aprenden ustedes en su clase de español?   (muchas cosas)

   _____

   6.   ¿Quiere usted tener mi libro?   (sí)

   _____

   7.   ¿Desea usted vivir en su escuela?   (no)

   _____

   8.   ¿Trae usted su cama a la escuela?   (no)

   _____

   9.   ¿Van ustedes al cine con su profesor de español?   (sí)

   _____

   10.   ¿Cuándo hablan ustedes por teléfono con sus amigos?   (todos los días)

   _____

F.   Complete the Spanish sentences according to the English.

   1.   Our records are very old.

   _____ son muy viejos.

   2.   Where are your (*fam. sing.*) books?

   ¿Dónde están _____?

   3.   Their class is interesting.

   _____ es interesante.

   4.   My friends live in the country.

   _____ viven en el campo.

   5.   Does your father have his newspapers?

   ¿Tiene su padre _____?

6. Where do you buy your shirts?

    ¿Dónde compráis _____?

7. Our mother works in the city.

    _____ trabaja en la ciudad.

8. Her shoes are very expensive.

    _____ son muy caros.

9. Do you have your ticket?

    ¿Tiene usted _____?

10. His books are on the table.

    _____ están en la mesa.

11. My house has seven rooms.

    _____ tiene siete habitaciones.

12. Our parents are not home.

    _____ no están en casa.

13. Do you have your money?

    ¿Tiene _____?

14. Their church is new.

    _____ es nueva.

15. What is his answer?

    ¿Cuál es _____?

18
Numbers from 0 to 1999

Numbers From 0 to 99

0	**cero**	6	**seis**
1	**uno, un, una**	7	**siete**
2	**dos**	8	**ocho**
3	**tres**	9	**nueve**
4	**cuatro**	10	**diez**
5	**cinco**		

11	**once**	16	**dieciséis (diez y seis)**
12	**doce**	17	**diecisiete (diez y siete)**
13	**trece**	18	**dieciocho (diez y ocho)**
14	**catorce**	19	**diecinueve (diez y nueve)**
15	**quince**		

20	**veinte**	25	**veinticinco (veinte y cinco)**
21	**veintiuno (veinte y uno)**	26	**veintiséis (veinte y seis)**
22	**veintidós (veinte y dos)**	27	**veintisiete (veinte y siete)**
23	**veintitrés (veinte y tres)**	28	**veintiocho (veinte y ocho)**
24	**veinticuatro (veinte y cuatro)**	29	**veintinueve (veinte y nueve)**

30	**treinta**	70	**setenta**
35	**treinta y cinco**	73	**setenta y tres**
40	**cuarenta**	80	**ochenta**
47	**cuarenta y siete**	86	**ochenta y seis**
50	**cincuenta**	90	**noventa**
58	**cincuenta y ocho**	99	**noventa y nueve**
60	**sesenta**		
62	**sesenta y dos**		

1. *One* is **un** before a masculine noun, **una** before a feminine noun: **un** libro, **una** casa. The Spanish words for 21, 31, 41, etc., also obey this rule:

> veinti**ún** (veinte y **un**) **cuadernos**   cuarenta y **un hombres**
> veinti**una** (veinte y **una**) **plumas**   sesenta y **una mujeres**

2. The numbers 16 to 19 and 21 to 29 may be written one word or as three words:

> **diecisiete**
> *or* } páginas
> **diez y siete**

> **veintinueve**
> *or* } chicos
> **veinte y nueve**

Remember that the following words take accent marks: **dieciséis, veintiún, veintidós, veintitrés, veintiséis.**

3. Except for 1, 21, 31, etc., Spanish number-words do not change in gender: **cuatro** casas, **cincuenta** hombres, etc.

Practice A: Write the Spanish words for the numbers in parentheses. Where two blanks are given, write the number in two ways. (Be careful to notice the gender of nouns preceded by 1, 21, 31, etc.)

1. (19) _____ _____ casas

2. (61) _____ hombres

3. (11) _____ personas

4. (35) _____ alumnos

5. (1) _____ chico

6. (12) _____ flores

7. (91) _____ estrellas

8. (15) _____ museos

9. (14) _____ parques

10. (42) _____ programas

11. (21) _____ _____ días

12. (9) _____ lenguas

13. (86) _____ países

14. (1) _____ padre

15. (75) _____ mercados

16. (17) _____ _____ años

17. (23) _____ _____ manzanas

18. (10) _____ profesores

19. (13) _____ escuelas

20. (1) _____ niña

Numbers From 100 to 1999

100	**cien, ciento**	500	**quinientos, quinientas**
103	**ciento tres**	600	**seiscientos, seiscientas**
156	**ciento cincuenta y seis**	700	**setecientos, setecientas**
		800	**ochocientos, ochocientas**
200	**doscientos, doscientas**	900	**novecientos, novecientas**
201	**doscientos uno**		
		1000	**mil**
300	**trescientos, trescientas**	1009	**mil nueve**
398	**trescientos noventa y ocho**	1034	**mil treinta y cuatro**
		1114	**mil ciento catorce**
400	**cuatrocientos, cuatrocientas**	1575	**mil quinientos setenta y cinco**
426	**cuatrocientos veinte y seis**	1999	**mil novecientos noventa y nueve**

Cien, Ciento

cien vasos	100 glasses
cien sillas	100 chairs
ciento un muchachos	101 boys
ciento una muchachas	101 girls
ciento cuarenta y siete dólares	147 dollars

4. Exactly 100 of anything is expressed by **cien**:

—¿Cuántos(-as) tiene Ud.?	"How many do you have?"
—Tengo **cien**.	"I have 100 (of them)."

5. In numbers 101 to 199, **ciento** is used.

6. 101 followed by a masculine noun is **ciento un**; 101 followed by a feminine noun is **ciento una**. The form **ciento uno** is used only in counting or when referring to a masculine noun that is understood but not expressed:

—¿Cuántos libros tiene Ud.?	"How many books do you have?
—Tengo **ciento uno**.	"I have 101 (of them)."

—cientos, —cientas

trescientos **hombres**	300 men
trescientas **mujeres**	300 women
mil novecient**os** once **edificios**	1911 buildings
mil novecient**as** once **páginas**	1911 pages
mil quinient**os** **un chicos**	1501 boys
mil quinient**as** **una chicas**	1501 girls

7. The numbers 200 to 900 end in **-os** if followed by a masculine noun, and in **-as** if followed by a feminine noun. Note that this gender agreement occurs even when other number-words come between the hundreds and the noun:

setecient**os** veinte y tres dólar**es**

trescient**as** cuarenta y cinco **casas**

8. The conjunction **y** (*and*) occurs only between the tens and units digits:

	cuarenta **y** cinco	45
but:	tres mil siete	3007

Practice B: Before each noun, write the Spanish words for the number in parentheses.

1. (113) _____ libros

2. (121) _____ días

3. (257) _____ años

4. (314) _____ palabras

   5. (501) _____ alumnos

   6. (836) _____ automóviles

   7. (100) _____ personas

   8. (1018) _____ cajas

   9. (1751) _____ casas

   10. (1999) _____ platos

   ### Arithmetical Expressions

¿Cuántos son tres y (más) ocho?	How much is 3 + 8? (How much are 3 and 8?)
Tres y (más) ocho son once.	3 + 8 = 11.
Diez menos cuatro son seis.	10 − 4 = 6.
Siete por cuatro son veintiocho.	7 × 4 = 28.

9. In Spanish, *plus* (+) is **y** or **más**, *minus* (−) is **menos**, *times* (×) is **por** and *equals* (=) is **son**.

   Practice C: Write the following operations in Spanish words.

   EXAMPLE: **19 − 13 = 6**   Diecinueve menos trece son seis.

   1. 5 × 6 = 30.   _____

   2. 25 − 23 = 2.   _____

   3. 14 + 37 = 51.   _____

   4. 4 × 5 = 20.   _____

   5. 46 + 17 = 63.   _____

▲ EXERCISES ▲

A. Show how you would express the telephone numbers of some of your friends. Express each number in two ways as shown in the example.

   EXAMPLE: Felipe: **El número de teléfono de Felipe es 953-1097.**
   a. nueve–cinco–tres–uno–cero–nueve–siete
   b. nueve–cincuenta y tres–diez–noventa y siete

   1. Roberto: 431-2649

      a. _____

      b. _____

   2. Gloria: 725-2323

      a. _____

      b. _____

   3. Benito: 698-4261

      a. _____

      b. _____

   4. Magdalena: 284-3011

      a. _____

      b. _____

   5. Sofía: 556-6857

      a. _____

      b. _____

B. Write out the following addresses.

   EXAMPLE: 375 18th Street: calle dieciocho, número trescientos setenta y cinco

   1. 597 42nd St. _____

   2. 752 98th St. _____

   3. 409 56th St. _____

   4. 311 23rd St. _____

   5. 910 65th St. _____

C. Show how the following people applying for a job would give their social security number.

   EXAMPLE: Mi número del seguro social es: 096-24-8504
               cero—nueve—seis—dos—cuatro—ocho—cinco—cero—cuatro

   1. 113–23–0942 _____

   2. 075–09–4567 _____

   3. 254–49–0889 _____

   4. 115–06–2354 _____

   5. 001–52–7891 _____

D. Answer the following questions in complete Spanish sentences, writing all numbers as *words*.

   1. ¿Cuántos días hay en un año?

   _____

2. ¿Cuántos alumnos hay en su clase de español?

_____

3. ¿Cuántos huevos hay en una docena?

_____

4. ¿Cuántos meses hay en cuatro años?

_____

5. ¿Cuántos años hay en un siglo?

_____

6. ¿Cuántos días tiene el mes de enero?

_____

7. ¿Cuál es el número de teléfono de su escuela?

_____

8. ¿Cuántos son diez por nueve?

_____

9. ¿Cuántas teclas (_keys_) tiene una computadora?

_____

10. ¿En qué año estamos?

_____

11. ¿Cuántos segundos hay en tres minutos?

_____

12. ¿Cuántas horas hay en una semana?

_____

13. ¿Cuántos son setecientos cincuenta y ocho más novecientos noventa y dos?

_____

14. ¿Cuántos zapatos hay en treinta y un pares?

_____

15. ¿En qué año nació Ud. (_were you born_)?

Yo nací en _____.

E. Complete each sentence in Spanish writing all numbers as _words_.

1. In my school there are 1576 pupils: 872 girls and 704 boys.

En mi escuela hay _____ alumnos:

_____ muchachas y _____

muchachos.

2. I have 61 dollars.

Tengo _____ dólares.

3. 1898 is the year of the Spanish-American War.

_____ es el año de la guerra entre España y

los Estados Unidos.

4. George Washington was elected president in 1789.

Jorge Washington fue elegido presidente en

_____.

5. This book has 288 pages.

Este libro tiene _____ páginas.

6. García Márquez, the Nobel Prize winner of literature, was born in 1928.

García Márquez, el ganador del premio Nobel de literatura, nació en

_____.

7. The vacation lasts 71 days.

Las vacaciones duran _____ días.

8. In our city there are 1654 streets.

En nuestra ciudad hay _____ calles.

9. My coat costs $113.

Mi abrigo cuesta _____ dólares.

10. There are 100 céntimos in a peseta.

Hay _____ céntimos en una peseta.

F. For the mathematical whizzes. Continue the following series in spelled-out Spanish numbers.

1. 4, 7, 10, 13, _____, _____, _____,

_____, _____, _____.

2. 3, 6, 10, 15, _____, _____, _____,

_____, _____.

3. 2, 4, 8, _____, _____, _____,

_____, _____.

4. 984, 492, _____, _____.

5. 1, 9, 17, _____, _____, _____,

_____, _____.

19
Days, Months, Dates, Seasons

■▶ Los Días De La Semana

FEBRERO					
lunes		3	10	17	24
martes		4	11	18	25
miércoles		5	12	19	26
jueves		6	13	20	27
viernes		7	14	21	28
sábado	1	8	15	22	
domingo	2	9	16	23	

lunes	Monday	**viernes**	Friday
martes	Tuesday	**sábado**	Saturday
miércoles	Wednesday	**domingo**	Sunday
jueves	Thursday		

—**¿Qué día es hoy?**
—**Hoy es jueves.**

What day is (it) today?
Today is Thursday.

El viernes vamos al cine.
No vamos a la escuela **los sábados** y **los domingos.**

On Friday we are going to the movies.
We do not go to school on Saturday and Sunday ("on Saturdays and on Sundays").

Vamos a la escuela **los lunes, los martes, los miércoles, los jueves y los viernes.**

We go to school on Monday, Tuesday, Wednesday, Thursday, and Friday ("on Mondays, on Tuesdays, on Wednesdays, ...").

1. *On* followed by a day of the week is expressed by **el** in Spanish if the day is in the singular. If the day is in the plural, **los** is used.

2. In English, the names of the days are often used in the singular even when they refer to more than one day. For example, on *Saturday* may mean either a particular Saturday or every Saturday. To express that idea in Spanish, you must decide which meaning is intended:

   We are going to the movies *on Saturday.*   Vamos al cine **el sábado.**
   We go to the movies *on Saturday.*   Vamos al cine **los sábados.**

3. The names of the five weekdays end in **-s** in both the singular and the plural: **el jueves, los jueves**.

122

4. The Spanish names for the days of the week are not capitalized as in English.

5. The week in Hispanic countries starts on Monday.

Practice A: Complete the Spanish sentences.

1. On Wednesdays we do not watch TV.

_____ no miramos la televisión.

2. They generally visit their grandparents on Friday.

Generalmente visitan a sus abuelos _____.

3. What are you doing on Sunday?

¿Qué haces _____?

4. On Monday my uncle is coming to our house.

_____ mi tío viene a nuestra casa.

5. We play soccer on Thursdays.

Jugamos al fútbol _____.

Los Meses Del Año

enero	January	**julio**	July
febrero	February	**agosto**	August
marzo	March	**septiembre**	September
abril	April	**octubre**	October
mayo	May	**noviembre**	November
junio	June	**diciembre**	December

6. As with the names of the days, the Spanish names of the months are not capitalized.

Practice B: Complete each sentence with the name of the appropriate month.

1. Celebramos la Navidad en el mes de _____.

2. El primer mes de año es _____.

3. No vamos a la escuela en los meses de _____ y _____.

4. El tercer mes del año es _____.

5. El otoño empieza en el mes de _____.

La Fecha

¿Cuál es la fecha (de hoy)?	What is the date (today)?
Hoy es **el primero de mayo**.	Today is May 1st ("the first of May").
Viene **el** dos de junio.	He is coming on June 2nd.
Es **el veintiuno de noviembre**.	It is November 21st.
Hoy es el trece **de** abril de dos mil tres.	Today is April 13th, 2003.

7. The preposition **de** is used to separate the month from the number: August 5 = el cinco **de** agosto.

8. With the exception of **el primero**, the cardinal numbers (**dos, seis, veinte**, etc.) are used in dates.

9. *On* before a date is expressed by **el** in Spanish.

10. Unlike English, which expresses the year in abbreviated form (1937 = <u>nineteen thirty-seven</u>), Spanish expresses the year fully:

$$1937 = \textbf{mil novecientos treinta y siete}$$
("one thousand nine hundred thirty-seven")

Practice C: Write the following dates in Spanish words.

EXAMPLE: **(on) June 19, 1762** el diecinueve de junio de mil setecientos sesenta y dos

1. (on) July 1, 1929 _____

2. (on) January 5, 1876 _____

3. (on) October 30, 1684 _____

4. (on) November 28, 1513 _____

5. (on) August 12, 1706 _____

Las Estaciones Del Año

(Review the weather expressions listed on page 88.)

| **la primavera** spring | **el otoño** autumn (fall) |
| **el verano** summer | **el invierno** winter |

En **el** verano generalmente hace calor. It is generally warm in the summer (the summertime).
La primavera es una estación bonita. Spring (The springtime) is a very pretty season.

11. The names of the seasons in Spanish are generally preceded by the definite article (**el** or **la**). The seasons are masculine except for **la primavera**.

Practice D: Write the Spanish name of the season.

1. _____ Hace mucho frío.

2. _____ Estación que viene después de la primavera.

3. _____ Empieza el veinte y uno de septiembre.

4. _____ Termina el veinte de junio.

5. _____ Hace mucho calor.

▲ EXERCISES ▲

A. Make the statements true by changing the words in italics. Write the correct words in the blank spaces at the right.

1. En *el invierno* vamos a la playa a nadar.   _____

2. *Marzo* es el segundo mes del año.   _____

3. Si hoy es martes, mañana es *domingo*.   _____

4. *Enero* viene después de marzo.   _____

5. Hace frío en el mes de *agosto*.   _____

6. En *el verano* llevamos mucha ropa.   _____

7. *La primavera* comienza en septiembre.   _____

8. *Los jueves y los viernes* no vamos a la escuela.   _____

9. En el año hay doce *semanas*.   _____

10. En *noviembre* comenzamos las vacaciones de verano.   _____

11. *El mes* tiene siete días.   _____

12. *Julio* tiene veintiocho días.   _____

13. El año tiene cuatro *meses*.   _____

14. *El otoño* termina el veinte de junio.   _____

15. Si ayer fue (was) *viernes*, hoy es domingo.   _____

═══ HOLY WEEK (SEMANA SANTA) IN SEVILLE ═══

Every year, from Palm Sunday to Easter Sunday, the city of Seville (Sevilla) in southern Spain celebrates *Semana Santa*, or Holy Week. During this week the inhabitants of Seville (los sevillanos) dress up in the most elegant fashion. In the streets there are processions that accompany the famous *pasos*, or *floats* that represent religious scenes. Thousands of spectators line the streets to see the floats pass by. The culminating point of these parades occurs on the famous narrow street called *Sierpes*. The paraders pass very carefully through this street in order not to damage the floats. When the paraders leave *Calle Sierpes*, they pass by the City Hall bound for the Cathedral where they receive blessings. Afterward they return to their own parishes with the floats. The route that each float must follow is fixed in advance and the march to the Cathedral takes about twelve hours. Even before and after Semana Santa there are many fairs, carnivals, bullfights, and horseriding spectacles. For several weeks Seville is the most exciting and crowded city in Spain.

B.   Answer each question with a complete Spanish sentence.

   1.   ¿En qué estación hace buen tiempo generalmente?

   _____

   2.   ¿En qué mes celebras tu cumpleaños?

   _____

   3.   ¿Asisten ustedes a la escuela los sábados y los domingos?

   _____

   4.   ¿En qué fecha celebramos el día de la independencia de los Estados Unidos?

   _____

   5.   ¿En qué estación hay muchas flores en los jardines?

   _____

   6.   ¿Cuántos meses tienen treinta días? ¿Cuáles son?

   _____

   7.   ¿Cuántos meses tienen treinta y un días? ¿Cuáles son?

   _____

   8.   ¿Qué mes tiene veinte y ocho días?

   _____

   9.   ¿En qué mes volvemos a la escuela después de las vacaciones de verano?

   _____

   10.   ¿Hace calor generalmente en el invierno?

   _____

   11.   ¿En que fecha celebramos el Año Nuevo?

   _____

   12.   ¿Qué días mira usted la televisión?

   _____

   13.   ¿Qué día es mañana?

   _____

   14.   ¿Cuál es la fecha de hoy?

   _____

   15.   ¿Hay mucha nieve en julio?

   _____

C. Write a complete sentence in Spanish describing the following pictures. Utilize the guides as shown in the example.

EXAMPLE:

En _____ **los** _____ _____ .
sobre el hielo. (patinar = to skate**)**
En el invierno los muchachos patinan sobre el hielo.

1.

En la _____ hace _____ .

2.

JUNE 1983						
SUN	MON	TUE	WED	THU	FRI	SAT
Mexico			1	2	3	4
5	6	7	8	9	10	11
12	13	14	15	16	17	18
19	20	21	22	23	24	25
26	27	28	29	30		

El _____ vamos _____ .

3.

_____ y _____ son meses del _____ .

4.

Carlitos celebra su _____ el _____.

5.

Nací _____.

6.

Los meses del _____ son _____, _____,

_____ y _____.

7.

JUNE 1983						
SUN	MON	TUE	WED	THU	FRI	SAT
			1	2	3	4
5	6	7	8	9	10	11
12	13	14	15	16	17	18
19	20	21	22	23	24	25
26	27	28	29	30		

¿Qué hacen ustedes _____?

8.

Visitamos a _____ los _____.

9.

La Segunda Guerra Mundial empezó _____.

10.

Volvemos a la _____ en _____.

20
Clock Time

¿Qué hora es?	What time is it?
Es la una.	It is one o'clock.
Son las dos (tres, cuatro, etc.).	It is two (three, four, etc.) o'clock.

1. To tell time in Spanish, start with **Son las** and add the number of the hour. The exception is one o'clock: **Es la una.**

"A Quarter Past" and "Half Past"

Es la una **y cuarto**.	It is a quarter past one.
Es la una **y media**.	It is half past one.
Son las ocho **y cuarto**.	It is 8:15.
Son las diez **y media**.	It is 10:30.

2. To express a quarter past the hour, add **y cuarto** to the hour; to express half past the hour, add **y media** to the hour.

Practice A: Write in Spanish.

1. 9:15. _____

2. 12:30. _____

3. 7:30. _____

4. 1:15. _____

5. 1:30. _____

Expressing Minutes After the Hour

Es la una **y diez**.	It is ten (minutes) past one. (It is 1:10.)
Son las nueve **y veinte**.	It is twenty (minutes) past nine. (It is 9:20.)
Son las dos **y diecisiete**.	It is seventeen (minutes) after two. (It is 2:17.)

3. To express time past or after the hour (but not beyond the half-hour), add **y** and the number of minutes.

Practice B: Write in Spanish the time shown on the following digital clocks.

1. `6:25`

_____

2. `1:13`

_____

3 `11:11`

_____

4. `3:02`

_____

5. `9:28`

_____

Expressing Time Past the Half-Hour

Son las diez **menos cuarto**.	It is a quarter to ten. (It is 9:45.)
Son las tres **menos cinco**.	It is five (minutes) to three. (It is 2:55.)
Es la una **menos veinte**.	It is twenty (minutes) to one. (It is 12:40.)

4. To express time after the half-hour, start with the next hour and subtract the number of minutes from the next hour. Remember to start with the coming hour. (*It is* 11:50 is the same as *It is ten minutes to twelve:* **Son las doce menos diez.**)

Practice C: Write in Spanish.

1. It is twelve minutes to four. _____

2. It is 7:43. _____

3. It is 12:52. _____

4. It is 9:38. _____

5. It is a quarter of two. _____

Expressing "A.M." and "P.M." in Spanish

Son las seis **de la mañana**.	It is 6:00 A.M.
Es la una **de la tarde**.	It is 1:00 P.M.
Son las diez y veinte **de la noche**.	It is 10:20 P.M.
Es mediodía.	It is 12:00 noon.
Es medianoche.	It is 12:00 midnight.

5. Between 12:01 A.M. and noon, we add **de la mañana** to the time to indicate A.M.

6. Between 12:00 noon and nightfall, we add **de la tarde** to indicate P.M. From nightfall to midnight, we add **de la noche** to indicate P.M.

7. *Noon* is **mediodía**; *midnight* is **medianoche**.

8. In Spanish-speaking countries, it is actual darkness that determines whether the afternoon has ended. Thus, if there is still light in the sky, 7:30 P.M. will be expressed as "las siete y media **de la tarde**."

Practice D: Write in Spanish.

1. It is 10:30 A.M. _____

2. It is 5:10 P.M. _____

3. It is 11:45 P.M. _____

4. It is 12:00 noon. _____

5. It is 6:50 P.M. (*not dark yet*). _____

"At" + Time of Day

¿**A qué hora** llegas a casa?	At what time do you arrive home?
Vuelvo a casa **a las cinco**.	I return home at 5:00.
La clase empieza **a la una y diez**.	The class begins at 1:10.
A mediodía almorzamos en la escuela.	At noon we have lunch in school.
A medianoche dormimos.	At midnight we are sleeping.

9. To express *at* with the hour, use **a**: **a la una** (*at one o'clock*), **a las dos** (*at two o'clock*), etc.

10. A common mistake is to confuse the answers to ¿**A qué hora?** and ¿**Qué hora es?** The answer to the first question requires **a** ("¿A qué hora vienes? "Vengo **a** las tres."). The answer to the second questions begins with **Es** or **Son** ("¿Qué hora es?" "**Son** las tres.").

Practice E: Write in Spanish.

1. At four fifteen _____ llego a casa muy cansado(a).

2. At 7:30 _____ salgo para la escuela.

3. At 1:55 P.M. _____ empieza mi clase de inglés.

4. At 10:14 A.M. _____ estoy en mi clase de historia.

5. At midnight _____ estoy durmiendo.

Other Time Expressions

Son las ocho **en punto**.	It is eight o'clock sharp.
Llegamos **a tiempo**.	We are arriving on time.
Es tarde.	It is late.
Es temprano.	It is early.
Estudiamos **por la mañana (por la tarde, por la noche)**.	We study in the morning (in the afternoon, in the evening).

11. The phrases **por la mañana, por la tarde**, etc., refer to parts of the day and are not used after expressions of clock time.

◢ EXERCISES ◣

A.   ¿Qué hora es? Reply with a complete sentence, giving the time indicated on each clock.

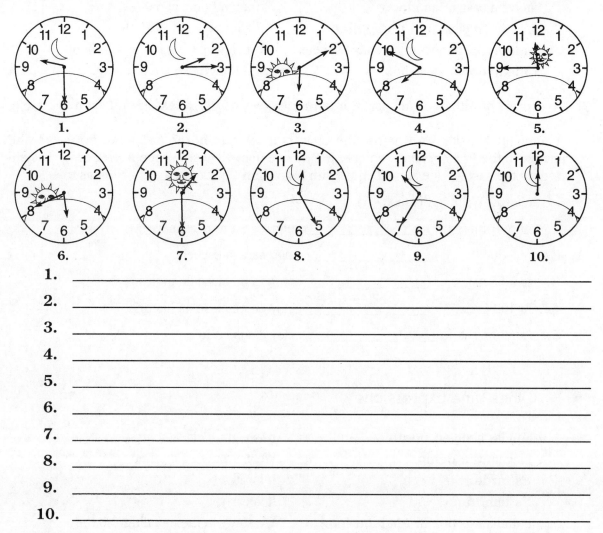

1. _____

2. _____

3. _____

4. _____

5. _____

6. _____

7. _____

8. _____

9. _____

10. _____

B.   Change each of the following sentences as in the example.

    EXAMPLE: Son las ocho de la noche.   (subtract 5 hours)
        Son las tres de la tarde.

    1.   Son las seis y media.   (add a half hour)

    _____

    2.   Son las tres menos veinte.   (subtract 15 minutes)

    _____

    3.   Es medianoche.   (add twelve hours)

    _____

4. Son las doce menos tres de la noche.   (add five minutes)

_____

5. Es la una de la tarde.   (subtract a half hour)

_____

6. Son las dos de la mañana.   (change to 12 hours later)

_____

7. Es la una de la tarde.   (change to 12 hours earlier)

_____

8. Son las ocho y veinticinco.   (add 20 minutes)

_____

9. Son las cinco y media de la tarde.   (subtract 12 hours)

_____

10. Son las once de la mañana.   (add one hour)

_____

C. Your Mexican pen-pal is curious about your schedule and time-zone differences in the US. Answer his/her questions in complete Spanish sentences.

1. ¿A qué hora almuerzas en la escuela?

_____

2. ¿Empieza a tiempo tu clase de español?

_____

3. ¿A qué hora termina tu clase de español?

_____

4. ¿A qué hora te levantas para ir a la escuela?

_____

5. ¿A qué hora comienza tu programa favorito de televisión?

_____

6. ¿Qué hora es en Los Ángeles cuando es la una de la tarde en Nueva York?

_____

7. ¿Qué hora es en Boston cuando son las seis de la tarde en San Francisco?

_____

8. ¿A qué hora te acuestas los viernes?

_____

9. ¿Qué haces tú a medianoche generalmente?

_____

10. ¿Estudias tus lecciones por la tarde o por la noche?

_____

D. In items 1–3 below, read the description of each situation and the first line of dialogue, then choose the most likely response that the second speaker would make. Circle the letter of your choice.

1. Es sábado. Raquel y su madre se preparan para ir al centro y tienen que tomar el autobús de las diez.

   LA MADRE DICE: Vamos, Raquel, es tarde.

   RAQUEL CONTESTA: *a.* No, mamá; sólo son las nueve y media.
                      b. Es medianoche, mamá.
                      c. Son las diez y veinte; tenemos tiempo.

2. Todos los días la familia Pérez mira las noticias en la televisión a las seis de la tarde. Ahora son las cinco y media. Todos están sentados a la mesa.

   MAMÁ DICE: Vamos a terminar la comida. Quiero ver las noticias en la televisión.

   PAPÁ CONTESTA: *a.* Sí, ya empieza el programa.
                      b. El programa va a terminar en cinco minutos.
                      c. Pero el programa comienza en treinta minutos.

3. Esta noche a las nueve, hay un baile en la escuela. José va a acompañar a Susana. Ahora son las nueve y cuarto. José llega a casa de Susana.

   SUSANA DICE: Hola, José. ¿Sabes qué hora es?

   JOSÉ CONTESTA: *a.* Sí, llego a tiempo.
                      b. Sí, es un poco tarde.
                      c. Sí, es muy temprano.

=========== **LA QUINCEAÑERA** ===========

The most important birthday for a Hispanic girl is her fifteenth, equivalent to the sixteenth of the American girl. On this date, the *quinceañera* (girl celebrating her fifteenth birthday) receives special gifts from her godparents. Generally the occasion is celebrated with a big party, just like the *sweet sixteen* party in the United States.

REVIEW EXERCISES: CHAPTERS 15-20

A. Rewrite each sentence, replacing the word in italics with the word in parentheses. Make all necessary changes of gender and number.

EXAMPLE: *Alberto* **es nuestro buen amigo.   (Susana)**
Susana es nuestra buena amiga.

  1. Esta *señora* es una amiga de mi padre.   (señor)

_____

  2. La tercera *lección* es muy difícil.   (ejercicio)

_____

  3. No tenemos ninguna *fruta*.   (dinero)

_____

  4. Ese restaurante sirve malas *comidas*.   (platos)

_____

  5. Esos *edificios* son grandes y hermosos.   (casas)

_____

  6. Voy a tomar el primer *tren*.   (lección de guitarra)

_____

  7. ¿Quiere Ud. estos *guantes*?   (abrigo)

_____

  8. Escribo con esa *pluma*.   (lápiz)

_____

  9. Javier quiere llevar mi *corbata*.   (calcetines)

_____

10. Voy al cine con mi *tía*.   (amigos)

_____

11. ¿Tienen Uds. nuestros *libros*?   (revista)

_____

12. Tengo buenos *zapatos*.   (camisas)

_____

13. Están sentados en los primeros *asientos*.   (sillas)

_____

14. Algún *hombre* viene esta noche.   (mujer)

_____

15. Quiero hablar con tus *padres*.   (hermana)

_____

B. Complete the sentences, writing all numbers as words.

   1. El tercer mes del año es _____.

   2. En los meses de _____ y _____ hace calor.

   3. Hay siete días en la _____.

   4. Abril y octubre son _____ del _____.

   5. A las diez de la _____ nos acostamos.

   6. A las siete de la _____ nos levantamos.

   7. Si hoy es martes, mañana es _____.

   8. Celebramos la Navidad el veinticinco de _____.

   9. Los _____ y los _____ nos levantamos tarde.

 10. Ahora son las seis y cuarto. Media hora más tarde (*later*) son _____.

 11. Ahora son las nueve menos diez. Quince minutos más tarde son _____.

 12. Si hoy es el treinta de septiembre, mañana es el _____ de
_____.

 13. El mes de _____ tiene veintiocho días.

 14. Hay _____ días en el mes de enero.

 15. En un dólar hay _____ centavos.

 16. Hay _____ estados en los Estados Unidos.

 17. Este año es _____.

 18. Yo nací (*was born*) en mil novecientos ochenta y dos. Ahora tengo _____
años.

 19. Doscientos y trescientos son _____.

 20. Catorce por diez son _____.

C. Your teacher will read aloud four statements in Spanish. Write the Spanish name of the season most closely associated with each statement.

1. _____   3. _____

2. _____   4. _____

D. Your teacher will read aloud five statements in Spanish. Write the Spanish name of the month that is usually associated with each statement.

1. _____   4. _____

2. _____   5. _____

3. _____

E. In the blank at the left, write the letter of the "activity" in column B that commonly occurs at the time expressed in column A.

A	B
_____ **1.** Son las siete de la mañana.	*a.* Dormimos.
_____ **2.** Son las tres de la tarde.	*b.* Nos despertamos.
_____ **3.** Es mediodía.	*c.* Cenamos.
_____ **4.** Es medianoche.	*d.* Almorzamos.
_____ **5.** Son las seis de la tarde.	*e.* Salimos de la escuela.

F. Answer each question with a complete Spanish sentence.

1. ¿Cuándo hace buen tiempo?

_____

2. ¿Es diciembre el primer mes del año?

_____

3. ¿Habla usted español con su profesor(a) de inglés?

_____

4. ¿Desea usted ver mi casa?

_____

5. ¿Cuántas semanas hay en dos años?

_____

6. ¿Cuántos años hay en cinco siglos?

_____

7. ¿En qué año nació (*was born*) su padre?

_____

8. ¿Cuántos alumnos hay en su escuela?

    _____

9. ¿En qué estación hace mal tiempo generalmente?

    _____

10. ¿Qué días no van ustedes a la escuela?

    _____

11. ¿Cuál es la fecha de mañana?

    _____

12. ¿A qué hora cena su familia?

    _____

13. ¿A que hora se levanta usted para ir a la escuela?

    _____

14. ¿Se acuesta usted a las tres de la tarde?

    _____

15. ¿Va usted a casa a mediodía para almorzar?

    _____

G. Read each paragraph and answer the questions that follow. Before you begin, review the following expressions:

Hispanoamérica, Spanish America (= all the Spanish-speaking countries of the Western Hemisphere)
el santo, the saint (**San** before a male saint's name, **Santa** before a female saint's name)
además de, besides
el cumpleaños, the birthday
por ejemplo, for example
hispano, Hispanic (= Spanish-speaking; refers to Spain or Spanish America or both)
significar, to mean
lo contrario, the opposite
cenar, to have supper
entre, between
la costumbre, the custom
la nota, the (school) grade, mark
por eso, therefore
el mundo, the world

1. En España y en los países de Hispanoamérica muchas personas celebran el día de su santo además de su cumpleaños. Por ejemplo, si un muchacho se llama Jorge, él celebra el día de San Jorge—el veintitrés de abril—. Si una muchacha se llama Bárbara, ella celebra el día de su santo el cuatro de diciembre.

Complete the sentences:

a. El 23 de abril es el día de _____.

b. El 4 de diciembre es el día de _____.

c. Los chicos de los países hispanos celebran el día de su _____ y el

día de su _____.

2. ¿Sabe usted que cuando es invierno en los Estados Unidos, es verano en la Argentina? Esto significa que las estaciones argentinas son lo contrario de nuestras estaciones. Por ejemplo:

a. Cuando celebramos la Navidad en los Estados Unidos, generalmente hace frío,

pero en la Argentina hace _____.

b. Cuando es primavera en la Argentina, aquí es _____.

3. En los países hispanos las familias generalmente cenan muy tarde: entre las nueve y las diez de la noche. Esta costumbre no es como nuestra costumbre en los Estados Unidos. Nosotros generalmente cenamos entre las seis y las siete de la tarde.

In the blank provided, write *Sí* if the statement is true, *No* if it is false.

a. Muchos norteamericanos generalmente cenan a las seis y

media de la tarde.   _____

b. Los hispanos tienen la costumbre de cenar a las nueve o a

las diez de la mañana.   _____

c. Los norteamericanos y los hispanos cenan a la misma hora.   _____

4. En las escuelas españolas los alumnos reciben notas de cero a diez. En los Estados Unidos los alumnos reciben notas de cero a cien. Por ejemplo, en nuestro sistema una nota de setenta corresponde a una nota de siete en el sistema español.

a. Una nota de ochenta en el sistema norteamericano corresponde a una nota de

_____ en el sistema español.

b. Una nota de cinco en el sistema español corresponde a una nota de

_____ en nuestro sistema.

5. El doce de octubre es una fecha muy importante en España, en Hispanoamérica y en los Estados Unidos. El 12 de octubre de mil cuatrocientos noventa y dos Cristóbal Colón descubrió (*discovered*) el Nuevo Mundo. Por eso todos celebramos este día, llamado el Día de la Raza o el Día de la Hispanidad en el mundo hispano.

In the blank provided, write *Sí* if the statement is true, *No* if it is false.

a. Colón descubrió el Nuevo Mundo en 1942.   _____

b. El Día de la Raza es el doce de octubre.   _____

c. Celebramos este día solamente en el Nuevo Mundo.   _____

Part 5
The Preterit Tense

><><><><><><><><><><><><><><><><><><><

21
-AR Verbs in the Preterit Tense

trabajar, to work

yo	traba*jé* anoche	I worked last night.
tú	trabaj*aste*	you worked
Ud.	trabaj*ó*	you worked
él	trabaj*ó*	he worked
ella	trabaj*ó*	she worked
nosotros (-as)	trabaj*amos*	we worked
vosotros(-as)	trabaj*asteis*	you worked
Uds.	trabaj*aron*	you worked
ellos	trabaj*aron*	they worked
elllas	trabaj*aron*	they worked

1. The preterit tense is equivalent to the English past tense.

2. To form the preterit tense of **-AR** verbs, add the following endings to the stem of the infinitive:

    -é, -aste, -ó, -amos, -asteis, -aron

    Note: The 3rd person singular of the preterit ends in **-o** like the first person of the present. The difference is the accent mark in the preterit.

3. The **nosotros (-as)** form of the preterit of **-AR** verbs is identical to the **nosotros (-as)** form in the present tense.

    Practice A: Express each sentence in two ways.

    EXAMPLE: Hablamos inglés.   We speak English.   We spoke English.

    1. Estudiamos en casa.   _____   _____

    2. Contestamos bien.   _____   _____

3. No comenzamos la tarea. _____   _____

4. No trabajamos mucho. _____   _____

5. Terminamos la tarea. _____   _____

4. Stem-changing verbs of the **-AR** conjugation do not undergo any stem change in the preterit tense:

	Present Tense		Preterit Tense
cerrar	yo **cierro**		yo cerré
mostrar	yo **muestro**		yo mostré

Practice B: Using the subject in italics, write the preterit forms of the verbs indicated below the blanks.

EXAMPLE: *ella*	ayudó	habló	cerró
	(ayudar)	**(hablar)**	**(cerrar)**
1. *Uds.*	_____	_____	_____
	(mostrar)	(visitar)	(estudiar)
2. *yo*	_____	_____	_____
	(contestar)	(pensar)	(hablar)
3. *nosotros*	_____	_____	_____
	(encontrar)	(escuchar)	(mirar)
4. *José*	_____	_____	_____
	(trabajar)	(recordar)	(explicar)

◼️ Did + Verb in the Past Tense

Mi hermana **no estudió** anoche.   My sister *did not study* last night.
¿**Encontró Ud.** su traje ayer?   *Did you find* your suit yesterday?

5. As in all other tenses, a Spanish sentence is made negative simply by adding the word **no** directly before the verb; to form a question, place the subject after the verb. Notice that "did" is not used in Spanish.

6. Common adverbial expressions used with the preterit tense are:

ayer	yesterday
anoche	last night
ayer por la mañana (tarde)	yesterday morning (afternoon)
la semana pasada	last week
el mes pasado	last month
el año pasado	last year
el verano pasado	last summer
hace cinco años (tres días, etc.)	five years (three days, etc.) ago

Practice C: Change from Spanish into English or vice versa.

1. Mi padre no trabajó ayer. _____

2. ¿Estudiaron los muchachos anoche? _____

3. Mary did not take the book yesterday morning. _____

4. Did John close the door last night? _____

Practice D: Write the English meaning of each sentence.

EXAMPLE: a. **Miro la casa.**   I am looking at the house.
           b. **Miró la casa.**   He (She, You) looked at the house.

1. a. Explico la lección. _____

   b. Explicó la lección. _____

2. a. No pago el dinero. _____

   b. No pagó el dinero. _____

3. a. Compro un disco. _____

   b. Compró un disco. _____

▲ EXERCISES ▲

A. Complete each sentence by writing the appropriate form of the verb that is indicated below the blank.

EXAMPLE: **Mis amigos bailaron anoche pero yo _____*pasé*_____ la noche en casa.**
                                              (pasar)

1. Ayer el profesor enseñó el pretérito. ¿_____ los alumnos con atención?
                                             (escuchar)

2. Ellos compraron un coche el mes pasado. El coche _____ 14,000 dólares.
                                             (costar)

3. Yo pienso que la película _____ a las siete anoche.
                                 (empezar)

4. Mi padre llegó a casa a las seis y media y luego nosotros _____.
                                                 (cenar)

5. ¿Estudiaron Uds. la lectura que el profesor _____ ayer por la tarde?
                                             (explicar)

6. ¿Terminó ella sus tareas? No, porque _____ la televisión.
                                        (mirar)

7. El profesor explicó el ejercicio y luego nosotros _____ en las computadoras.
                                         (trabajar)

8. Anoche en la fiesta Ana y Roberto cantaron y yo _____ toda la noche.
                                        (bailar)

9. Mi padre habló pero yo no _____ mucho.
                                  (escuchar)

10. El verano pasado mis tíos visitaron a la familia y _____ muchos regalos para todos.
                                       (comprar)

B. Write the italicized verb in the preterit tense. Be sure to keep the same subject.

Use the following guide:

	Present	Preterit
yo	-o	-é
tú	-as	-aste
Ud., él, ella	-a	-ó
nosotros	-amos	-amos
vosotros	-áis	-asteis
Uds., ellos, ellas	-an	-aron

EXAMPLE: **Este año *viajo* por España. El año pasado** _____*viajé*_____ **por Sudamérica.**

1. Ahora *compro* pan. Ayer _____ leche.

2. La familia *almuerza* a la una hoy. Ayer _____ a las doce.

3. ¿Qué *piensas* tú de la escuela? ¿Qué _____ de la película?

4. No *estudiamos* esta mañana. Ayer por la mañana _____ por dos horas.

5. Mis padres *visitan* a nuestros abuelos en el verano. El año pasado _____ a nuestros tíos.

6. Yo *hablo* español con mi amigo Federico López. El semestre pasado _____ con Juana Fernández.

7. Este año *pagáis* mucho dinero por la ropa. El año pasado _____ menos dinero.

8. ¿Cuánto tiempo *pasa* Felipe en España este verano? ¿Y cuánto tiempo _____ allí el verano pasado?

9. Mi hermana *toma* café esta mañana. Anoche ella _____ té.

10. Ahora *miro* la televisión en mi casa. Ayer por la tarde _____ la televisión en la casa de Pedro.

C. Answer each question with a complete Spanish sentence.

1. ¿Cuántas horas estudió usted anoche?

   _____

2. ¿Trabajaron sus padres en una tienda el mes pasado?

   _____

3. ¿Quién explicó la lección de español ayer en su clase?

   _____

4. ¿Quiénes cantaron y bailaron anoche en la televisión?

   _____

5. ¿Qué compró su madre ayer en la tienda?

   _____

6. ¿Recordó usted el número de teléfono de su mejor amigo(a)?

   _____

7. ¿Contestó usted a todas las preguntas del profesor ayer?

   _____

8. ¿Hablaron ustedes con el profesor esta mañana cuando entraron en la clase?

   _____

9. ¿A qué hora tomó Ud. el desayuno esta mañana?

   _____

10. a. ¿Cuánto costó su camisa favorita?

    _____

    b. ¿Cuánto costaron sus zapatos favoritos?

    _____

D. Complete the Spanish sentences.

   1. What did they buy last night?

      ¿Qué _____ anoche?

   2. Yesterday I worked eight hours.

      Ayer _____ ocho horas.

   3. We did not look at television last night.

      _____ la televisión anoche.

   4. Last year she visited our school.

      El año pasado _____ nuestra escuela.

   5. The lesson began at 10:20.

      La lección _____ a las diez y veinte.

   6. Did John close the windows?

      ¿_____ las ventanas?

   7. The dress cost seventy-five dollars.

      El vestido _____ setenta y cinco dólares.

   8. We ate lunch in the city yesterday.

      _____ en la ciudad ayer.

   9. When did you (*tú*) speak with the teacher?

      ¿Cuándo _____ con el profesor?

   10. I did not answer very well in class yesterday afternoon.

       _____ muy bien en la clase ayer por la tarde.

22
-ER and -IR Verbs
in the Preterit Tense

aprender, to learn

yo aprend*í* mucho ayer	I learned a lot yesterday.
tú aprend*iste*	you learned
Ud. aprend*ió*	you learned
él aprend*ió*	he learned
ella aprend*ió*	she learned
nosotros(-as) aprend*imos*	we learned
vosotros(-as) aprend*isteis*	you learned
Uds. aprend*ieron*	you learned
ellos aprend*ieron*	they learned
ellas aprend*ieron*	they learned

escribir, to write

yo escrib*í* la carta	I wrote the letter
tú escrib*iste*	you wrote
Ud. escrib*ió*	you wrote
él escrib*ió*	he wrote
ella escrib*ió*	she wrote
nosotros(-as) escrib*imos*	we wrote
vosotros(-as) escrib*isteis*	you wrote
Uds. escrib*ieron*	you wrote
ellos escrib*ieron*	they wrote
ellas escrib*ieron*	they wrote

1. **-ER** and **-IR** verbs have the same set of preterit endings:

-í, -iste, -ió, -imos, -isteis, -ieron

These endings are added to the stem of the infinitive.

Practice A: Using the indicated subjects, write the preterit form of each verb.

1. yo _____ _____
  (beber) (dividir)

2. nosotros _____ _____
  (salir) (responder)

3. Juan _____ _____
  (vivir) (comprender)

2. Stem-changing verbs of the **-ER** conjugation do not undergo any stem change in the preterit tense:

	Present Tense	Preterit Tense
<u>entend</u>er	yo **entiend**o	yo <u>entend</u>í
<u>volv</u>er	yo **vuelv**o	yo <u>volv</u>í

(Stem-changing **-IR** verbs, such as **dormir** and **sentir**, also have stem changes in the preterit tense but they are beyond the scope of this book.)

Practice B: Using the indicated subjects, write the preterit forms of the given verbs.

1. el niño _____   **2.** ellos _____
                    (perder)   (volver)

3. tú no _____   **4.** yo _____
                  (entender)   (mover)

3. The verb **ver** has the regular preterit endings but the accent marks are omitted:

vi, viste, vio, vimos, visteis, vieron

◄ EXERCISES ►

A. Complete each sentence by writing the appropriate form of the preterit tense of the verb in parentheses.

EXAMPLE: **(salir) Ramón** ____*salió*____ **de casa a las nueve.**

1. (aprender)   ¿Dónde _____ tú el español?

2. (recibir)   Ayer nosotros _____ la carta.

3. (vivir)   ¿Dónde _____ ustedes el año pasado?

4. (correr)   Marta y Elena _____ por el parque.

5. (partir)   ¿A qué hora _____ el tren anoche?

6. (volver)   Mi familia _____ a casa muy tarde.

7. (llover)   Ayer _____ todo el día.

8. (perder)   Yo _____ mi pluma esta mañana.

9. (abrir)   ¿Quién _____ las ventanas?

10. (ver)   El no _____ la película con nosotros.

B. Laura is an exchange student from Costa Rica staying with an American family. She is helping George, one of the children, with his Spanish homework, in which he has to change some sentences in the present to the preterit. Rewrite each sentence as if you were George. Follow the example.

EXAMPLE: **¿Qué comen Uds.? (esta mañana)**   ¿Qué *comieron* Uds. esta mañana?

1. Yo no *veo* la pizarra.   (ayer)   _____

2. En abril *llueve* mucho.   (el año pasado)   _____

3. ¿A qué hora *sales* tú?   (ayer)   _____

4. *Bebéis* mucha leche.   (la semana pasada)   _____

5. ¿Quién *vende* las cintas?   (anoche)   _____

6. No *comprendemos* esta lección.   (esta mañana)   _____

7. *Escribo* en mi cuaderno.   (hace poco)   _____

8. ¿Dónde *viven* sus amigos?   (hace un año)   _____

9. No *recibimos* el dinero.   (el mes pasado)   _____

10. Jorge *ve* la película.   (hace tres días)   _____

C. Answer each question as indicated in parentheses. Follow the example.

EXAMPLE: **¿Cuándo recibiste mi paquete? (por la mañana)**
          Yo recibí tu paquete por la mañana.

1. ¿A qué hora salieron los chicos ayer por la tarde?   (a las cinco y media)

_____

2. ¿Cuánto dinero perdió José en la calle?   (diez dólares)

_____

3. ¿Quién escribió a los abuelos?   (nadie)

_____

4. ¿Con quién comieron ustedes anoche?   (con Paco)

_____

5. ¿Cuántos animales vieron Uds. en el zoo el domingo pasado?   (muchos)

_____

6. ¿Quién vivió en la casa de al lado el año pasado?   (una familia mejicana)

_____

7. ¿Qué bebieron Uds. después de la cena?   (café)

_____

8. ¿Qué vendieron Uds. en la fiesta de la escuela?   (refrescos y comida)

_____

9. ¿Cuándo llovió aquí?   (la semana pasada)

_____

10. ¿Quiénes entendieron el discurso del presidente?   (todos los alumnos)

_____

D. Add a Subject. With a partner play the game of "add a subject." One partner reads the original sentence and then adds a new subject. The other partner restates the sentence as shown in the example. Rewrite each sentence, forming a new subject by adding the words in parentheses.

EXAMPLE: **Ana volvió a casa temprano.   (y María)**
Ana y María volvieron a casa temprano.

1. Héctor corrió rápidamente por la calle.   (y yo)

_____

2. Mi madre no vio la película anoche.   (y mi tía)

_____

3. Yo viví en Buenos Aires el año pasado.   (y mi primo)

_____

4. Los profesores escribieron las palabras.   (y los alumnos)

_____

5. Usted describió la pintura muy bien.   (y Gilberto)

_____

E. Complete the Spanish sentences.

1. Where did they live last year?

¿Dónde _____ el año pasado?

2. When did she sell the house?

¿Cuándo _____ la casa?

3. We did not understand the lesson.

_____ la lección.

4. What did you (vosotros) lose last night?

¿Qué _____ anoche?

5. It rained a lot yesterday.

_____ mucho ayer.

6. I learned the verbs very well.

   _____ los verbos muy bien.

7. We didn't write letters last week.

   _____ cartas la semana pasada.

8. What did they see there?

   ¿Qué _____ allí?

9. Did the train leave at 4:00?

   ¿_____ el tren a las cuatro?

10. Why didn't she open the window?

   ¿Por qué _____ la ventana?

F. Circle the letter of the answer that best completes the sentence.

   EXAMPLE: **José dice al profesor que no comprendió la lección muy bien. Es porque**

   ⓐ no estudió en casa anoche.
   b. aprendió toda la lección.
   c. llovió toda la noche.

1. Anita entró en la escuela esta mañana y
   a. salió del cine.
   b compró la casa.
   c. saludó a sus amigas.

2. Mi padre trabajó todo el día y
   a. almorzó con nosotros a las siete.
   b. volvió a casa muy cansado.
   c. recibió buenas notas.

3. Rosa y Ramón miraron la televisión anoche y
   a. vivieron en España.
   b. vieron buenos programas.
   c. perdieron todo su dinero.

4. Ricardo abrió la puerta y
   a. su amigo entró.
   b. María vendió la casa.
   c. la familia almorzó.

5. La familia Pérez viajó por España durante el mes de agosto y
   a. vio muchas ciudades americanas.
   b. volvió en septiembre.
   c. habló francés con los habitantes.

ZIPAQUIRÁ

A great wonder of Latin America is the huge cathedral of Zipaquirá, situated about 35 miles from Bogotá, Colombia. This cathedral was constructed out of a salt mine exploited by the Chibcha Indians, who used this treasure to dominate the neighboring tribes. It is said that this mine could provide the whole world with salt for a hundred years. The idea of building a cathedral inside the mine originated with one of the miners. The project was begun in 1950 and was completed in four years. The distance from the entrance to the door of the cathedral is 1575 feet. The cathedral is supported by fourteen enormous columns of salt, one of which measures 120 feet at the base. Until 1975 automobiles were permitted to enter the cathedral. They entered through the lower part and went out through a tunnel. This was finally prohibited because the vibrations, the gases, and the weight of the automobiles had a damaging effect on the structure. Today you can visit the cathedral on foot only.

23
Irregular Verbs in the Preterit Tense—U-Group

	yo	tú	Ud. él, ella	nosotros(-as)	vosotros(-as)	Uds. ellos ellas
andar, to walk	**anduve**	**anduviste**	**anduvo**	**anduvimos**	**anduvisteis**	**anduvieron**
estar, to be	**estuve**	**estuviste**	**estuvo**	**estuvimos**	**estuvisteis**	**estuvieron**
poder, to be able	**pude**	**pudiste**	**pudo**	**pudimos**	**pudisteis**	**pudieron**
poner, to put, to set	**puse**	**pusiste**	**puso**	**pusimos**	**pusisteis**	**pusieron**
saber, to know	**supe**	**supiste**	**supo**	**supimos**	**supisteis**	**supieron**
tener, to have	**tuve**	**tuviste**	**tuvo**	**tuvimos**	**tuvisteis**	**tuvieron**

1. These preterit forms have no accent marks.

2. Verbs in this group have preterit stems containing the letter **u**:

andar	estar	poder	poner	saber	tener
anduv-	**estuv-**	**pud-**	**pus-**	**sup-**	**tuv-**

3. The endings that are added to these special stems are:

    -e, -iste, -o, -imos, -isteis, -ieron

4. The preterit of **tener** sometimes means *got, received*:

    Tuvo una carta de su madre.   She got (received) a letter from her mother.

5. The preterit tense of **saber** means *found out* (learned):

    Supimos que vienen esta noche.   We found out (We learned) that they are coming tonight.

6. The irregular preterit forms of **conducir**, *to lead, to drive*, are similar to those of the other verbs in this group except that **–ieron** becomes **–jeron** in the third person plural:

    conduje, condujiste, condujo, condujimos, condujisteis, condujeron

◢ EXERCISES ◣

A. Mr. Negative: Little Pedro delights in being contrary. For every statement he hears, he changes it to the negative. For each statement that follows, change it to the negative as in the following example.

EXAMPLE: Yo anduve por la calle.   Yo no anduve por la calle.

   1. Mi hermano puso sus libros en la mesa.

   _____

   2. Estuvimos en casa anoche.

   _____

   3. Mi padre condujo el coche muy despacio.

   _____

   4. Pedro tuvo una carta ayer.

   _____

   5. Pudiste jugar en el gimnasio.

   _____

B. Pedro's sister Vilma loves to turn everyone's statements into a question. How would she turn each of the following into a question? Follow the example.

EXAMPLE: María estuvo en la escuela ayer.   ¿Estuvo María en la escuela ayer?

   1. Elena pudo salir a las tres.

   _____

   2. Supimos la información en seguida.

   _____

   3. Mis amigos estuvieron en el cine anoche.

   _____

   4. Yo no puse mi ropa en la cama esta mañana.

   _____

   5. Uds. anduvieron por todo el edificio.

   _____

C. How fast can you change present to preterit? First change the italicized verb to the preterit and write it in the space provided. Then recite the new sentence aloud.

EXAMPLE: ¿Quién puede ver la casa?   pudo

   1. *Conducimos* el coche por la ciudad.   _____

   2. ¿Dónde *estáis* vosotros?   _____

3. Pedro *anda* por la ciudad.   _____

4. No *sé* la dirección.   _____

5. *¿Pueden* ellas venir con nosotros?   _____

D. In a complete Spanish sentence, answer each question as indicated in parentheses.

    EXAMPLE: **¿Por dónde condujeron Uds. el coche?   (por el parque)**
        Condujimos el coche por el parque.

    1. ¿Dónde estuviste anoche?   (en el cine)

    _____

    2. ¿Qué pusieron Uds. en los bolsillos?   (el dinero)

    _____

    3. ¿Quién anduvo por tres horas?   (José)

    _____

    4. ¿Cuántas cartas tuvo Ud. ayer?   (cuatro)

    _____

    5. ¿Qué no pudieron los alumnos aprender hoy?   (los verbos irregulares)

    _____

Independence Square, Quito, Ecuador.

E. Complete the Spanish sentences.

    1. Were you able to see the movie last night?

       ¿_____ ustedes ver la película anoche?

    2. Who drove the car yesterday?

       ¿_____ el coche ayer?

    3. They were not at home last week.

       _____ en casa la semana pasada.

    4. I got the information yesterday.

       _____ la información ayer.

    5. Where did she put her watch?

       ¿Dónde _____ su reloj?

24
Irregular Verbs in the Preterit Tense— I-Group and TRAER

	yo	tú	Ud. él ella	nosotros(-as)	vosotros(-as)	Uds., ellos ellas
decir, to say, to tell	dije	dijiste	dijo	dijimos	dijisteis	dijeron
hacer, to do, to make	hice	hiciste	hizo	hicimos	hicisteis	hicieron
querer, to want	quise	quisiste	quiso	quisimos	quisisteis	quisieron
venir, to come	vine	viniste	vino	vinimos	vinisteis	vinieron
traer, to bring	traje	trajiste	trajo	trajimos	trajisteis	trajeron

1. Each of these five verbs has a special preterit stem:

decir	hacer	querer	venir	traer
dij-	**hic-**	**quis-**	**vin-**	**traj-**

2. Except for **traer**, the preterit stems of this group contain the letter **i**.

3. The preterit forms of these verbs have no accent marks.

4. The endings that are added to their special stems are the same as those for the verbs of the previous lesson:

-e, -iste, -o, -imos, -isteis, -ieron

Exceptions: The forms **dijeron** and **trajeron** end in **-eron**.

5. The third-person singular of the preterit of **hacer** is **hizo**. The **c** changes to **z** to keep the same sound before the **-o** ending.

 EXERCISES

A. Each of the following sentences will make sense with one of the two verb forms. Read each sentence, decide which of the two forms is correct, and underline it.

1. ¿(Hicieron–Vinieron) Uds. planes para las vacaciones?

2. Anoche yo no (dije–quise) estudiar.

3. ¿No (dijeron–trajeron) los niños la verdad?

4. Mi abuelo (quiso–vino) anoche a las nueve.

5. No (traje–dije) mis libros a la escuela.

B. Rewrite the sentences, changing the subjects and verbs in italics from the singular to the plural or vice versa. You can use the following table as guide:

Singular	Plural
yo	nosotros(-as)
tú	vosotros(-as) or Uds.
Ud	Uds.
él	ellos
ella	ellas

1. *¿Hicieron Uds.* la tarea anoche? _____

2. No *quise* ir al cine ayer. _____

3. *¿Trajisteis* la camisa azul? _____

4. *Ellos vinieron* temprano esta mañana. _____

5. ¿Qué *dijo ella*? _____

C. *Time Machine*: Imagine being in a time machine that takes you back to the past. Write the form of the verb in the preterit and then recite the new sentence.

EXAMPLE: **¿A qué hora *vienes*?** viniste

1. ¿Qué *dicen* tus amigos? _____

2. Yo *vengo* temprano. _____

3. ¿Qué *traes* tú a la fiesta? _____

4. No *quiere* escribir la carta. _____

5. Juanito no *hace* la tarea. _____

D. Jorge's mother has gone out for a while leaving Jorge to mind the younger children. She asks him questions about what occurred in her absence. How would Jorge answer each question? Use the cues provided as in the example.

EXAMPLE: **¿Qué hiciste tú?** **(mis tareas)** Hice mis tareas.

1. ¿Qué trajeron a casa Carlos y Juana? (la comida para el perro)

_____

2. ¿Qué quisiste ver en la televisión? (mi programa favorito)

_____

3. ¿Cuándo hizo María sus tareas?   (a las cinco)

_____

4. ¿Qué dijeron los abuelos por teléfono?   (que desean visitarnos pronto)

_____

5. ¿A qué hora vino Ramón a casa?   (a las ocho)

_____

E.   Here are several examples of the conversations between members of the González family last night. Write their equivalents in Spanish.

1. She came early this afternoon.   _____

2. What did you (*tú*) want to see there?   _____

3. They did not bring the CD's yesterday.   _____

4. Did you (*vosotros*) do the exercise this morning?   _____

5. We did not say that (*eso*).   _____

25
Irregular Verbs in the Preterit Tense: CAER, CREER, LEER, OÍR; DAR, SER, IR

▰ Preterit Tense of Caer, Creer, Leer, Oír

	yo	tú	Ud. él, ella	nosotros(-as)	vosotros(-as)	Uds. ellos ellas
caer, to fall	**caí**	**caíste**	**cayó**	**caímos**	**caísteis**	**cayeron**
creer, to believe	**creí**	**creíste**	**creyó**	**creímos**	**creísteis**	**creyeron**
leer, to read	**leí**	**leíste**	**leyó**	**leímos**	**leísteis**	**leyeron**
oír, to hear	**oí**	**oíste**	**oyó**	**oímos**	**oísteis**	**oyeron**

1. In this group of verbs, the preterit endings of the third-person singular and plural change **i** to **y**. In the ending of the other forms, the **i** bears an accent mark.

   Practice A: Write the preterit form of the verb.

   EXAMPLE: ustedes oyen   oyeron

   1. nosotros leemos _____

   2. tú no caes _____

   3. ella cree _____

   4. usted oye _____

   5. vosotros leéis _____

▰ Preterit Tense of Dar, Ser, Ir

dar, to give	**di, diste, dio, dimos, disteis, dieron**
ser, to be } **ir**, to go }	**fui, fuiste, fue, fuimos, fuisteis, fueron**

2. **Dar** is conjugated in the preterit tense as if it were a regular **–ER** or **–IR** verb. The forms **di** and **dio** do not need accent marks.

3. The preterit forms of **ser** and **ir** are identical. The forms **fui** and **fue** do not need accent marks. When a preterit form of **ser** or **ir** appears in a sentence, the meaning of the sentence will indicate which of the two verbs is being used. Here are some examples:

EXAMPLES: *a.* **Fuimos** al cine anoche.   We went to the movies last night.
                Fuimos buenos amigos.   We were good friends.

            b. Mi tío Juan **fue** un gran hombre.   My uncle John was a great man.
                Mi tío Juan **fue** a Madrid.   My uncle John went to Madrid.

Practice B: Translate into English.

1. Fuimos a la escuela.   _____

2. ¿Quién fue ese hombre?   _____

3. ¿Fuiste al cine anoche?   _____

4. Ellos fueron buenos amigos.   _____

▲ EXERCISES ▲

A. Underline the verb form that completes the meaning of the sentence.

    1. ¿(Cayeron—Oyeron) ustedes la música ayer?

    2. (Leímos—Fuimos) dos libros el mes pasado.

    3. El chico (cayó—creyó) de la cama anoche.

    4. ¿(Diste—Fuiste) el dinero a tu padre?

    5. Ana y José (oyeron—fueron) a México la semana pasada.

B. Write the preterit form of each verb in parentheses.

    1. (leer) ¿_____ Ud. ese libro anoche?

    2. (dar) Juan y Elena _____ los papeles al profesor.

    3. (ir) ¿Adónde _____ ella ayer?

    4. (oír) Mi amigo y yo _____ la historia.

    5. (ser) ¿Quiénes _____ esas mujeres?

C. An alleged criminal is given a lie-detector test, but he fails because he does not tell the truth in answering any of the questions. Answer each question according to the cue "sí" or "no" as the alleged criminal did.

    1. ¿Cayó Ud. en la calle la semana pasada?

      Sí, _____.

    2. ¿Fue Ud. presidente de los Estados Unidos?

      Sí, _____.

    3. ¿Dio Ud. una pistola a su amigo anoche?

      No, _____.

    4. ¿Leyó Ud. cuatro novelas ayer?

      Sí, _____.

    5. ¿Fue Ud. al sitio del crimen anoche?

      No, _____.

D. Now the same lie-detector test is administered to the alleged accomplice of the alleged criminal. Have him/her answer in the "nosotros" form.

    1. ¿Cayeron Uds. en la calle la semana pasada?

      _____

    2. ¿Fueron Uds. presidentes de los Estados Unidos?

      _____

    3. ¿Dieron Uds. pistolas a sus amigos?

      _____

    4. ¿Leyeron Uds. cuatro novelas ayer?

      _____

    5. ¿Fueron Uds. al sitio del crimen anoche?

      _____

E. Can you switch tenses in Spanish?

EXAMPLES: I run I ran   **Do you see?** Did you see?

    In the following sentences, change each italicized verb in the present to the preterit and write the new verb in the space provided. Then recite the new sentence aloud.

    1. ¿Qué *crees* tú?   _____

    2. No *dan* la respuesta correcta. _____

    3. ¿Cuántos libros *leen* ellos?   _____

4. *¿Vais* a España?   _____

5. Ella *es* mi buena amiga.   _____

F.   Write the Spanish equivalents of each of the following sentences.

1. We went home late last night.   _____

2. Did he hear the music?   _____

3. I did not give the money to my father.   _____

4. Was he your friend?   _____

5. We did not read the novel.   _____

6. Did you (*tú*) believe the story?   _____

7. Did you (*vosotros*) read the lesson?   _____

8. We did not believe what (*lo que*) they said.   _____

9. Who was that man?   _____

10. What did your cousin say?   _____

REVIEW EXERCISES: CHAPTERS 21-25

A.   Your teacher will read aloud an incomplete sentence in Spanish. Circle the letter of the expression that correctly completes the sentence.

1. a. el periódico
    b. el desayuno

2. a. a la escuela
    b. al cine

3. a. salí de la escuela
    b. entré en la escuela

4. a. vimos una película
    b. escuchamos la radio

5. a. en la calle
    b. en la cama

6. a. estuvo enferma
    b. quiso visitar el museo

7. a. comí mis libros
    b. bebí jugo de naranja

8. a. visitaron a nuestra familia
    b. bailaron en su coche

9. a. volvió a casa
    b. entró en la sala

10. a. tres meses
    b. dos horas

B. Rosa keeps a diary of her daily activities and generally writes it in the present tense. Rewrite the italicized verb forms in the preterit.

El Diario De Rosa

Voy _____ a una fiesta en casa de María con mis amigos Carlota y
                    1

Bárbara. *Tomamos* _____ el autobús para llegar allí. Mucho muchachos
                              2

y muchachas *vienen* _____ a esta fiesta y *traen* _____
                                3   4

regalos para María. María *da* _____ las gracias a todos y la fiesta
                                            5

empieza _____ . Todos *están* _____ contentos.
                      6   7

Comemos _____ muchos pasteles y dulces y *bebemos*
                        8

_____ muchos refrescos. Todos los muchachos *son*
            9

_____ muy guapos, especialmente Ramón, que *baila*
          10

_____ muy bien. Yo *bailo* _____ tres veces con él.
          11   12

Ramón y yo *charlamos* _____ un rato; él *habla* _____
                                  13   14

de su equipo de fútbol y yo *hablo* _____ de mis lecciones de piano. A las
                                          15

once *tenemos* _____ que salir, y *vuelvo* _____ a casa.
                        16   17

Ramón me *acompaña* _____ y *decimos* _____ adiós
                              18   19

cerca de mi casa. *Quiero* _____ ver otra vez a Ramón.
                                20

C. Carlos and Paquita tell about their visit to a movie. Assume that only one of them went. Rewrite each verb in italics in the "yo" form.

Una Visita Al Cine

Ayer *quisimos* _____ ver una película en el Cine Ritz pero no *pudimos*
                          1

_____ salir de casa antes de terminar las tareas. *Salimos*
          2

_____ de casa a las cuatro de la tarde. Como *tuvimos*
          3

_____ frío, *llevamos* _____ sombrero, abrigo y
          4   5

guantes. *Anduvimos* _____ hacia la esquina, *subimos*
                                  6

_____ al autobús y *fuimos* _____ a la calle
          7   8

veintiocho. Al bajar, *corrimos* _____ hacia el cine y *entramos*
                                  9

_____ en el teatro. *Vimos* _____ una buena película
          10   11

y *comimos* _____ muchos dulces. *Estuvimos* _____
                  12   13

en el cine dos horas y media. Cuando *salimos* _____ del teatro,
                                            14

encontramos _____ a José Molina y a Lola Méndez. *Hablamos*
                        15

_____ con ellos un rato y luego *volvimos* _____ a
          16   17

casa. Hoy *quisimos* _____ ir a cine otra vez porque *leímos*
                        18

_____ en el periódico acerca de una buena película nueva, pero
          19

decidimos _____ ir a verla el sábado.
                  20

D. In items **1** to **5** below, read the description of each situation and the first line of dialogue, then choose the most likely response that the second speaker would make. Circle the letter of your choice.

Before you begin, review the following words and expressions:

ya, already	el **jugador**, player
cenar, to have supper	el **abrigo**, coat
añadir, to add	**conducir**, to drive

el **partido**, game	**obtener**, to obtain (conjugated like **tener**)
el **equipo**, team	el **permiso de conducir**, driver's license
ganar, to win	**dar un paseo**, to take a ride

1. Anoche papá volvió a casa muy tarde y estuvo muy cansado.

    —La familia ya terminó de cenar—le dijo mamá, y ella añadió:

MAMÁ: Llegaste a casa tarde y estás cansado. ¿Quieres comer algo?

PAPÁ: a. No, ya tomé el desayuno.
             b. No trabajé hoy.
             c. No, ya comí en la ciudad.

2. Anoche Marta y Juan fueron a ver un partido de básquetbol en su escuela. El equipo de su escuela ganó el partido.

JUAN: Nuestro equipo jugó muy bien esta noche.

MARTA: a. Sí, fue un partido magnífico.
                 b. Sí, y los jugadores leyeron novelas.
                 c. Sí, y vimos un buen programa de televisión.

3. Ayer Rafael y su madre fueron a la ciudad para comprar un abrigo. Cuando volvieron a casa la madre dijo:

LA MADRE: Este abrigo costó mucho dinero.

RAFAEL: a. Y vendimos mi sombrero.
                 b. Sí, y es muy barato.
                 c. Pero yo quise comprar el otro que costó menos.

4. Ayer el profesor de español dio un examen muy difícil. Todos los alumnos hablaron del examen.

ROSA: Este examen fue imposible. Nadie pudo contestar a las preguntas.

CARLOS: a. El profesor oyó música.
                 b. Yo no comprendí nada.
                 c. Y José perdió su dinero en el parque.

5. Alberto aprendió a conducir el coche de su padre, y obtuvo un permiso de conducir. Habla con su amigo Juan.

ALBERTO: Ya tengo mi permiso de conducir. Vamos a dar un paseo.

JUAN: a. Buena idea. Él se llama Pedro.
                 b. Sí, cantaron en la iglesia anoche.
                 c. Muy bien. Vamos a visitar a Rosita.

Part 6
Pronouns

⋈⋈⋈⋈⋈⋈⋈⋈⋈⋈⋈⋈⋈⋈⋈⋈⋈⋈⋈⋈⋈

26
Prepositional and "Personal" A

Column A	Column B
¿Qué ve usted?	**¿A quién** ve usted?
What do you see?	*Whom* do you see?
Yo veo la pizarra.	Yo veo **a** <u>Teresa</u>.
I see the chalkboard.	I see Theresa.
¿Qué no comprenden ustedes?	**¿A quién** no comprenden ustedes?
What don't you understand?	*Whom* don't you understand?
No comprendemos el ejercicio.	No comprendemos **al** <u>profesor.</u>
We don't understand the exercise.	We don't understand the teacher.
¿Qué visita Ramón?	**¿A quiénes** visita Ramón?
What is Raymond visiting?	*Whom* is Raymond visiting?
Ramón visita las ciudades.	Ramón visita **a** <u>sus abuelos</u>.
Raymond is visiting the cities.	Raymond is visiting his grandparents.

1. In the sentences of column A above, the nouns that receive the action of the verb denote *things* (**la pizarra, el ejercicio, las ciudades**). They answer the question *What?* In the sentences of column B, the nouns that receive the action denote *persons* (**Teresa, el profesor, sus abuelos**). They answer the question *Whom?*

2. In Spanish, when the noun receiving the action of the verb denotes a person or persons, the noun is preceded by **a**. This word is called "the personal **a**" and is not translated into English.

   Practice A: Write the personal *a* in the blank before the noun wherever it is required. (Remember: *a* + *el* = *al*. If this is the form required, write *al* in the blank and cross out the article *el* that it replaces.)

167

1. ¿Ven Uds. _____ nuestra casa?

2. Invitamos _____ el amigo de Juan.

3. No comprendo _____ José.

4. Describimos _____ el país.

5. Visitan _____ el médico.

6. ¿Conoces tú _____ los hombres?

7. Traemos _____ las cartas.

8. No oigo _____ la mujer.

9. No puedo encontrar _____ el coche.

10. Yo recuerdo _____ las chicas.

11. Quiero ayudar _____ mi madre.

12. Escucho _____ el maestro.

tener + PERSONAL OBJECT

Tengo tres hermanos.　　María **tiene** un abuelo.
I have three brothers.　　　Mary has a grandfather.

3. **Tener** generally does not take the personal **a** before a personal object.

"Personal A" and Prepositional A

Column A	Column B
¿A quién ven Uds.?	**¿A quién** hablan Uds.?
Whom do you see?	*To whom* are you speaking?
Vemos **a** Roberto.	Hablamos **a** Roberto.
We see Robert.	We are speaking to Robert.

4. In the sentences of column A, the word **a** is not translated into English since it is the "personal **a**." In the sentences of column B, the word **a** is a preposition meaning *to*; hence, it must be translated into English.

5. **¿A quién? (¿a quiénes?)** may mean either *whom*? or *to whom*?, depending on whether **a** is "personal" or a preposition.

　　Practice B: Translate into English.

1. ¿Qué da Ud. a Juan? _____

2. No comprenden a los profesores. _____

3. Quieren ver a las niñas. _____

4. No escribimos cartas a nuestros amigos. _____

_____

5. Voy a visitar a mis abuelos. _____

6. ¿A quién escribes la carta? _____

7. ¿A quién no comprenden ellos? _____

◢ EXERCISES ◣

A. Paco and Paca are twin brother and sister who are ready to go to a party at their friend Roberto's home. They are so alike that they even say similar things. In the following example Paco makes a statement and Paca makes a similar statement, making <u>one</u> change. In each sentence that follows make the changes as in the example.

EXAMPLE: PACO: No conozco muy bien la casa de Roberto.
PACA: (la familia de Roberto) Yo no conozco muy bien a la familia de Roberto.

1. PACO: Yo prefiero ver un programa de televisión.

PACA: (mi amiga Berta) _____

2. PACO: No quiero oír a Jaime Rodríguez.

PACA: (los discos de Roberto) _____

3. PACO: Vamos a encontrar comida buena allí.

PACA: (los padres de Roberto) _____

4. PACO: No quiero escuchar a la hermana de Roberto.

PACA: (las historias de Roberto) _____

5. PACO: No entiendo las conversaciones de los amigos de Roberto.

PACA: (Roberto) _____

B. Answer each question as indicated in parentheses.

EXAMPLES: **¿A quién ve Ud.? (el hombre)**   **¿Qué quieren tomar Uds.? (el helado)**
Yo veo al hombre.   Nosotros queremos tomar el helado.

1. ¿A quién visitan Uds. hoy?   (nuestro tío)

_____

2. ¿Qué desea escribir Ud.?   (la carta)

_____

3. ¿A quiénes ves tú?   (los profesores)

_____

4. ¿A quién describe ella?   (su amiga)

_____

5. ¿Qué necesita hacer Ud.?   (el trabajo)

_____

6. ¿A quiénes llaman Uds.?   (las muchachas)

_____

7. ¿A quién entienden ellos?   (Alberto)

_____

8. ¿Qué dice Ud.?   (la verdad)

_____

9. ¿A quién saluda él?   (su amigo)

_____

10. ¿Qué terminan ellas?   (la tarea)

_____

C. Complete in Spanish.

1. a. I am describing the book. Yo describo _____.

    b. I am describing the boy. Yo describo _____.

2. a. I know the girl. Yo conozco _____.

    b. I know the city. Yo conozco _____.

3. a. Whom do you see? ¿_____ ves tú?

    b. What do you see? ¿_____ ves tú?

4. a. We do not believe the story. No creemos _____.

    b. We do not believe the man. No creemos _____.

5. a. Is he visiting my house? ¿Visita él _____?

    b. Is he visiting my father? ¿Visita él _____?

6. a. She does not understand the teacher. Ella no comprende _____.

    b. She does not understand the lesson. Ella no comprende _____.

7. a. Do you see many friends? ¿Ves tú _____.

    b. Do you have many friends? ¿Tienes tú _____.

8. a. Do they hear the noise? ¿Oyen ellos _____.

    b. Do they hear the children? ¿Oyen ellos _____.

9. a. To whom is he speaking? ¿_____ habla él?

    b. Whom is he helping? ¿_____ ayuda él?

10. a. He is speaking to John. Él habla _____.

    b. He is helping John. Él ayuda _____.

27
Direct Object Pronouns LO, LA, LOS, LAS: Referring to Things

▰▶ LO, LA

1. a. **Juan tiene el libro.**   John has the book.
    b. Juan **lo** tiene.   John has it.

2. a. Yo veo **la casa**.   I see the house.
    b. Yo **la** veo.   I see it.

1. The underlined words are *direct objects* of the verbs in the sentences.

    The direct object answers the question *what?* For example, in the sentence "John has the book," we can identify the direct object by asking, "John has *what?*" Answer: "the book." Hence, *the book* is the direct object of the verb *has*.

2. In sentences 1a and 2a above, the direct object is a *noun phrase* (**el libro; la casa**). In sentences 1b and 2b, the direct object is a *pronoun* (**lo; la**).

3. If the direct object is masculine singular, the object pronoun that replaces it is **lo**; if the direct object is feminine singular, it is replaced by **la**:

Ellos miran **el programa interesante**.   They are watching the interesting program.
Ellos **lo** miran.   They are watching it.

Él no estudia **la lección difícil**.   He does not study the difficult lesson.
Él no **la** estudia.   He does not study it.

4. The object pronoun comes directly before the verb. This is the case even if the subject of the verb is not expressed:

Hago **el trabajo**.   I do the work.
Lo hago.   I do it.

    Practice A: Rewrite each sentence, using the new verb given in parentheses.

EXAMPLE: **Juan lo compra. (vende)**   Juan lo vende.

  1. Nosotros la vemos.   (comprendemos) _____

  2. Ellos lo escriben.   (describen) _____

3. Ella lo hace.   (quiere)   _____

4. Juanito la lee.   (escribe)   _____

5. La explico.   (enseño)   _____

■▬▬▶   *LOS, LAS*

Mi padre lee **los periódicos**.   My father reads <u>the newspapers</u>.
Mi padre **los** lee.   My father reads <u>them</u>.

Luis compra **las revistas**.   Louis is buying <u>the magazines</u>.
Luis **las** compra.   Louis is buying <u>them</u>.

5. If the direct object is masculine plural, the object pronoun that replaces it is **los**; if it is feminine plural, it is replaced by **las**.

6. The form **los** is also used when referring to a group of nouns of "mixed" genders: Yo miro **el libro** y **la revista**; yo **los** miro.

Practice B: Complete the sentence by writing the object pronoun (*lo, la, los* or *las*) that can be substituted for the words in italics.

EXAMPLE: Nosotros leemos *las revistas.*   Nosotros _____*las*_____ leemos.

1. El profesor enseña *los verbos.*   El profesor _____ enseña.

2. Ella quiere *las cintas.*   Ella _____ quiere.

3. Yo escribo *la tarea.*   Yo _____ escribo.

4. Mi padre compra *el video.*   Mi padre _____ compra.

5. Ana ve *la casa* y *el jardín.*   Ana _____ ve.

Practice C: We learned in note 4, page 171, that the position of the object pronoun is not affected by the absence of an expressed subject. Rewrite each sentence so that it includes the direct object pronoun indicated in parentheses.

1. (la) Tomamos ahora.   _____

2. (los) Aprendo hoy.   _____

3. (las) Escribe ahora.   _____

4. (lo) Leen todos los días.   _____

5. (las) Compras con frecuencia.   _____

Position of Object Pronouns in Negative and Interrogative Sentences

Yo no comprendo <u>la frase</u>.	I do not understand <u>the sentence</u>.
Yo no <u>la</u> comprendo.	I do not understand <u>it</u>.
¿Desea usted <u>el libro</u>?	Do you want <u>the book</u>?
¿<u>Lo</u> desea usted?	Do you want <u>it</u>?

7. Whether the sentence is affirmative, negative, or interrogative, the direct object pronouns **lo, la, los,** and **las** *directly* precede the verb. (For exceptions, see Chapter 36.)

Practice D: Rewrite the sentence so that it includes the direct object pronoun indicated in parentheses.

1. (las)   No comprendo. _____

2. (lo)   ¿Beben ustedes? _____

3. (la)   ¿Quieres tú? _____

4. (los)   Ellos no escriben. _____

5. (lo)   ¿Hablamos? _____

Summary of Direct Object Pronouns

it, *m.*	**lo**	
it, *f.*	**la**	directly preceding the verb
them, *m.*	**los**	
them, *f.*	**las**	

◆ EXERCISES ◆

A. Make each sentence negative.

EXAMPLE: Yo lo tomo.   Yo no lo tomo.

1. Mi padre lo gana. _____

2. Elena la canta. _____

3. Las compramos. _____

4. Los venden. _____

5. José lo tiene. _____

B. Rewrite each statement as a question.

EXAMPLE: **Él lo habla.** ¿Lo habla él?

1. Juanita los tiene. _____
2. Mis amigos las visitan. _____
3. Tú lo haces. _____
4. Yo las quiero. _____
5. Ellos la traen. _____

C. Complete the sentence by writing the object pronoun (*lo, la, los,* or *las*) that can be substituted for the words in italics.

EXAMPLE: **Mi padre lee *el periódico.*** Mi padre ____lo____ lee.

1. El profesor explica *la lección.* El profesor _____ explica.
2. Mi hermana usa la computadora. Mi hermana _____ usa.
3. ¿Sabes tú *los verbos?* ¿_____ sabes tú?
4. Yo no tengo *el dinero.* Yo no _____ tengo.
5. Aprendemos *las palabras.* _____ aprendemos.
6. ¿Quiere Ud. *el diccionario?* ¿_____ quiere Ud.?
7. Mi madre prepara *la comida.* Mi madre _____ prepara.
8. No visitan *el museo.* No _____ visitan.
9. ¿Ven ellos *la escuela?* ¿_____ ven ellos?
10. Compramos *los discos* compactos. _____ compramos.

D. Rewrite each sentence, substituting an object pronoun for the words in italics.

EXAMPLE: **¿Ve ella *la película?*** ¿La ve ella?

1. Yo no como *las hamburguesas.* _____
2. Mis amigos leen el libro. _____
3. ¿Venden Uds. *los vestidos?* _____
4. Compramos *la carne.* _____
5. María estudia *los verbos.* _____

E. Lupe is very indecisive. Every time she is asked a question, she answers affirmatively, but then changes her mind and answers negatively. In the spaces provided write Lupe's two responses as in the example.

EXAMPLE: **¿Escribe Ud. el ejercicio?**   Sí, yo lo escribo.
No, yo no lo escribo.

1. ¿Usa Ud. el diccionario?   _____

_____

2. ¿Cantan ellos la canción?   _____

_____

3. ¿Tiene Juan los papeles?   _____

_____

4. ¿Beben Uds. la limonada?   _____

_____

5. ¿Escribe ella las cartas?   _____

_____

F. Underline the correct pronoun-verb combination that best completes the sentence.

EXAMPLE: **Juanito necesita una pluma y** (<u>la compra</u>, lo compra, las vende).

1. José tiene la computadora y (lo usa, la usa, la lee).

2. María estudia la lección y (la aprende, lo aprende, la vende).

3. Yo abro el libro y (los mato, lo leo, las leo).

4. Mi padre prepara la comida y (lo pone, la pone, la canta) en la mesa.

5. Tú traes los paquetes a casa y (los visitas, las bebes, los abres).

G. Complete in Spanish. In the following dialogs the first person makes a statement or asks a question, and the second person either comments on the statement or answers the question. Write the second person's comment or question as shown in the example.

EXAMPLE: **My father has the money.**   Mi padre tiene el dinero.
But you spend it.   Pero tú lo gastas.

1. My brother speaks Spanish.   Mi hermano habla español.

My sister speaks it too.   _____

2. They are selling the books.   Ellos venden los libros.

And we are buying them.   _____

3. I see the house.   Yo veo la casa.

We see it too.   _____

4. The teacher prepares the lessons.   El profesor prepara las lecciones.
    But I don't study them.   _____

5. Where is my shirt?   ¿Dónde está mi camisa?
    I have it.   _____

6. The dessert is on the table.   El postre está en la mesa.
    Are they eating it?   _____

7. Do you have the tickets?   ¿Tienes los billetes?
    I'm buying them.   _____

8. Do you want to watch TV?   ¿Quieres mirar la televisión?
    No, I'm turning it off (*apagar*).   _____

9. We're taking the bus.   Tomamos el autobús.
    I'm taking it too.   _____

10. Who has the magazines?   ¿Quién tiene las revistas?
    John has them.   _____

28
Direct Object Pronouns LO, LA, LOS, LAS: Referring to Persons

■■ I. "Him," "Her," "Them"

Yo veo **a Juan**.	I see *John*.
Yo **lo** veo.	I see *him*.
No comprendemos **a la profesora**.	We don't understand *the teacher*.
No **la** comprendemos.	We don't understand *her*.
¿Conoce Ud. **a estos señores**?	Do you know *these gentlemen*?
¿**Los** conoce Ud.?	Do you know *them*?
Visito **a mis amigas Lupe y Lola**.	I am visiting *my friends Lupe and Lola*.
Las visito.	I am visiting *them*.

1. In the preceding chapter, we learned how the object pronouns **lo**, **la**, **los**, and **las** can be substituted for noun phrases referring to *things*. As shown in the sentences above, the four object pronouns can also refer to *persons*:

$$\left.\begin{array}{ll} \textbf{lo} = it \ (m.) \ \text{or} \ him & \textbf{los} \ (m.) \\ \\ \textbf{la} = it \ (f.) \ \text{or} \ her & \textbf{las} \ (f.) \end{array}\right\} = them \ \text{(things or persons)}$$

2. The form **los** is also used when referring to a "mixed" group of males and females: Yo veo a **María** y a **Jorge**; yo **los** veo.

   Some examples of how the direct object pronouns are used:

Comprendo **la lección**. Comprendo **a la profesora**.	}	**La** comprendo.	{ I understand *it*. I understand *her*.
Escuchamos **el cuento**. Escuchamos **a Paco**.	}	**Lo** escuchamos.	{ We listen to *it*. We listen to *him*.
Ella ve **las casas**. Ella ve **a las chicas**.	}	Ella **las** ve.	She sees *them*.
¿Conoce Ud. **estos países**? ¿Conoce Ud. **a estos chicos**?	}	¿**Los** conoce Ud.?	Do you know *them*?

177

Practice A: Complete the sentence by writing the direct object pronoun that can be substituted for the words in italics.

EXAMPLES: **Esteban tiene *los libros.***   Esteban _____*los*_____ tiene.

   Yo visito a mis amigos.   Yo _____*los*_____ visito.

1. María estudia *las lecciones.*   María _____ estudia.

2. José saluda *a la profesora.*   José _____ saluda.

3. Vemos *a los profesores.*   _____ vemos.

4. ¿No conoces *a Juan?*   ¿No _____ conoces?

5. Ellos miran *el programa musical.*   Ellos _____ miran.

6. Yo conozco *a las alumnas y a su profesor.*   Yo _____ conozco.

II. "You"

No **lo** oigo, señor Pérez.   I don't hear *you*, Mr. Pérez.

La entiendo, señora Mendoza.   I understand *you*, Mrs. Mendoza.

Yo **los** invito a mi fiesta, señores González.   I invite *you* to my party, Mr. and Mrs. González.

Muchachas, ¿dónde están Uds.? No **las** veo.   Where are you, girls? I don't see *you*.

3. The direct object pronouns **lo**, **la**, **los**, and **las** can also mean *you*. They are used with this meaning when speaking to persons addressed as **usted** or **ustedes**.

4. a. **Lo** is used when speaking to a male, **la** when speaking to a female.
    b. Many Spanish-speaking people use the form **le** instead of **lo** to mean *you* (*m.*) or *him* as a direct object:

    Yo **le** veo.   { I see you (*m.*).
                            I see him.

    Ellos **le** comprenden.   { They understand you (*m.*).
                                  They understand him.

    In this book, however, only **lo** will be used in such cases.

5. **Los** is used when speaking to two or more males or to a "mixed" group of males and females, **las** when speaking to two or more females.

6. In English, *you* may be either a subject or an object pronoun. In the sentence "You see John," *You* is a subject pronoun and is translated as **Tú, Usted,** or **Ustedes**; in the sentence "John sees you," *you* is a direct object pronoun and is translated as **lo, la, los,** or **las,** depending on whether the *you* is male or female, singular or plural.

    Practice B: Complete each sentence with an appropriate object pronoun meaning you.

    1. ¿Quién es usted, señor? Yo no _____ conozco.

    2. Señoritas, nosotros _____ invitamos a la fiesta.

3. Creo que _____ conozco; ustedes son los hermanos de Juan, ¿verdad?

4. Cuando usted habla, señora, siempre _____ escucho.

Note:

Lo veo	*I see it.* (el libro)	
	I see him.	**Lo veo a él.**
	I see you. (m. sing.)	**Lo veo a Ud.**
La vemos.	*We see it.* (la casa)	
	We see her.	**La vemos a ella.**
	We see you. (f. sing.)	**La vemos a Ud.**
Los (las) oímos.	*We hear them.* (things)	
	We hear them. (people)	**Los (las) oímos a ellos (ellas).**
	We hear you. (pl.)	**Los (las) oímos a Uds.**

Since the object pronouns **lo, la, los, las** may refer to things or people, we may add **a él, a ella, a Ud.**, etc. to clarify the meanings when referring to people.

Practice C: Add **a él, a ella, a ellos, a ellas, a Ud., a Uds.** where necessary. Rewrite the sentence if you add **a él**, etc.

EXAMPLES: I don't hear it.   No lo oigo.

_____

I don't hear him.   No lo oigo.
                          No lo oigo a él.

1. Do they understand him?   ¿Lo comprenden?

_____

2. We don't see them. (las casas)   No las vemos.

_____

3. I'm visiting her.   La visito.

_____

4. I don't hear you.   No lo oigo.

_____

5. She knows him.   Ella lo conoce.

_____

6. They don't believe it.   No lo creen.

_____

7. We don't understand you.   No los comprendemos.

_____

8. Do they hear you?   ¿Los oyen ellos?

_____

9. I don't see them. (los edificios)   No los veo.

_____

10. We are buying it.   Lo compramos.

_____

=== **LA MITAD DEL MUNDO** ===

A very interesting site, called _La Mitad del Mundo_ (the Middle of the World), is found at about fifteen miles from Quito, Ecuador. At this place there is a monument that marks the equator, and at that point one can cross the equator, placing one foot in the Northern Hemisphere and the other foot in the Southern Hemisphere. There is a plaque on the monument with the inscription 0° 0′ 0″. This is a very popular attraction for tourists from all parts of the world.

▲ EXERCISES ▲

A. Complete the sentence by writing the object pronoun (_lo, la, los,_ or _las_) that can be substituted for the words in italics.

EXAMPLE: **No oímos** _al profesor._   No ____lo____ oímos.

1. ¿Encuentran Uds. a _sus amigos?_   ¿_____ encuentran Uds.?

2. Saludamos _a los jugadores._   _____ saludamos.

3. No veo _a mi padre._   No _____ veo.

4. ¿Conoces _a Francisca?_   ¿_____ conoces?

5. ¿Oyen Uds. _el ruido?_   ¿_____ oyen Uds?

6. Comprendo muy bien _la situación._   _____ la comprendo muy bien.

7. ¿Por qué no ayudas _a tus padres?_   ¿Por qué no _____ ayudas?

In **8-10,** complete the sentence by using the appropriate direct object pronoun that means "you."

8. Señora Méndez, ¿puede Ud. hablar más alto? No _____ oigo.

9. Cuando Ud. habla rápidamente, señor García, no _____ entendemos.

10. Señoritas, ¿vienen Uds. a la clase? El profesor _____ busca.

B. Rewrite each sentence, substituting an object pronoun for the words in italics.

EXAMPLES: **Yo veo** _a María._   Yo la veo.
   ¿Tienen Uds. _el dinero?_   ¿Lo tienen Uds.?

1. No comprendo _al profesor._   _____

2. ¿Conocen Uds. _a estos señores?_   _____

3. Saludamos *a Lola*.   _____

4. No escuchan *a Juana y María*.   _____

5. No compro *la calculadora*.   _____

6. ¿Quién conoce *a ese hombre*?   _____

7. No escuchamos *el disco*.   _____

8. ¿Cuándo visita Ud. *a sus tíos*?   _____

9. Ellas ven *a sus amigas*.   _____

10. ¿Tienes tú *las cintas*?   _____

C. In the following exercise your friend makes a statement and then asks you if that also happens to you, as shown in the example. In the blanks provided, supply the follow-up questions.

EXAMPLES: **No veo a José.**   ¿Lo ves tú?
           Yo no ayudo a la profesora. ¿La ayudas tú?

1. Yo no conozco a esa mujer.   _____

2. No escucho a los adultos.   _____

3. Yo no visito a mi abuelo.   _____

4. No uso la computadora.   _____

5. Yo no leo los libros de aventuras. _____

D. In the following exercise, one person asks a question and the other(s) answer(s) affirmatively using an object pronoun. Write the answer to each question as shown in the example.

EXAMPLE: **¿Conoce Ud. a Roberto?** Sí, (yo) lo conozco.

1. ¿Entiende Ud. a los actores?   _____

2. ¿Oyen Uds. las cintas?   _____

3. ¿Describe Ud. a su profesor?   _____

4. ¿Miran Uds. a Luis?   _____

5. ¿Ve Ud. los edificios?   _____

E. Complete the reply to each question as shown in the example (*me* = me, *nos* = us).

EXAMPLE: **¿Me conoce Ud.?** Sí, señor, yo _____lo conozco_____ .

1. ¿Me escucha Ud.?   Sí, señora, yo _____ .

2. ¿Nos conoce Ud.?   Sí, señores, yo _____ .

3. ¿Nos invitan Uds.?   Sí, señoritas, nosotros _____ .

4. ¿Me comprenden Uds.?   Sí, señor, nosotros _____ .

5. ¿No me oye Ud.?   No, señora, yo no _____ .

F. Follow the instructions in exercise D. But this time answer negatively as in the example.

EXAMPLE: **¿Tienen Uds. el dinero?** No, no lo tenemos.

1. ¿Oyen Uds. la música?   _____

2. ¿Comprende Ud. al profesor?   _____

3. ¿Ves tú a tu hermana?   _____

4. ¿Ayuda Ud. a sus padres?   _____

5. ¿Abren Uds. las ventanas?   _____

G. Complete each sentence in Spanish.

1. I have the tapes and I'm bringing them.

   Tengo las cintas y _____ .

2. He sees his friend and he greets him.

   Ve a su amigo y _____ .

3. I know you, John, and I don't believe it.

   Yo _____ , Juan, y _____ .

4. We understand the children and we help them.

   Nosotros comprendemos a los niños y _____ .

5. I always hear you, Mrs. López, but sometimes I don't understand you.

   Yo siempre _____ señora López, pero algunas veces

   _____ .

6. I remember Mary but I don't know her well.

   Yo recuerdo a María pero _____ bien.

7. We are meeting our uncle at the airport and are taking him home. [to take (someone somewhere) = *llevar*]

   Encontramos a nuestro tío en el aeropuerto y _____ a casa.

8. When she has money, she spends it. (to spend = *gastar*)

Cuando ella tiene dinero, _____.

9. The children see the toys and want them.

Los niños ven los juguetes y _____.

10. Do you call your aunts and do you visit them often?

¿Llaman Uds. a sus tías y _____ a menudo?

H. In items **1-5** below, read the description of each situation and the first line of dialog, then choose the most likely response that the second speaker would make. Circle the letter of your choice.

1. Francisco y Vicente hablan de un viaje que desean hacer a España.

FRANCISCO: Mi profesor de español dice que España es un país muy hermoso.

VICENTE: a. Es verdad. Mis padres la visitan todos los años.
                   b. Sí, yo la visito todos los domingos.
                   c. Sí, mis tíos la escriben todos los sábados.

2. Tomás y Gerardo caminan por la calle y ven a unas amigas.

TOMÁS: ¿Ves a Graciela y a Lupita?

GERARDO: a. Sí, los veo.
                   b. Sí, las veo muy bien.
                   c. Sí, las comprendo bien.

3. Usted mira un programa de televisión y su padre entra en la sala.

EL PADRE: ¿Miras otra vez la televisión?

USTED: a. Sí, mamá, los miro.
                   b. Sí, papá, la miro.
                   c. Sí, papá, los miro.

4. La profesora habla con los estudiantes.

LA PROFESORA: ¿Me escuchan Uds. con cuidado cuando explico las lecciones?

LOS ESTUDIANTES: a. Sí, señora, los escuchamos con cuidado.
                   b. Sí, señora, las escucho con cuidado.
                   c. Sí, señora, la escuchamos con cuidado.

5. El señor Gómez decide comprar un coche.

LA SEÑORA GÓMEZ: ¿Por qué compras este coche?

EL SEÑOR GÓMEZ: a. Lo compro porque es práctico.
                   b. La compro porque no cuesta mucho dinero.
                   c. No lo compro porque no me gusta.

29
Indirect Object
Pronouns LE and LES

I. "(to) Him," "(to) Her," "(to) Them"

LE

Yo hablo a **José**.*	I speak to *Joseph*.
Yo **le** hablo.	I speak to *him*.
Yo hablo a **María**.*	I speak to *Mary*.
Yo **le** hablo.	I speak *to her*.

Yo doy el libro a **Juan**.*	I give *John* the book. I give the book *to John*.
Yo **le** doy el libro.	I give *him* the book. I give the book *to him*.

LES

Escribimos **a los hombres**.*	We write *to the men*.
Les escribimos.	We write *to them*.
¿Quién da los libros **a las chicas**?*	Who gives the books *to the girls*?

¿Quién **les** da los libros?	Who gives *them* the books? Who gives the books *to them*?

1. In the sentences above, the Spanish pronouns **le** and **les** are *indirect object pronouns*. They answer the question *to whom?* Note their meanings in those sentences:

     le = to him, to her   **les** = to them (*m. & f.*)

2. Note that **le** and **les** can be substituted for phrases beginning with the preposition **a** (meaning *to*) such as **a José, a los profesores, a las muchachas bonitas, a mis amigos,** etc.

3. Keep in mind that the pronouns *him, her,* and *them* are sometimes direct objects, sometimes indirect objects. For example, the pronoun *her* is a direct object in the sentence "I see her" but an indirect object in the sentence "I give her the book." In the first case, *her* = **la**; in the second, *her* = **le**.

*It is very common in spoken and written Spanish to use the object pronouns *le* and *les* with the phrases they refer to, e.g., **yo le hablo a José, les escribimos a los hombres,** etc. For the purpose of this First-year Workbook, this usage will not be required.

Practice A: Complete the Spanish sentences.

1. She shows her the books.   Ella _____ muestra los libros.

2. She shows the books to her.   Ella _____.

3. She shows him the books.   Ella _____ muestra los libros.

4. She shows the books to him.   Ella _____.

Practice B: Complete the Spanish sentences.

1. They write to her.   Ellos _____ escriben.

2. She writes to him.   Ella _____ escribe.

3. (them = los muchachos)

   He writes to them.   Él _____ escribe.

4. (them = las señoritas)

   She writes to them.   Ella _____ escribe.

The Roman aqueduct at Segovia, Spain. The imposing aqueduct of Segovia, built by the Romans almost 2000 years ago, continued to supply water to the city until 1958.

Practice C: Complete the Spanish sentences. Be careful to distinguish between direct and indirect object pronouns.

1. We invite her to the party.   _____ invitamos a la fiesta,

2. We tell her the truth.   _____ decimos a la verdad.

(In 3 and 4, them = los amigos)

3. I see them every day.   _____ veo todos los días.

4. I show them the picture.   _____ muestro el cuadro.

(In 5 and 6, them = las muchachas)

5. We greet them.   _____ saludamos.

6. We give them the tickets.   _____ damos los billetes.

II. "(to) You"

LE

Ellos **le** hablan.	They speak *to you* (*m. & f.*).
Yo **le** doy el libro.	{ I give *you* the book. { I give the book to *you*.

LES

Los chicos no **les** escriben.	The boys don't write to you (*pl., m. & f.*).
Ellos **les** muestran las fotos.	{ They show *you* (*pl.*) the photos. { They show the photos *to you* (*pl.*).

4. *To you* (*plural*) = **les** in Spanish America. In Spain, however, *to you* (*formal plural*) = **les** and *to you* (*familiar plural*) = **os** (see note 3, page 191).

5. In English, *you* may be either a subject or an object pronoun. In the sentence "You give him the book," *You* is a subject pronoun and is expressed in Spanish as **usted** or **ustedes**; in the sentence "He gives you the book," *you* is an indirect object pronoun and is expressed as either **le** or **les**, depending on whether the "you" is singular or plural.

6. Unlike the direct object pronouns (Chapter 28), the forms **le** and **les** do not indicate gender and therefore can refer to persons of either gender.

Practice D: Complete each sentence with an appropriate object pronoun meaning (*to*) *you*. The names in parentheses indicate the persons addressed as "you."

1. (Juan y María)   Yo _____ doy los billetes.

2. (el Sr. García)   Yo _____ muestro mi composición.

3. (los Sres. Rivera) Nosotros _____ explicamos el problema.

4. (la Sra. Pérez)   Juan _____ escribe una carta.

7. **Note:** The meanings of the indirect object pronouns may be clarified by adding any of the following: **a Ud., a él, a ella, a Uds., a ellos, a ellas.**

Yo **le** escribo.	I write to you.	Yo **le** escribo *a Ud.*
	I write to him.	Yo **le** escribo *a él.*
	I write to her.	Yo **le** escribo *a ella.*
Les damos el dinero.	We give them the money.	Les damos el dinero *a ellos (ellas).*
	We give you the money.	Les damos el dinero *a Uds.*

Practice E: Expand each sentence as in the following example.

EXAMPLE: **Doy los libros.** I give her the books.
Le doy los libros a ella.

1. Mandamos cartas. We are sending them letters.

_____

2. ¿Dices la verdad? Are you telling her the truth?

_____

3. No presto el dinero. I'm not (lending you [pl.]) the money.

_____

4. Traen los discos. They're bringing you (sing.) the records.

_____

5. Pagamos un dólar. We're paying him one dollar.

_____

▲ EXERCISES ▲

A. Make each sentence negative.

EXAMPLE: **Ella les trae el dinero.** Ella no les trae el dinero.

1. Yo les doy los libros.   _____

2. ¿Quién le escribe la carta?   _____

3. Nosotros les prestamos dinero. _____

4. Luisa le manda el paquete.   _____

5. Ramón les trae las cintas.   _____

B. Change each statement to a question.

EXAMPLE: **Ud. le da el libro.** ¿Le da Ud. el libro?

1. Él les sirve la comida.   _____

2. Yo le digo la verdad.   _____

3. Marta les habla en inglés.   _____

4. Ellos le pagan dos dólares.   _____

5. Tú les describes la casa.   _____

C. Answer affirmatively.

EXAMPLE: **¿Les vende Ud. la casa?** Sí, les vendo la casa.

1. ¿Le mandan Uds. los disquetes?   _____

2. ¿Les habla Ud. en español?   _____

3. ¿Le dice Ud. la verdad?   _____

4. ¿Les escriben Uds. cartas?   _____

5. ¿Le presta Ud. dinero?   _____

D. Answer negatively.

EXAMPLES: **¿Le da Ud. la pluma?**   No, no le doy la pluma.
           ¿Le traen Uds. el paquete? No, no le traemos el paquete.

1. ¿Le repite Ud. la pregunta?   _____

2. ¿Les muestra Ud. el cuadro?   _____

3. ¿Le pagan Uds. el sándwich?   _____

4. ¿Les explica Ud. la regla?   _____

5. ¿Le cantan Uds. una canción?   _____

E. Answer affirmatively, as shown in the following examples. [*me* = (to) me, *nos* = (to) us]

EXAMPLES: **¿Me dicen Uds. la verdad?** Sí, le decimos la verdad.
           ¿Nos presta Ud. el libro? Sí, les presto el libro.

1. ¿Me da Ud. la revista?   _____

2. ¿Nos habla Ud. de María?   _____

3. ¿Me venden Uds. los libros? _____

4. ¿Nos trae Ud. los billetes? _____

5. ¿Me sirven Uds. la comida? _____

F. Answer each question affirmatively and negatively, using an indirect object pronoun.

    EXAMPLE: **¿ Le escribe Ud. la carta?** Sí, le escribo la carta.
                                          No, no le escribo la carta.

1. ¿Le manda Ud. la tarjeta? _____

_____

2. ¿Les lee Ud. el cuento? _____

_____

3. ¿Le vende Ud. la casa? _____

_____

4. ¿Les prestan Uds. el dinero? _____

_____

5. ¿Le escribes tú la nota? _____

_____

G. Write the Spanish equivalents. Clarify each sentence.

1. I am singing to her.   Yo le canto a ella.

    a. I am speaking to her. _____

    b. I am reading to her. _____

    c. I am writing to her. _____

2. We send flowers to them.   Les mandamos flores a ellos.

    a. We send flowers to her. _____

    b. We send him flowers. _____

3. Are you telling him the truth?   ¿Le dice Ud. la verdad a él?

    a. Are you telling her the truth? _____

    b. Are you telling them the truth? _____

4. He is not sending them the video.   No les manda el video a ellas.

   a. He is not lending them the video. _____

   b. He is not giving them the video. _____

   c. He is not bringing her the video. _____

5. (The words in parentheses indicate the persons addressed as "you.")

   EXAMPLE: (Mr. Smith) He gives you the book.   Le da el libro a Ud.

   a. (Mr. and Mrs. Jones)
     They give you the gifts. _____

   b. (Miss Pérez)
     They send you a letter. _____

   c. (the boys)
     They speak to you in Spanish. _____

30
The Object Pronouns
ME, TE, NOS, and OS

Yo estoy aquí. ¿**Me** oye Ud.?	I am here. Do you hear **me**?
Ella **me** da cinco dólares.	She gives **me** five dollars.
Tú hablas muy rápido; no **te** comprendo.	You speak very fast; I don't understand **you**.
Ellos no **nos** comprenden.	They don't understand **us**.
Él **nos** presta los discos.	He lends **us** the records.
Vosotros sois los amigos de Juan; **os** conocemos bien.	You are John's friends; we know **you** well.
Ellos **me** hablan.	They speak **to me**.
te	**to you**
nos	**to us**
os	**to you** (*pl.*)

1. **Me**, **te**, **nos**, and **os** may be used as both direct and indirect object pronouns.

2. Like all other object pronouns, **me**, **te**, **nos**, and **os** precede the verb. (For exceptions, see Chapter 36.)

3. **Os**, the object-pronoun form of **vosotros**, is used in Spain only. The forms **vosotros** and **os** are not used in Spanish America, where two or more persons are addressed as **ustedes** even when the speaker is on familiar terms with them. (For the object pronouns corresponding to **ustedes**, see Chapter 28, page 178, and Chapter 29, page 186.)

◀ EXERCISES ▶

A. Make each sentence negative.

EXAMPLE: **Mis amigos me ven.**   Mis amigos no me ven.

1. El profesor nos habla. _____

2. Yo te traigo los discos. _____

3. ¿Quién me entiende? _____

4. Te mandan los videos. _____

5. Ellos os dicen la verdad. _____

B. Rewrite each statement as a question.

EXAMPLE: **Ellos nos comprenden.** ¿Nos comprenden ellos?

1. Uds. me prestan el dinero.   _____

2. Tú nos visitas en el hospital.   _____

3. Yo te doy la cinta.   _____

4. Ellas me saludan en español.   _____

5. Ellos no os oyen.   _____

C. Complete the answer to each question as shown in the following examples.

EXAMPLES: **¿Quién me ve?**   Papá _____ te ve _____ .

            ¿Quién nos habla? El profesor _____ os habla _____ .

1. ¿Quién nos escribe?   Mamá _____ .

2. ¿Quién me paga el dinero?   Paco _____ .

3. ¿Quién nos manda flores?   Vuestro tío _____ .

4. ¿Quiénes me traen los libros? José y Mariana _____ .

5. Quiénes nos saludan?   Las chicas _____ .

D. Answer the questions as shown in the following examples.

EXAMPLES: **¿Te ven todos los días?**   Sí, me ven todos los días.
            ¿Me comprenden ellos ahora?   Sí, ellos te comprenden ahora.

1. ¿Me sirven el desayuno?   _____

2. ¿Te explican la lección?   _____

3. ¿Me oyen los niños?   _____

4. ¿Te visitan Lola y Javier? _____

5. ¿Me mira Luis?   _____

E. Express in Spanish as shown by the models.

1. I see you now.   Yo te veo ahora.

    a. I am visiting you now.   _____

    b. I am speaking to you now. _____

    c. I hear you now.   _____

2. They see us.   Nos ven.

    a. They ask us.   _____

    b. They write to us.   _____

    c. They describe us.   _____

3. Does he see me?   ¿Me ve él?

    a. Does he hear me?   _____

    b. Does he answer me?   _____

    c. Does he speak to me?   _____

4. She is not talking to me.   Ella no me habla.

    a. She isn't writing to me.   _____

    b. She isn't reading to me.   _____

    c. She isn't visiting me.   _____

5. What are you bringing me?   ¿Qué me traes?

    a. What are you bringing us?   _____

    b. What are they bringing you?   _____

    c. What are they bringing us?   _____

31
Object Pronouns With
GUSTAR: "To Like"

"I Like"

Me gusta la escuela.	I like the school.
Me gustan los profesores.	I like the teachers.
Me gusta estudiar.	I like to study.

1. *I like* is expressed in Spanish by **me gusta** or **me gustan**.

2. Use **me gusta** if what is liked is in the singular or is an infinitive; use **me gustan** if what is liked is in the plural.

   Practice A: Use *Me gusta* or *Me gustan*.

   1. _____ los libros.

   2. _____ comer.

   3. _____ mi sombrero.

   4. _____ sus amigos.

   5. _____ mirar la televisión.

"You Like," "He (She) Likes," etc.

Te gusta el café.	You like (the) coffee.
No **te** gustan las flores.	You don't like (the) flowers.
Le gusta leer.	{ You like to read. He/She likes to read.
Le gustan las revistas.	{ You like the magazines. He/She likes the magazines.
Nos gusta el programa.	We like the program.
Nos gustan las casas.	We like the houses.
Os gusta viajar.	You (*pl.*) like to travel.
Os gustan los discos compactos.	You like the CD's.
No **les** gusta la película.	They/You (*pl.*) don't like the film.
Les gustan los cuentos.	They/You (*pl.*) like the stories.

3. In all cases, we use **gusta** if what is liked is singular or is an infinitive; we use **gustan** if what is liked is plural.

4. The verb **gustar** means *to please* or *to be pleasing* (*to someone*). Thus, when we say "I like it" in Spanish, we are really saying "It is pleasing to *me*." That is why we use the indirect object pronouns **me, te, le, nos, os,** and **les.**

Summary of the Use of GUSTAR

I like   **me gusta, me gustan**

	familiar		formal
you like	**te gusta, os gusta**	or	**le gusta, les gusta**
	te gustan, os gustan	or	**le gustan, les gustan**

he (she) likes **le gusta, le gustan**

we like   { **nos gusta**
              { **nos gustan**

they like   { **les gusta**
              { **les gustan**

Practice B: Underline the correct form.

1. We like to eat.
   (Nos gusta, Nos gustan, Les gusta) comer.

2. She does not like the books.
   (No les gusta, No le gusta, No le gustan) los libros.

3. They like the ice cream.
   (Les gustan, Les gusta, Le gusta) el helado.

4. You like to dance.
   (Te gustan, Te gusta, Les gustan) bailar.

5. I don't like the shirts.
   (No me gustan, No me gusta, Me gustan) las camisas.

Forming Questions With GUSTAR

Te gustan las frutas.	You like (the) fruit.
¿Te gustan las frutas?	Do you like the fruit?
No les gusta el vestido.	They don't like the dress.
¿No les gusta el vestido?	Don't they like the dress?

5. A statement with **gustar** can be changed to a question without changing the word order. Only the punctuation (¿ . . . ?) or the tone of voice indicates that the sentence is a question.

Practice C: Rewrite as a question.

1. Me gustan los postres. _____

2. Les gusta andar. _____

3. Le gustan los animales. _____

4. Nos gusta la ciudad. _____

5. No te gustan los libros. _____

Clarifying the Meaning of *Le* or *Les*

¿**le** gusta(n)?	do *you* like?	= ¿**le** gusta(n) **a usted**?*
	does *he* like?	= ¿**le** gusta(n) **a él**?
	does *she* like?	= ¿**le** gusta(n) **a ella**?
no **les** gusta(n)	*you* (*pl.*) don't like	= no **les** gusta(n) **a ustedes**
	they (*m.*) don't like	= no **les** gusta(n) **a ellos**
	they (*f.*) don't like	= no **les** gusta(n) **a ellas**

*or ¿**A usted le** gusta(n)? Same with the following.

6. Each of the object pronouns **le** and **les** has several possible meanings. If emphasis or greater clarity is required, the intended meaning can be precisely expressed by adding one of the following phrases: **a usted, a él, a ella, a ustedes, a ellos,** and **a ellas**:

—¿**Les** gusta el libro?	Do they like the book?
—**Le** gusta **a él** pero no le gusta **a ella**.	He likes it but she does not.
—¿No **le** gustan **a usted** los cuadros?	Don't you like the pictures?

Llama at waterhole in the Andes of Chile.

Practice D: In the Spanish sentences, clarify the meaning of **le** or **les** by writing the appropriate phrase in the blank.

1. They like the movie.   _____ les gusta la película.

2. She does not like to skate.   _____ no le gusta patinar.

3. Do you like to work?   ¿Le gusta trabajar _____?

4. He likes the candy.   _____ le gustan los dulces.

5. Do you like the books.   ¿Les gustan los libros _____?

How to Express "It" and "Them" When Using GUSTAR

—¿Le gusta a Ud. el sombrero?   Do you like the hat?
—Sí, me gusta.   Yes, I like *it*.

—¿Les gusta a Uds. la casa?   Do you like the house?
—No, no nos gusta.   No, we do not like *it*.

—¿Te gustan las cintas?   Do you like the tapes?
—Sí, me gustan.   Yes, I like *them*.

7. When statements such as *I like it* and *we like them* are translated into Spanish, the words *it* and *them* are not expressed since they become the *subject* of the verb. For example, I like *it* = "*it* pleases me," we like *them* = "*they* please us." (The word *it*, as *subject*, is usually not expressed in Spanish.)

Practice E: Express in Spanish.

1. I like them.   _____

2. Do you like it?   _____

3. We do not like it.   _____

4. They like them.   _____

5. She does not like them. _____

◤ EXERCISES ◢

A. **Nacho negativo.** Nacho is a contrary individual who negates everything he hears. Write Nacho's contradictions as shown in the following example.

   EXAMPLE: **Me gustan las frutas.**   No me gustan las frutas.

1. Les gusta viajar.   _____

2. Nos gustan las noticias.   _____

3. A ella le gustan las bebidas. _____

4. Te gusta trabajar.   _____

5. A él le gusta el fútbol.   _____

B.   Choose **gusta** or **gustan**.

    1. No me _____ las verduras.

    2. ¿Te _____ jugar al tenis?

    3. Les _____ el país.

    4. A ella no le _____ los exámenes.

    5. Nos _____ tocar el piano.

    6. A Ud. le _____ los deportes, ¿verdad?

    7. A ellos no les _____ la clase.

    8. Me _____ enseñar.

    9. ¿Les _____ las plantas?

  10. No nos _____ la televisión.

C.   Nacho and his sister Nidia are going shopping for gifts for their brother and sister. The clerk
in the store asks them questions about the likes and dislikes of the recipients in order to
help them decide what to buy. Give Nidia's affirmative response and Nacho's negative response as shown in the following example.

    EXAMPLE: **¿Le gusta a ella la lana?**   Sí, le gusta la lana.
                                               No, no le gusta la lana.

    1. ¿Le gusta a ella llevar faldas?   _____

                                             _____

    2. ¿Les gusta a ellos llevar pantalones?   _____

                                             _____

    3. ¿Le gusta a él el algodón?   _____

                                             _____

    4. ¿Les gustan a ellos los pañuelos?   _____

                                             _____

    5. ¿Le gustan a él los deportes?   _____

                                             _____

D. Answer each question as shown in the example, replacing the words in italics with an unexpressed pronoun. (In your answers to **3** and **4**, omit the phrases "a ella" and "a ellas.")

EXAMPLE: **¿Te gusta** *la fiesta?* Sí, ___*me gusta*___ . (Yes, I like it.)

1. ¿Le gustan a Ud. *los carnavales?*   No, _____.

2. ¿Te gusta ir *al centro?*   Sí, _____.

3. ¿Le gusta a ella *el coche nuevo?*   No, _____.

4. ¿Les gustan a ellas *los restaurantes?*   Sí, _____.

5. ¿Os gusta *andar por el parque?*   No, _____.

E. The editor's word processor has gone haywire. Rearrange each sentence so that it makes sense. Arrange the words so that they form a sentence.

1. gustan los me artículos

_____

2. ¿ bailar Ud. gusta a le ?

_____

3. nos estudiar gusta no

_____

4. ¿ gustan fiestas te las ?

_____

5. invierno no ellos gusta a les el

_____

F. Complete in Spanish.

1. I like the movies   _____ el cine.

2. Do you like the ties?   ¿_____ a Ud. las corbatas?

3. They do not like to travel.   _____ viajar.

4. Does she like your dress?   ¿_____ su vestido?

5. We do not like them.   _____.

6. Do they like summer?   ¿_____ el verano?

7. I do not like the shoes.   _____ los zapatos.

8. He likes the animals.   _____ los animales.

9. Don't you like it?   ¿_____ a Uds.?

10. We like to watch television.   _____ mirar la televisión.

32
Reflexive Pronouns

Yo me miro y me admiro.

me, myself	**nos**, ourselves
te, yourself	**os**, yourselves

se { yourself, himself, herself, itself, yourselves, themselves

1. Reflexive pronouns are also object pronouns. Therefore, they directly precede the conjugated verb.

◼ Reflexive Verbs

lavarse, to wash oneself

yo *me* **lavo**	I wash (am washing) myself
tú *te* **lavas**	you wash (are washing) yourself
Ud. *se* **lava**	you wash (are washing) yourself
él *se* **lava**	he washes (is washing) himself
ella *se* **lava**	she washes (is washing) herself
nosotros(-as) *nos* **lavamos**	we wash (are washing) ourselves
vosotros(-as) *os* **laváis**	you wash (are washing) yourselves
Uds. *se* **lavan**	you wash (are washing) yourselves
ellos *se* **lavan**	they wash (are washing) themselves
ellas *se* **lavan**	they wash (are washing) themselves

2. The so-called reflexive verbs are verbs that are commonly used with reflexive-pronoun objects. They are identified in vocabulary lists by the pronoun **se** attached to the infinitive.

3. Reflexive verbs are conjugated like other verbs, except that their conjugated forms are preceded by reflexive pronouns.

4. In English, the reflexive pronouns *myself, yourself, herself,* etc., are often omitted; for example, "I am washing" may mean "I am washing *myself* " or "I am washing the *dishes (clothes,* etc.)," depending on the situation. Spanish, however, almost never omits the reflexive pronoun when the meaning is reflexive: "I am washing (*myself* understood)" = yo **me** lavo.

Common Reflexive Verbs

1. **acostarse** (**ue**), to go to bed
   Anita **se acuesta** a las diez.   Anita goes to bed at ten o'clock.

2. **bañarse**, to bathe (oneself)
   Yo **me baño** todos los días.   I bathe every day.

3. **despertarse** (**ie**), to wake up
   ¿A qué hora **te despiertas** los sábados?   At what time do you wake up on Saturdays?

4. **lavarse**, to wash (oneself), to get washed
   ¿**Se lava** Ud. las manos antes de comer?   Do you wash your hands before eating?

5. **levantarse**, to rise, to get up, to stand up
   Se levantan a las seis.   They get up at six o'clock.

6. **llamarse**, to be called (named)
   Ese muchacho **se llama** Juan.   That boy is called John. (That boy's name is John.)

7. **peinarse**, to comb one's hair
   Mis amigos siempre **se peinan**.   My friends are always combing their hair.

8. **ponerse**, to put on (clothes)
   Me pongo el sombrero cuando hace frío.   I put on my hat when it is cold.

9. **quedarse**, to remain, to stay
   ¿**Se quedan** Uds. en casa esta tarde?   Are you staying at home this afternoon?

10. **quitarse**, to take off (clothes)
    Nos quitamos el abrigo en casa.   We take off our coats at home.

11. **sentarse**(**ie**), to sit down
    ¿Dónde **se sienta** su padre?   Where does your father sit?

Observe:

a. Many reflexive verbs are also stem-changing verbs. (See verbs 1, 3, and 11.)

b. Many reflexive verbs have meanings that are not expressed reflexively in English. For example, note that the reflexive pronouns *myself, yourself,* etc., are not used in the English equivalents of verbs 8, 9, and 11.

c. When the object of a reflexive verb is an article of clothing or a part of the body, as in examples 4, 8, and 10, the definite article (**el, la, los, las**) is used rather than the possessive adjective (**mi, mis, su, sus**, etc,).

d. If the subject of the reflexive verb is plural, as in example 10, the article of clothing or part of the body remains in the singular unless each of the persons included in the subject has "more than one":

	Nos quitamos **el abrigo**.	We take off our coats.
but:	Nos quitamos **los guantes**.	We take off our gloves.

"Nos quitamos *los abrigos*" would imply that each of us is wearing two or more coats!

◤ EXERCISES ◢

A. Write *Sí* if the statement is true or makes sense. *No* if it is false or does not make sense.

_____ **1.** Me lavo la cara con agua y jabón.

_____ **2.** Cuando entramos en la casa, nos ponemos el sombrero.

_____ **3.** Por la mañana nos acostamos.

_____ **4.** Los alumnos se acuestan en la escuela.

_____ **5.** Me despierto a las siete de la mañana.

_____ **6.** El profesor se baña en la clase.

_____ **7.** La mujer se llama José.

_____ **8.** Me siento a la mesa para comer.

_____ **9.** Me quedo en casa cuando hace mal tiempo.

_____ **10.** Nos quitamos los guantes cuando hace frío.

B. Do the following exercise with a partner. One partner makes the statement and the other partner changes it to a question. Then reverse roles. Each partner should then complete the blank spaces.

EXAMPLE: **Luis se pone el abrigo.** ¿Se pone Luis el abrigo?

1. Nosotros nos quitamos la camisa. _____

2. El profesor se sienta detrás de la mesa. _____

3. Se lavan la cara por la mañana. _____

4. Yo me quedo en casa hoy. _____

5. El niño se peina rápidamente. _____

C. Nacho is at it again. In the spaces provided write what Nacho would say to change each sentence to the negative. Follow the example.

EXAMPLE: **José se pone los guantes.** José no se pone los guantes.

1. Ella se llama Ana.   _____
2. Nos quedamos en el parque.   _____
3. Me levanto tarde.   _____
4. ¿Se despierta Ud. tarde?   _____
5. Los niños se acuestan temprano. _____

D. In each blank, write the verb in the form required by the new subject.

EXAMPLE: **Yo me llamo Martín.**   Usted _____*se llama*_____ Susana.

1. ¿Quién se acuesta tarde?
   ¿Quiénes _____ ahora?
2. Mi padre no se sienta aquí.
   Mis padres _____ allí.
3. Rosa se pone el vestido nuevo.
   Nosotras _____ el vestido nuevo también.
4. ¿A qué hora se levanta él?
   ¿Cuándo _____ tú?
5. Yo me despierto a las seis y cuarto.
   Juanito _____ a las siete y cuarto.
6. Nosotros nos lavamos despacio esta mañana.
   Los niños _____ rápidamente.
7. ¿Cómo se llaman ellos?
   ¿Cómo _____ ella?
8. Elena y Martín se peinan cinco veces al día.
   Yo _____ todo el día.
9. Mis amigos y yo nos quitamos los guantes.
   Tú _____ el sombrero.
10. Yo no me quedo aquí ahora.
    Mi padre y yo _____ en la ciudad.

E. Do this exercise with a partner: one partner asks the question and the other gives the answer. Then reverse roles. Then each partner must write the answers in the blanks.

1. ¿Con qué se lava Ud.?
   _____ con agua y jabón.
2. ¿A qué hora se despiertan sus padres?
   Mis padres _____

3. ¿Cuántas horas te quedas en la escuela?

_____

4. ¿Se acuesta Ud. temprano o tarde?

_____

5. ¿Se pone Ud. los guantes en el verano?

_____

6. ¿Cómo se llama su tío favorito?

Mi tío _____

7. ¿Cuántas veces al día se peina Ud.?

_____

8. ¿Se levantan Uds. tarde los domingos?

_____

9. ¿Quién se sienta al lado de Ud. en la clase de español?

_____ a mi lado.

10. ¿Te bañas en la sala o en el cuarto de baño?

_____

F.   Write the Spanish equivalents as shown by the models in italics.

1. The children go to bed early.   _Los niños se acuestan temprano._

   a. I go to bed late.   _____

   b. We go to bed at 10:00.   _____

2. At what time does she get up?   _¿A qué hora se levanta ella?_

   a. At what time do you (Ud.) get up?   _____

   b. At what time does Robert get up?   _____

3. Where are you sitting?   _¿Dónde se sienta usted?_

   a. Where do I sit?   _____

   b. Where do you (vosotros) sit?   _____

4. Their name is Rodríguez.   _Se llaman Rodríguez._

   a. Her name is González.   _____

   b. My name is Pérez.   _____

5. We're not staying here.   _No nos quedamos aquí._

   a. They aren't staying there.   _____

   b. You (Tú) aren't staying at home.   _____

33
Pronouns That Go With Prepositions

Prepositions

a, to   **para**, for
con, with   **sin**, without
de, of, from   **sobre**, on, on top of, above, over
en, in

cerca de, near   **detrás de**, behind, in back of
debajo de, under   **lejos de**, far from
delante de, in front of

El video es **para mí**.	The video is for me.
¿Dónde estás tú? Vamos **sin ti**.	Where are you? We are going without you.
Usted vive en mi calle. Yo vivo **cerca de usted**.	You live on my street. I live near you.
Él compra el libro. El libro es **para él**.	He buys the book. The book is for him.
Ella vive en California. Vivimos **lejos de ella**.	She lives in California. We live far from her.
Nosotros nos quedamos en casa. Van **sin nosotros**.	We are staying at home. They are going without us.
¿Queréis vosotros estas revistas? Son **para vosotros**.	Do you want these magazines. They are for you.
Ustedes son simpáticos. Tenemos confianza **en ustedes**.	You are nice. We have confidence in you.
Ellos son buenos amigos. Vamos **con ellos**.	They are good friends. We are going with them.
Ellas están allí. Juan está **delante de ellas**.	They are there. John is in front of them.

1. Pronouns that are objects of prepositions are the same as the subject pronouns except for **yo**, which becomes **mí**, and **tú**, which becomes **ti**.

2. *With me* is expressed as one word in Spanish: **conmigo**. *With you* (familiar singular) is also expressed as one word: **contigo**.

Ella va al campo **conmigo**.   She is going to the country with me.
Yo voy al baile **contigo**.   I am going to the dance with you.

The forms **conmigo** and **contigo** are the same for both genders.

3. Keep in mind that the pronouns that follow prepositions are not the same as the direct and indirect object pronouns:

Ella **me** ve.   She sees me.

but:

Ella va sin **mí**.   She is going without me.

Titicaca.   Titicaca, the sacred lake of the Incas, is situated between Peru and Bolivia at an altitude of 12,580 feet above sea level. It is 110 miles long and 40 miles wide. The two best known islands in this lake are *Isla del Sol* and *Isla de la Luna*. Along the shores of this lake the pre-Hispanic cultures developed their advanced civilizations. On the small island of Suriqui, in the Bolivian part of the lake, the inhabitants build their famous *totoras* or reedboats by methods that date back thousands of years. Two brothers from Suriqui constructed the famous *balsa* (raft) in which the Norwegian navigator Thor Heyerdahl made his expeditions across the Atlantic Ocean in 1970 . At the extreme south of Lake Titicaca, forty-three miles from La Paz, Bolivia, is a site called Tiahuanaco, which contains the ruins of a pre-Inca civilization called los *aimaraes*. This civilization dates back to 700 A.D. This tribe was conquered by the Incas in the fifteenth century. At this site one can see monuments, aqueducts, temples, and huge monolithic stones. What stands out is the famous "Puerta del Sol," a large block of stone that weighs about ten tons, with the figure of the God Viracocha in the center. According to tradition, this site is where the city of La Paz was founded.

▲ EXERCISES ▲

A. Your friend questions every statement made to her. In the blanks that follow each statement change each group of italicized words to a prepositional pronoun as shown in the following example.

EXAMPLE: **Vienen a casa con *María*.**   ¿con ella?

1. El dinero no es para *Luis*.   _____

2. Estamos cerca de *los hombres*.   _____

3. Vamos a la fiesta sin *las chicas*.   _____

4. Recibo regalos de *mi madre*.   _____

5. Ellos viven lejos de *sus primos*   _____

B. Answer each question as shown in the following examples:

EXAMPLES: **¿Es para mí el libro?**   Sí, _____*es para Ud. (para ti)*_____.

            ¿Vienes tú conmigo?   No, _____*no vengo contigo*_____.

1. ¿Van ellos sin Ud.?   Sí, _____.

2. ¿Hablan Uds. de mí?   No, _____.

3. ¿Vive ella cerca de nosotros?   Sí, _____.

4. ¿Puedo bailar con Ud.?   No, _____.

5. ¿Tienen ellos confianza en Ud.?   Sí, _____.

C. Complete the Spanish translations.

1. They are traveling with me this summer.

    Ellos viajan _____ este verano.

2. Johnny, this drink is for you.

    Juanito, esta bebida es _____.

3. Without her I can't work.

    _____ no puedo trabajar.

4. What is in front of them?

    ¿Qué hay _____?

5. They are going to receive a letter from me.

    Van a recibir una carta _____.

6. My relatives live far from us.

    Mis parientes viven _____.

7. Mary, I want to go shopping with you.

    María, quiero ir de compras _____.

8. They have confidence in him.

    Tienen confianza _____.

9. The house is behind her.

    La casa está _____.

10. Gentlemen, do they live near you?

    Señores, ¿viven _____?

SUMMARY AND REVIEW EXERCISES: CHAPTERS 26-33

Note: The reflexive pronouns were omitted from this summary because a full display of their forms and uses would be beyond the scope of this book.

Summary of Pronoun Forms

Subject	Direct Object	Indirect Object	Prepositional
Yo veo la casa I see the house.	Ella **me** ve. She sees me.	**Me** dan dinero. They give me money.	El libro es para **mí**. The book is for me.
			Habla **conmigo.** He speaks with me.
Tú hablas bien. You speak well.	Yo **te** veo. I see you.	¿**Te** hablan? Do they speak to you?	Es para **ti**. It is for you.
			Hablo **contigo**. I'm speaking with you.
Ud. escribe bien. You write well.	Ana **lo (la)** ve. Ann sees you.	Yo **le** escribo. I'm writing to you.	Hablo con **Ud**. I'm speaking with you.
Él va a casa. He goes home.	**Lo** oímos. We hear him.	**Le** doy el libro. I give him the book.	Vamos sin **él**. We're going without him.
Ella está aquí. She is here.	¿**La** oye Ud.? Do you hear her?	**Le** doy mi pluma. I give her my pen.	Vivo cerca de **ella**. I live near her.

Subject	Direct Object	Indirect Object	Prepositional
("It" = el café.) Está caliente. It is hot.	**Lo** tomo con leche. I drink it with milk.	**Le** añado azúcar. I add sugar to it.	Beyond the scope of this book.
("It" = la ciudad.) Es muy grande. It is very large.	**La** visito. I visit it.	¿Qué **le** pasa? What's happening to it?	Beyond the scope of this book.
Nosotros vivimos aquí. We live here.	¿**Nos** comprenden? Do they understand us?	No **nos** dan el dinero. They don't give us the money.	Hablan de **nosotros(as)**. They speak of (about) us.
Vosotros tenéis el dinero. You have the money.	**Os** veo. I see you.	No **os** escriben. They don't write to you.	Vamos con **vosotros (-as)**. We are going with you.
Uds. son ricos. You are rich.	No **los (las)** vemos. We don't see you.	**Les** damos los libros. We give you the books.	Vivo cerca de **Uds.** I live near you.
Ellos estudian. They are studying.	**Los** oímos. We hear them.	No **les** presto dinero. I don't lend them money.	Voy con **ellos**. I go with them.
Ellas están aquí. They are here.	No **las** veo. I don't see them.	¿**Les** escribes? Do you write to them?	Hablo de **ellas**. I speak of (about) them.
("They" = los libros.) Están aquí. They are here.	¿**Los** vende Ud.? Are you selling them?	¿**Les** añade Ud. páginas? Do you add pages to them?	Beyond the scope of this book.
("They" = las flores.) Son muy bonitas. They are very pretty.	**Las** admiro. I admire them.	**Les** doy agua. I give them water.	Beyond the scope of this book.

▲ EXERCISES ▲

A. Complete the passage by using *yo* as the subject of the indicated verb.

Todas las mañanas _____ a las seis pero _____ a
　　　　　　　　　1. (despertarse)　　　　　　　　　　　　　　2. (levantarse)

las seis y cuarto. _____ al cuarto de baño donde _____
　　　　　　　　3. (pasar)　　　　　　　　　　　　　　　　　　　　4. (lavarse)

la cara y las manos. Luego _____ y _____ la ropa.
　　　　　　　　　　　　　5. (peinarse)　　　　　　　6. (ponerse)

B. Change the subject in exercise **A** to *mi hermano* and write the new verb forms in the blanks below.

1. _____   4. _____

2. _____   5. _____

3. _____   6. _____

C. Change the subject in exercise **A** to *mi hermano y yo* and write the new verb forms in the blanks below.

1. _____   4. _____

2. _____   5. _____

3. _____   6. _____

D. Rewrite each sentence, changing the pronoun in italics to a corresponding word or phrase to be chosen from the following:

nuestra profesora	el periódico	tus amigos
las chicas	Luis	mi pluma
los alumnos		

Use each choice only once. When necessary, add either a prepositional or a "personal" *a*, as in the following example.

EXAMPLE: *¿Le* **prestas el libro?**   ¿Prestas el libro a Juana?

1. ¿Quién *los* ve?   _____

2. Yo no *la* tengo.   _____

3. *Les* damos cinco dólares.   _____

4. Voy al cine con *él*.   _____

5. ¿*Lo* quieren Uds.?   _____

6. ¿No *les* hablas todos los días?   _____

7. *La* saludamos al entrar en la sala. _____

E. Rewrite the sentence, inserting the indicated Spanish object pronoun.

EXAMPLE: **(him) No vemos.**   No lo vemos.

1. (to me)   Escriben notas.   _____

2. (us)   ¿Describe Ud.?   _____

3. (them, *f.*) No visitamos hoy.   _____

4. (you, *fam. sing.*)   Entiendo perfectamente. _____

5. (her)   Pagamos cinco dólares. _____

6. (you, *m., formal sing.*)   ¿Recuerdan ellos bien? _____

7. (me)   ¿Comprendes tú ahora? _____

8. (to us)   Mi madre lee un cuento. _____

9. (it, *m.*)   ¿Quién tiene? _____

10. (them, *m.*)   Yo no oigo. _____

F. Add the words in parentheses to each of the following sentences, using *a* where necessary.

   EXAMPLE: **(Luis) yo no comprendo** _____*a Luis*_____ .

1. (Rosa)   Ellos no ven ——————————.

2. (el chico)   Doy dinero ——————————.

3. (el desayuno)   ¿Quién sirve ——————————.

4. (los hombres)   Papá invita ——————————.

5. (Felipe)   ¿Oyes tú ——————————?

6. (las gorras)   Compramos —————————— en el centro.

7. (su casa)   Mi tío vende ——————————.

8. (las chicas)   ¿Conocen Uds. ——————————?

9. (Teresa)   Digo la verdad ——————————.

10. (los mapas)   Usamos —————————— en la clase.

G. Your teacher will read aloud a question in Spanish. Circle the letter of the correct answer.

1. a. Veo la casa
    b. Veo a Carlos.

2. a. No, no lo comprendemos.
    b. Si, la comprendemos.

3. a. No, no los tomo.
    b. No, no lo tomo.

4. a. Sí, le doy el dinero.
    b. No, no les doy el dinero.

5. a. Sí, la conocemos.
    b. No, no los conocemos.

6. a. No, no me gusta.
    b. Sí, nos gusta mucho.

7. a. Nos gusta el edificio.
    b. Le gusta mi sombrero.

8. a. Sí, vienen conmigo.
    b. No, no vienen con él.

9. a. Sí, es para nosotros.
    b. Sí, es para ti.

10. a. Sí, yo lo oigo.
    b. No, no los oigo.

H. Fill each blank with the missing words, making any change that may be required by the change in subject.

> **Example:** **No me gustan los libros.** No _____*me gusta*_____ el libro.

1. ¿Te gusta mi corbata?   ¿_____ mis libros?

2. Nos gustan las flores.   _____ comer.

3. Me gusta cantar.   _____ todas mis clases.

4. No le gustan los metros.   _____ viajar en tren.

5. Les gusta mucho jugar.   _____ comprar ropa.

I. Read paragraphs **1–5** below and answer the questions that follow: Before you begin, review the following expressions:

al aire libre, in the open air, outdoors
al poco rato, in a little while.
el **andén**, platform
antiguo, old (= former)
el **bar**, small restaurant with a counter
la **bebida**, drink, beverage
el **beso**, kiss
el **calamar**, squid
el **camarero**, waiter
la **cuenta**, bill, check
dentro de inside (of)
el **despacho**, office
el **Escorial**, famous royal palace and mausoleum of Spain, not far from Madrid, built in the 16th century
estimar, to respect
la **gamba**, shrimp

el **gusto**, pleasure
la **horchata**, drink made with crushed almonds, sugar and water
la **limonada,** lemonade
limpio, clean
el **lugar**, place
el **metro**, subway
el **miedo**, fear
el **pasajero**, passenger
pasar, to spend (time)
el **refresco**, refreshment
la **sonrisa**, smile
la **tapa**, snack, hors d'oeuvre
el **Valle de los Caídos**, a memorial park in Spain, not far from Madrid, built in honor of the soldiers who died in the Spanish Civil War of 1936–39

1. Javier Rivera y su esposa Susana son profesores de español que viven en Nueva York. Todos los veranos los dos van a España para pasar las vacaciones. En España visitan muchas ciudades como Madrid, Salamanca, La Coruña, Toledo, etc. Cuando están en Madrid, les gusta visitar lugares muy interesantes como el Escorial y el Valle de los Caídos, que están cerca de Madrid.

   In the blank, write *Sí*, if the statement is true, *No* if it is false.

   a. Susana y Javier viven en España.   _____

   b. Susana y Javier enseñan español.   _____

   c. Los dos pasan el verano en Nueva York.   _____

   d. En España los dos van solamente a Madrid.   _____

   e. El Escorial no está lejos de Madrid.   _____

2. Susana y Javier están en Madrid. Un día dan un paseo por el centro de la ciudad. Hace calor y tienen hambre. En Madrid hay muchos cafés al aire libre. Cuando ven uno que les gusta, deciden entrar para tomar unos refrescos. Se sientan a una mesa y miran el menú.

Susana dice: —Javier, ¿ves al camarero?

—No—contesta Javier—, no lo veo.

—Ah, ahora lo veo allí cerca de esos turistas. Les sirve unas bebidas—dice Susana.

—¿Qué toman ellos, Susana?

—Creo que le camarero les sirve café y horchata. No me gusta la horchata.

Complete each sentence.

a. Hace calor en _____.

b. _____ y _____ quieren tomar unos refrescos en un

_____.

c. Susana y Javier no ven al _____.

d. El camarero _____ unas _____ a unos

_____.

e. Los turistas beben _____ y _____.

3. Esa noche Susana y Javier van a un bar para tomar tapas. Javier pide gambas porque le gustan mucho. Susana pide calamares y los come rápidamente. Piden limonada y lo beben con las tapas. El camarero les sirve con una sonrisa porque los conoce bien. Después el camarero les trae la cuenta y les dice: —Para ustedes, señores. Javier le paga y los dos salen del bar muy contentos.

Answer the following questions with a complete Spanish sentence.

a. ¿Cuándo van al bar Susana y Javier? _____

b. ¿Qué comen en el bar? _____

c. ¿Qué toman con las tapas? _____

d. ¿Quién conoce bien a Susana y a Javier? _____

e. ¿Para quiénes es la cuenta? _____

f. ¿Quiénes salen contentos del bar? _____

4. Susana y Javier quieren visitar la Universidad de Madrid. Para ir allá deben tomar el metro y un autobús. Los trenes del metro son limpios, y llegan con mucha frecuencia. Al poco rato llega el tren. Hay mucho espacio entre el tren y el andén, y Susana lo mira con miedo. Cuando tratan de subir al tren, Susana se cae. Todos los pasajeros la miran y un soldado la ayuda. Javier le da las gracias.

In the blank, write *Sí* if the statement is true, *No* if it is false.

a. Susana y Javier usan sólo el autobús para ir a la universidad.   _____

b. Susana y Javier quieren ir a la universidad.   _____

c. Susana y Javier deben esperar el tren durante mucho tiempo.   _____

d. Susana y Javier se caen.   _____

e. Los pasajeros no ven a Susana.   _____

f. El soldado ayuda a Susana.   _____

g. Javier da la gracias al soldado.   _____

5. Susana y Javier llegan a la entrada de la universidad en diez minutos. Salen del metro y ahora tienen que tomar el autobús para llegar a los edificios de la universidad. Quieren visitar a un antiguo profesor de Susana. Este profesor se llama Juan Hernández Moreno, y Susana y Javier lo estiman mucho. Los dos bajan del autobús y caminan hacia el despacho del profesor. El profesor no está allí y lo buscan. Por fin lo encuentran en su sala de clase. El profesor los ve y les dice: —Hola, amigos, ¿me buscan ustedes? Susana contesta: —Sí, señor, lo buscamos y deseamos hablar con usted. El profesor Hernández los invita a entrar y los presenta a su clase.

a. Susana y Javier están en el (metro, autobús, tranvía) diez minutos.

b. Juan Hernández Moreno es el (padre, profesor, médico) de Susana.

c. Susana y Javier estiman (el metro, la universidad, al profesor).

d. El profesor está en su (sala de clase, despacho, casa).

e. El profesor los presenta a (su mujer, su clase, su secretaria).

Part 7
Optional Chapters

><><><><><><><><><><><><><><><><><><

34
Polite Commands

■■▰ Formation of Polite Commands

tomar
    Tome Ud. (Tomen Uds.) la bebida.   Take the drink.

aprender
    Aprenda Ud. (Aprendan Uds.) la lección.   Learn the lesson.

abrir
    Abra Ud. (Abran Uds.) la puerta.   Open the door.

1. To form the polite command, use the first person singular of the present tense. Drop the **-o** ending of the yo form and replace it as follows:

			Singular	Plural
-AR	verbs:	Add	**-e** or	**-en**
-ER / **-IR**	verbs:	Add	**-a** or	**-an**

Here are some examples:

	Present Tense, **yo** Form			
hablar:	habl*o*	habl*e* Ud.	habl*en* Uds.	Speak.
escribir:	escrib*o*	escrib*a* Ud.	escrib*an* Uds.	Write.
conducir:	conduzc*o*	conduzc*a* Ud.	conduzc*an* Uds.	Lead. Drive.
dormir:	duerm*o*	duerm*a* Ud.	duerm*an* Uds.	Sleep.
hacer:	hag*o*	hag*a* Ud.	hag*an* Uds.	Do. Make.
salir:	salg*o*	salg*a* Ud.	salg*an* Uds.	Leave.

Practice A: For each verb, write the first person singular (*yo* form) of the present tense in the first column; in the second and third columns, write the *Ud.* and *Uds.* forms of the command.

EXAMPLE: **salir:**   salgo   salga Ud.   salgan Uds.

1. cantar _____ _____ _____

2. comer _____ _____ _____

3. venir _____ _____ _____

4. pensar _____ _____ _____

5. servir _____ _____ _____

6. poner _____ _____ _____

7. oír _____ _____ _____

8. ver _____ _____ _____

9. volver _____ _____ _____

10. decir _____ _____ _____

Practice B: Change each statement to a command.

EXAMPLE: **Usted canta bien.**   Cante usted bien.

1. Ustedes contestan en inglés. _____

2. Usted bebe leche. _____

3. Ustedes traducen la frase. _____

4. Usted viene ahora. _____

5. Ustedes tienen cuidado. _____

2. The pronouns **Ud.** and **Uds.**, which follow the verb in a command, may be expressed or omitted:

$$\left.\begin{array}{c} \textbf{¡Hable Ud!} \\ or \\ \textbf{¡Hable!} \end{array}\right\} \text{Speak!}$$

Irregular Polite Commands

dar, to give:	**dé** Ud.	**den** Uds.	Give.
estar, to be:	**esté** Ud.	**estén** Uds.	Be.
ir, to go:	**vaya** Ud.	**vayan** Uds.	Go.
saber, to know:	**sepa** Ud.	**sepan** Uds.	Know.
ser, to be:	**sea** Ud.	**sean** Uds.	Be.

3. The command form of **dar** has an accent mark in the singular: **dé Ud**. The plural form has no accent mark: **den Uds.**

Practice C: Complete the Spanish sentences.

1. Give John the book.   _____ Ud. el libro a Juan.

2. Be there at two o'clock.   _____ Uds. allí a las dos.
                                         (estar)

3. Go with them.   _____ Ud. con ellos.

4. Don't be silly.   No _____ Ud. tonto.
                                         (ser)

5. Know your lesson.   _____ Uds. su lección.

Negative Commands

Pase Ud. a la puerta.   Go to the door.
No pase Ud. a la puerta.   Do not (Don't) go to the door.
Traigan Uds. los discos compactos.   Bring the CD's.
No traigan Uds. los discos compactos.   Do not (Don't) bring the CD's.

4. To make a command negative, place **no** before the verb.

Practice D: Write the negative form of each command.

1. Vuelvan Uds. temprano mañana.   _____

2. Haga Ud. el trabajo ahora.   _____

3. Vayan Uds. a la escuela.   _____

4. Coma Ud. el pan.   _____

5. Vengan Uds. a casa.   _____

Forming Commands With Reflexive Verbs

levantarse, to rise, to get up

    Levántese Ud. (**Levántense** Uds.) a las ocho.   Get up at eight o'clock.

    No se levante Ud. (**No se levanten** Uds.) tarde.   Do not get up late.

sentarse, to sit down

    Siéntese Ud. (**Siéntense** Uds.) cerca de la mesa.   Sit near the table.

    No se siente Ud. (**No se sienten** Uds.) cerca   Do not sit near the window.
    de la ventana.

5. To form a command with a reflexive verb, attach **se** to the command form of the verb and place an accent mark on the originally stressed vowel (generally the third vowel back).

6. To make the command negative, place **se** between **no** and the verb.

Practice E: Change each affirmative command to the negative or vice versa.

EXAMPLES: **No se ponga Ud. el sombrero.**   Póngase Ud el sombrero.
             Quédense Uds. aquí.   No se queden Uds. aquí.

1. Vístanse Uds. en seguida.   _____

2. No se acueste Ud. tarde.   _____

3. Lávese Ud. la cara.   _____

4. No se quiten Uds. los guantes.   _____

5. Levántese Ud. temprano.   _____

▶ EXERCISES ◀

A. Rewrite each sentence, changing the singular command form to the plural or vice versa.

EXAMPLES: **Siéntense Uds. aquí.**   Siéntese Ud. aquí.
             No tome Ud. esa silla.   No tomen Uds. esa silla.

1. Estudien Uds. la lección.   _____

2. Conduzca Ud. despacio.   _____

3. Cuenten Uds. hasta veinte.   _____

4. No haga Ud. la tarea.   _____

5. No vengan Uds. tarde.   _____

6. Póngase Ud. los zapatos.   _____

7. Levántense Uds. mañana a las seis.   _____

8. No se lave Ud. la cara.   _____

9. Escriba Ud. a sus tíos.   _____

10. Beban Uds. mucha agua.   _____

B. In this exercise you are asking someone if he or she is doing something. The person who answers says yes and invites you to do the same as in the following example.

EXAMPLE: **¿Viene Ud. a casa?**   Sí, venga Ud. a casa también.

1. ¿Toma Ud. agua con la comida?   _____

2. ¿Escribe Ud. una carta?   _____

3. ¿Dice Ud. la verdad?   _____

4. ¿Sale Ud. a las tres?   _____

5. ¿Da Ud. regalos al profesor?   _____

C. Now, a member of a group of people is asking questions of one person not from the group. Answer as in the example.

EXAMPLE: **¿Habla Ud. despacio?**   Sí, hablen Uds. despacio también.

1. ¿Sabe Ud. la respuesta?   _____

2. ¿Pide Ud. dinero a sus padres?   _____

3. ¿Lee Ud. revistas?   _____

4. ¿Usa Ud. una calculadora?   _____

5. ¿Va Ud. al cine esta noche?   _____

D. Write the command form for **Uds.** for the following sentences. Follow the example.

EXAMPLE: **(acostarse) temprano todas las noches.**
Acuéstense Uds. temprano todas las noches.

1. (No despertarse) tarde los días de escuela.

_____

2. (lavarse) las manos antes de comer.

_____

3. (quedarse) en casa por la noche.

_____

4. (no levantarse) tarde para ir a la escuela.

_____

5. (ponerse) un abrigo en el invierno.

_____

E. Repeat Exercise D using **Ud.** instead of **Uds**. Follow the example.

  EXAMPLE: **(acostarse) temprano todas la noches.**
  Acuéstese Ud. temprano todas las noches.

  1. _____
  2. _____
  3. _____
  4. _____
  5. _____

F. Write in Spanish, using *Ud.* or *Uds.* as directed.

  1. Write the letter now. (*Uds.*)   _____

  2. Get up at 7:00 tomorrow. (*Ud.*)   _____

  3. Leave at four o'clock. (*Ud.*)   _____

  4. Go to school early. (*Ud.*)   _____

  5. Do not give the money to Mary. (*Ud.*) _____

  6. Do not stay at home. (*Uds.*)   _____

  7. Come here at once. (*Uds.*)   _____

  8. Don't eat the candy. (*Uds.*)   _____

  9. Tell the truth. (*Ud.*)   _____

  10. Study the verbs for tomorrow. (*Uds.*) _____

  11. Don't use a calculator. (*Uds.*)   _____

  12. Don't open the windows. (*Ud.*)   _____

  13. Don't go to bed late. (*Ud.*)   _____

  14. Sleep eight hours. (*Uds.*)   _____

  15. (Use ser.) Don't be lazy. (*Ud.*)   _____

35
Present Participles
With ESTAR

The Present Progressive Tense

mirar, to look at
 Estoy mirando la televisión ahora.   I am watching TV now.

comer, to eat
 Estamos comiendo el postre.   We are eating the dessert.

escribir, to write
 José **está escribiendo** una carta.   Joseph is writing a letter.

1. The Spanish present progressive consists of a form of **estar** + *a present participle.*

2. The present participle of a Spanish verb ends in **-ndo**. For **-AR** verbs, we add **-ando** to the stem of the infinitive. For **-ER** and **-IR** verbs, we add **-iendo** to the stem.

3. The Spanish present participle corresponds to the English present participle, which ends in *-ing.*

4. The **-o** ending of the present participle does not change for gender or number.

 Practice A: Complete each sentence by writing the present participle of the verb indicated below the blank.

 EXAMPLE: **Estamos** _____*aprendiendo*_____ **la lección.**
 (aprender)

 1. Yo estoy _____ café.
 (tomar)

 2. Los alumnos están _____ mucho aquí.
 (jugar)

 3. Estamos _____ en España.
 (vivir)

 4. El hombre está _____ vegetales.
 (vender)

 5. Tú estás _____ mucho dinero.
 (recibir)

 6. Mi familia y yo estamos _____ tarde.
 (comer)

Regular Present Participles With "Short" Stems

dar, to give   **dando**, giving   **ver**, to see   **viendo**, seeing

Present Participle That End in -YENDO

caer, to fall   **cayendo**, falling   **oír**, to hear   **oyendo**, hearing
creer, to believe   **creyendo**, believing   **traer**, to bring   **trayendo**, bringing
leer, to read   **leyendo**, reading

Present Participles With Stem Changes

decir, to tell, to say   **diciendo**, telling, saying   **servir**, to serve   **sirviendo**, serving
dormir, to sleep   **durmiendo**, sleeping

Negative Forms of the Present Progressive

Yo estoy abriendo la puerta.	I am opening the door.
Yo **no estoy** abriendo la puerta.	I am not opening the door.
Estamos leyendo ahora.	We are reading now.
No estamos leyendo ahora.	We are not reading now.

5. A statement in the present progressive tense is made negative by placing the word **no** directly before the form of **estar**.

Practice B: Rewrite each sentence in the negative.

EXAMPLE: **Ellos están saliendo ahora.**   Ellos no están saliendo ahora.

1. Rosa está jugando en el patio.   _____

2. Mi tío está sirviendo el almuerzo.   _____

3. Estamos leyendo la revista.   _____

4. Estoy escribiendo la carta.   _____

5. Ellos están durmiendo ahora.   _____

Forming Questions in the Present Progressive

Roberto está viajando por Europa.	Robert is traveling through Europe?
¿Está viajando Roberto por Europa?	Is Robert traveling through Europe?
Usted está leyendo la revista.	You are reading the magazine.
¿Está usted leyendo la revista?	Are you reading the magazine?

6. To form a question in the present progressive tense, place the subject after the present participle. If the subject is **usted** or **ustedes**, place it between the form of **estar** and the present participle.

Practice C: Rewrite each statement as a question.

EXAMPLE: Mis amigos están durmiendo.   ¿Están durmiendo mis amigos?

1. Ellos están visitando la ciudad. _____

2. Uds. están trabajando mucho. _____

3. María está comiendo en la cocina. _____

4. Yo estoy trayendo los libros. _____

5. El camarero está sirviendo la comida. _____

The Relation Between the Simple Present and the Present Progressive

I sing.	Yo canto.	*I am singing.*	{	Yo canto. Yo estoy cantando.
Raymond reads.	Ramón lee.	*Raymond is reading.*	{	Ramón lee. Ramón está leyendo.

7. The English present progressive tense can be expressed in Spanish in two ways:

a. by using the present tense.

b. by using the present progressive tense, that is, the present tense of **estar** + a present participle.

Practice D: Express the same thought by using *estar* + a present participle.

EXAMPLE: Yo estudio los verbos.   Yo estoy estudiando los verbos.

1. Vivimos en el campo. _____

2. Ella no dice la verdad. _____

3. ¿Hace usted la tarea? _____

4. Describo la película. _____

5. ¿Habla Felipe a su amigo? _____

6. ¿Trabajáis ahora? _____

LAS CUEVAS DE ALTAMIRA

In northern Spain, not far from the Bay of Biscay, is the little town of Santillana del Mar. This town is famous for being the site of the celebrated *Cuevas de Altamira*, which just until several years ago were a great tourist attraction.

Discovered in 1869, when a dog fell into one of the caves, they did not arouse much interest until 1875, when some explorations were begun. On entering the caves, one has to pass through some very narrow passageways where there are stalagmites and stalactites, which are common to any other caves that one visits. At the end of a path there is a cave with a very low ceiling. On looking at the ceiling, one is introduced to the marvel of the cave: pictures of animals—bulls, bison, deer, horses—all of them in color. The animals seem to be sleeping. It is believed that these animals were painted on the rocks in the cave about twenty thousand years ago by the prehistoric hunters who lived in the vicinity.

Some historians believe that the hunters loved the animals they painted. Others believe that they painted them in order to dominate them. It has never been established exactly how the hunters were able to paint these animals on the ceilings. Because of the danger existing inside the caves, visits today are limited only to groups, who must obtain permission to visit them.

 EXERCISES

A. Answer each question as indicated in parentheses and then add your own answer.

EXAMPLE: **¿Qué está Ud. comiendo ahora? (los dulces)**
Yo estoy comiendo los dulces ahora.
Yo estoy comiendo una hamburguesa ahora.

1. ¿Qué está leyendo ahora su clase de inglés? (una novela interesante)

   _____

   _____

2. ¿Dónde están Uds. estudiando español? (en la escuela)

   _____

   _____

3. ¿Quién está vendiendo los periódicos en la escuela? (un alumno)

   _____

   _____

4. ¿Están Uds. durmiendo ahora en la clase? (Sí)

   _____

   _____

5. ¿Quiénes están aprendiendo mucho? (los alumnos de esta clase)

   _____

   _____

6. ¿Qué está explicando el profesor a la clase? (la gramática española)

   _____

   _____

7.   ¿Está Ud. mirando la televisión en este momento? (no)

_____

_____

8.   ¿Quién está dando dinero a los hijos? (la madre)

_____

_____

9.   ¿Está viajando su familia por Europa? (no)

_____

_____

10. ¿Quiénes están corriendo por las calles? (los niños)

_____

_____

B. Complete the Spanish translations by using *estar* + a present participle.

1.   Who is using the computer?

     ¿Quién _____ la computadora?

2.   We are doing the exercises now.

     _____ los ejercicios ahora.

3.   Joan is not working at this time.

     Juana _____ en este momento.

4.   What are you buying today?

     ¿Qué _____ usted _____ hoy?

5.   They are covering the table.

     _____ la mesa.

6.   Where is he sleeping?

     ¿Dónde _____?

7.   I am having lunch (almorzar) in the dining room.

     _____ en el comedor.

8.   Are you bringing the CD's?

     ¿_____ tú _____ los discos compactos?

9.   The child is not telling the truth.

     El niño _____ la verdad.

10. We are hearing the music now.

     _____ la música ahora.

11. It is not snowing today; it is raining.

_____ hoy; _____.

12. Are they finishing dinner now?

¿_____ la comida ahora?

13. The pupils are reading interesting books in the library.

Los alumnos _____ libros interesantes en la biblioteca.

14. My parents are returning from the airport now.

Mis padres _____ del aeropuerto ahora.

15. Who is giving the information?

¿Quién _____ la información?

36
Position of Object Pronouns as Objects of Commands, Infinitives and Present Participles

(Review the formation of commands, Chapter 34, and the present participles, Chapter 35.)

Commands

Affirmative	Negative
Háble*le* Ud.	No **le** hable Ud.
Speak to him (her).	Don't speak to him (her).

Infinitives

Quiero hablar*te*.	I want to speak to you.
No pueden visitar*nos*.	They cannot visit us.

Present Participles

Estoy hablándo*le*.	I am speaking to him (her).
No estamos leyéndo*la*.	We are not reading it.

Note: When the infinitive or present participle is used with a conjugated verb, as shown in the examples that follow, the object pronouns may be placed before the conjugated verb, according to the rule.

EXAMPLES: **Quiero hablarte.** = Te quiero hablar.
Estoy hablándole. = Le estoy hablando.

For the scope of this text, we will not deal with this alternate method.

1. In affirmative commands, the object pronoun is attached to the verb. Verb and pronoun are written as one word, and an accent mark is placed on the originally stressed vowel.

2. In negative commands, the object pronoun is placed between **no** and the verb.

3. The object pronoun is attached to the infinitive.

4. The object pronoun is attached to the present participle, and an accent mark is placed over the originally stressed vowel.

5. Since the reflexive pronouns are also object pronouns, they follow the same rules:

Láve*se* usted.	Wash yourself. (See Chapter 34, page 217.)
Puedo quedar*me* aquí.	I can stay here.
Están despertándo*se*.	They are waking up.

► ◄ EXERCISES ► ◄

A. Rewrite the sentence so that it includes the object pronoun indicated in parentheses.

EXAMPLES: **(lo)** **Mire Ud.** Mírelo Ud.

(me) **Escriban Uds.** Escríbanme Uds.

(la) **Estoy haciendo.** Estoy haciéndola

(nos) **¿Vas a mandar el paquete?** ¿Vas a mandarnos el paquete?

1. (lo) Hagan Uds. _____

2. (les) Están escribiendo. _____

3. (te) No puedo ver. _____

4. (la) ¿Desea Ud. beber? _____

5. (nos) Diga Ud. la verdad. _____

6. (le) Presten Uds. el dinero. _____

7. (los) Estamos leyendo. _____

8. (le) No escriban Uds. una carta. _____

9. (nos) Lea Ud. un cuento. _____

10. (la) Quiero escribir. _____

11. (los) ¿Estás mirando? _____

12. (me) No hable Ud. _____

13. (les) ¿Quieres mandar el paquete? _____

14. (nos) No muestre Ud. el mismo cuadro. _____

15. (me) Preste Ud. unos lápices. _____

B. Rewrite each sentence, changing the italicized words to object pronouns.

EXAMPLE: **Estamos mirando *la película*.** Estamos mirándola.

1. No puedo ver *la casa*. _____

2. ¿Puede Ud. leer *las frases*? _____

3. Mande Ud. el dinero *a Luis*. _____

4. ¿Estás escribiendo *a María*? _____

5. No compren Uds. *los cuadernos*. _____

6. Queremos tomar *el desayuno* temprano. _____

7. ¿Quieres visitar *a Felipe*? _____

8. Estamos contando *el dinero*. _____

9. Describa Ud. *el país*. _____

10. No escuchen Uds. *la música*. _____

11. Lean Uds. *los artículos*. _____

12. Desean tomar *el café*. _____

13. No estoy abriendo *la puerta*. _____

14. Ponga Ud. *los libros* allí. _____

15. El maestro empieza a explicar la lección *a los alumnos*. _____

_____

C. (Review the reflexive pronouns, Chapter 32, page 200.) Complete the sentences as shown in the following example.

EXAMPLE: (lavarse) **Me lavo.**

             a. Quiero _____*lavarme*_____ .   b. Estoy _____*lavándome*_____ .

1. (ponerse) ¿Te pones el abrigo?

    a. ¿Quieres _____ el abrigo?   b. ¿Estás _____ el abrigo?

2. (levantarse) Ella se levanta.

    a. Ella quiere _____ .   b. Ella está _____ .

3. (acostarse) Nos acostamos.

    a. Queremos _____ .   b. Estamos _____ .

4. (sentarse) No me siento aquí.

    a. No quiero _____ aquí.   b. No estoy _____ aquí.

5. (quedarse) ¿Se quedan ustedes en casa ahora?

    a. ¿Quieren Uds. _____ en casa ahora?   b. ¿Están Uds. _____ en casa ahora?

D. Write in Spanish as shown by the models in italics.

1. Tell me the truth.   *Dígame Ud. la verdad.*
   a. Tell her the truth.   _____
   b. Tell us the truth.   _____
   c. Tell them the truth.   _____

2. Can you sell them?   *¿Puede Ud. venderlos?*
   a. Can you buy them?   _____
   b. Can you see them?   _____
   c. Can you send them?   _____
   d. Can you describe them?   _____

3. We are bringing it.   *Estamos trayéndolo.*
   a. We are drinking it.   _____
   b. We are writing it.   _____
   c. We are closing it.   _____

4. Do not send us the package.   *No nos mande Ud. el paquete.*
   a. Do not send him the package.   _____
   b. Do not send her the package.   _____
   c. Do not send them the package. _____

5. Finish them.   *Termínelos Ud.*
   a. Do them.   _____
   b. Read them.   _____
   c. Open them.   _____

E. Translate into Spanish as shown by the models in italics.

1. Does she see her?   *¿La ve ella?*
   a. Does she see him?   _____
   b. Does she see you?   _____
   c. Does she see me?   _____

2. If you visit him today, don't visit him tomorrow.
   Si Ud. lo visita hoy, no lo visite Ud. mañana.

   a. If you visit her today, don't visit her tomorrow.

   _____

   b. If you read them (*m.*) today, don't read them tomorrow.

   _____

3. If you don't speak to her today, speak to her tomorrow.
Si Ud. no le habla hoy, háblele Ud. mañana.

    a. If you don't speak to them today, speak to them tomorrow.

    _____

    b. If you don't speak to us today, speak to us tomorrow.

    _____

4. If they don't read it today, they can read it tomorrow.
Si no lo leen hoy, pueden leerlo mañana.

    a. If we don't read it today, we can read it tomorrow.

    _____

    b. I'm not studying it (*f.*) today but I can study it tomorrow.

    _____

37
The Future Tense

trabajar, to work

yo trabajar*é* mañana	I will work tomorrow
tú trabajar*ás*	you will work

Ud.			you		
él	} trabajar*á*		he	} will work	
ella			she		

nosotros(-as) trabajar*emos*	we will work
vosotros(-as) trabajar*éis*	you will work

Uds.			you (*pl.*)		
ellos	} trabajar*án*		they (*m.*)	} will work	
ellas			they (*f.*)		

volver, to return

yo volver*é* el mes próximo	I will return next month
tú volver*ás*	you will return

Ud.			you		
él	} volver*á*		he	} will return	
ellas			she		

nosotros(-as) volver*emos*	we will return
vosotros(-as) volver*éis*	you will return

Uds.			you (*pl.*)		
ellos	} volver*án*		they (*m.*)	} will return	
ellas			they (*f.*)		

abrir, to open

yo abrir*é* la puerta	I will open the door
tú abrir*ás*	you will open

Ud.			you		
él	} abrir*á*		he	} will open	
ella			she		

nosotros(-as) abrir*emos*	we will open
vosotros(-as) abrir*éis*	you will open

Uds.			you (*pl.*)		
ellos	} abrir*án*		they (*m.*)	} will open	
ellas			they (*f.*)		

1. For all conjugations, the Spanish future tense is formed by adding the following endings to the infinitive form of the verb:

    -é, -ás, -á, -emos, -éis, -án

2. The future tense in Spanish has the same meaning as the English future tense: *I will (shall) go, he will (shall) run*, etc.

    Practice A: Using the given subjects, write the future tense of the indicated verbs.

    EXAMPLE: Ella _____*ayudará*_____ .
    (ayudar)

    1. Los alumnos _____.   6. Nosotros no _____.
        (aprender)   (beber)

    2. ¿Quién _____?   7. ¿_____ Uds.?
        (mirar)   (dormir)

    3. Juan y yo _____.   8. Jaime _____.
        (partir)   (subir)

    4. Yo _____.   9. Yo no _____.
        (contestar)   (escribir)

    5. ¿Cuándo _____ ella?   10. ¿Quiénes _____?
        (regresar)   (patinar)

Irregular Verbs in the Future Tense

Group 1

poder, to be able   **podré, podrás, podrá, podremos podréis, podrán**
querer, to want   **querré, querrás, querrá, querremos, querréis, querrán**
saber, to know   **sabré, sabrás, sabrá, sabremos, sabréis, sabrán**

3. In these three verbs, the **e** of the **-er** ending of the infinitive is dropped before the future tense endings are added.

    Practice B: Using the given subjects, write the future tense of the indicated verb.

    EXAMPLE: usted   ___*podrá*___   ___*querrá*___   ___*sabrá*___
    (poder)   (querer)   (saber)

    1. Yo no   _____   _____   _____
        (poder)   (saber)   (querer)

    2. ¿Quiénes _____?   _____?   _____?
        (saber)   (poder)   (querer)

    3. Nosotros _____   _____   _____
        (querer)   (saber)   (poder)

Group 2

poner, to put, to place	pondré, pondrás, pondrá, pondremos, pondréis, pondrán
salir, to leave, to go out	saldré, saldrás, saldrá, saldremos, saldréis, saldrán
tener, to have	tendré, tendrás, tendrá, tendremos, tendréis, tendrán
venir, to come	vendré, vendrás, vendrá, vendremos, vendréis, vendrán

4. In the verbs of this group, the **e** and the **i** of the **-er** and **-ir** endings of the infinitive change to **d** before the future-tense endings are added.

Practice C: Using the given subjects, write the future tense of the indicated verbs.

1. yo no _____   _____   _____   _____
            (venir)   (tener)   (salir)   (poner)

2. ¿quién _____ ? _____ ? _____ ? _____
            (poner)   (salir)   (venir)   (tener)

3. nosotros _____   _____   _____   _____
              (salir)   (venir)   (poner)   (tener)

Group 3

decir, to say, to tell	diré, dirás, dirá, diremos, diréis, dirán
hacer, to do, to make	haré, harás, hará, haremos, haréis, harán

5. The future stem of **decir** is **dir-**, and the future stem of **hacer** is **har-**.

Practice D: Using the given subjects, write the future tense of the indicated verbs.

1. María y yo _____   _____
                  (decir)   (hacer)

2. los muchachos no _____   _____
                        (hacer)   (decir)

3. ella _____   _____
            (decir)   (hacer)

Keep in mind: All Spanish verbs, whether regular or irregular in the future tense, take the same endings: **-é, -ás, -á, -emos, -éis, -án.**

6. The immediate future. Observe the following sentences:

Voy a comer ahora.	I am going to eat now.
Van a ver una película esta noche.	They are going to see a movie this afternoon.
¿Qué vas a hacer esta tarde?	What are you going to do this afternoon?

7. Future time is frequently expressed in Spanish by using **-ir** + the infinitive, and denotes an intention to do something fairly soon.

Practice E: Rewrite each sentence using the immediate future.

EXAMPLES: **Veré la televisión.**   Voy a ver la televisión.
 ¿Saldrán Uds. temprano?   ¿Van Uds. a salir temprano?

1. Haremos nuestras tareas.   _____

2. No tomaré agua con la comida.   _____

3. ¿Qué dirán ellos a la profesora? _____

4. ¿Escribirás una carta?   _____

5. Mi padre traerá una pizza a casa. _____

Machu Picchu, "Lost City" of the Incas. Machu Picchu, high in the Peruvian Andes, may have been the capital of the Incas before the Spaniards arrived in the New World. Its picturesque ruins were discovered in 1911, and hordes of tourists have been visiting it ever since, despite the arduous climb.

▲ EXERCISES ▲

A. Write the form of the verb that would be used with the new subject.

> **EXAMPLE:** *Ella* **traerá los libros mañana.** *Yo* ___traere___ .

1. *¿Quién* cubrirá la mesa esta noche. *¿Quiénes* _____?

2. *La clase* no terminará la lección hoy. *Los alumnos* no _____.

3. *¿A qué hora volverán ellos?* *¿A qué hora* _____ *vosotros?*

4. *Nosotros* iremos a casa temprano. *Mi tío* _____.

5. *Los amigos* andarán por el parque hoy. *Luis* _____.

6. *¿Cuántas horas dormirás tú por la mañana?* *¿Cuántas horas* _____ *usted?*

7. Mañana *mi padre y yo* haremos muchas cosas. Mañana *mi hermano* _____.

8. *Yo* no podré estudiar esta noche. *Ella no* _____.

9. *Las chicas* tendrán muchos regalos esta noche. *Mi hermana* _____.

10. *¿A qué hora vendrán ustedes a casa esta noche.* *¿A qué hora* _____ *tú?*

B. Write the appropriate form of the future tense of the verb in parantheses.

> **EXAMPLE:** **(trabajar)** Mi padre ___trabajará___ en la cuidad.

1. (jugar) Los amigos _____ en el parque mañana.

2. (vivir) ¿Dónde _____ ellos el año próximo.

3. (estar) Los músicos _____ en el concierto.

4. (leer) Nosotros no _____ la revista.

5. (comer) ¿Qué _____ la familia esta noche?

6. (mirar) ¿Cuándo _____ tú la televisión?

7. (conducir) ¿Quién _____ el coche esta noche?

8. (poder) ¿Quiénes _____ ir al baile?

9. (venir) ¿A qué hora _____ Uds.?

10. (hacer) Nosotros no _____ el trabajo mañana.

11. (saber)   ¿_____ ellas la respuesta?

12. (tener)   Mañana mi padre _____ mucho dinero.

13. (decir)   ¿Qué _____él a su padre?

14. (querer)   Mi amigo y yo _____ ir al partido de fútbol.

15. (salir)   ¿A qué hora _____ vosotros de la escuela hoy?

C. Answer each question as indicated in parentheses. Write a complete Spanish sentence in each case.

1. ¿Qué servirá su madre esta noche?   (arroz con pollo)

   _____

2. ¿Irá usted al campo el verano próximo?   (sí)

   _____

3. ¿Qué libros leerán ustedes en la clase de inglés?   (dos novelas)

   _____

4. ¿A qué hora llegará usted a casa esta tarde?   (a las cuatro)

   _____

5. ¿Qué escribirá usted a su abuelo?   (una carta)

   _____

6. ¿Vivirán ustedes en Puerto Rico el año próximo?   (no)

   _____

7. ¿Qué escucharás tú en la radio esta noche?   (la música rock)

   _____

8. ¿A qué hora saldrán ustedes de la escuela esta tarde?   (a las tres y media)

   _____

9. ¿Podrá usted mirar la televisión esta noche?   (sí)

   _____

10. ¿Sabrá su clase todos los verbos mañana?   (no)

    _____

11. ¿Cuánto dinero tendrás tú el mes próximo?   (cien dólares)

    _____

12. ¿Quién hará su tarea esta noche?   (mi padre)

    _____

13. ¿Cuánto dinero pondrá usted en el banco el viernes próximo?   (cincuenta dólares)

    _____

14. ¿Dirá usted siempre la verdad a sus amigos?   (sí)

_____

15. ¿Qué dira Ud. mañana a su profesor (profesora) de español?   (Buenos días)

_____

D. Complete the Spanish translations.

1. Will she speak with us later?

¿_____ con nosotros más tarde?

2. We won't sell the house this year.

_____ la casa este año.

3. What will they serve at the party?

¿Qué _____ en la fiesta?

4. At what time will you return tonight?

¿A qué hora _____ tú esta noche?

5. I'll go to the store tomorrow.

_____ a la tienda mañana.

6. Who will drive the car this week?

¿Quién _____ el coche esta semana?

7. What will you drink now?

¿Qué _____ ustedes ahora?

8. Where will we spend (_pasar_) the summer?

¿Dónde _____ el verano?

9. The class will begin in five minutes.

La clase _____ en cinco minutos.

10. The students will leave school at 1:30 today.

Los estudiantes _____ de la escuela hoy a la una y media.

11. I will not be able to go tonight.

_____ ir esta noche.

12. When will they make their plans for the summer?

¿Cuándo _____ sus planes para el verano?

13. They will know the answers if they study.

_____ las respuestas si estudian.

14. My brother will put a lot of money in the bank.

   Mi hermano _____ mucho dinero en el banco.

15. Will you tell the truth at the meeting?

   ¿_____ vosotros la verdad en la sesión?

E. You like to do things promptly without delay. Show this by answering the following questions your mother or father asks you.

   EXAMPLE: **¿Harás tu cama hoy?** Sí, mamá (papá), voy a hacer mi cama en seguida.

   1. ¿Sacarás la basura esta noche? _____

   2. ¿Pasearás al perro esta tarde? _____

   3. ¿Estudiarás tus lecciones hoy? _____

   4. ¿Vendrás a casa temprano esta noche? _____

   5. ¿Comerás todo el almuerzo esta tarde? _____

38
The Imperfect Tense

TO THE STUDENT: This very important tense is being introduced to you in your first year of Spanish so that you may be exposed to it early in your studies of the language. In some cases it is easy to distinguish this tense from the preterit. In other cases the distinction between the two tenses may not be so obvious. In this lesson the authors have tried to prepare an introduction to the imperfect tense in the least complicated way possible, leaving the more difficult distinctions for the second and third years of your study. For those of you who need further explanations and are too impatient to wait for next year, consult your Spanish teacher.

    Formation of the Imperfect Tense

All verbs in Spanish except three (**ser, ir, ver**) are formed regularly according to the models shown below:

	-AR Verbs	*-ER* and *-IR* Verbs	
	pensar, to think	**correr**, to run	**dormir**, to sleep
	I was thinking I used to think (I thought)	I was running I use to run (I ran)	I was sleeping I used to sleep (I slept)
yo	pens*aba*	corr*ía*	dorm*ía*
tú	pens*abas*	corr*ías*	dorm*ías*
Ud., él, ella	pens*aba*	corr*ía*	dorm*ía*
nosotros (-as)	pens*ábamos*	corr*íamos*	dorm*íamos*
vosotros(-as)	pens*abais*	corr*íais*	dorm*íais*
Uds., ellos, ellas	pens*aban*	corr*ían*	dorm*ían*

1. The imperfect tense, except for the three verbs (**ser, ir, ver**), is formed by adding to the stem the endings shown in bold type above.

2. Note that the first **a** of the ending **ábamos** has an accent mark

3. Reflexive verbs function as in the other tenses, e.g., **Yo me levantaba, tú te sentías,** etc.

   Practice A: Write the form of the imperfect tense for each subject given.

   1. ellas: estar _____   vivir _____   entender _____
   2. Tú: vestirse _____   comenzar _____   aprender _____
   3. nosotros: perder _____   visitar _____   copiar _____
   4. Ud.   sentir _____   ponerse _____   salir _____
   5. José: despertarse _____   pedir _____   beber _____

The Irregular Verbs *SER, IR, VER*

Ser, ir, and **ver** are the only irregular verbs in the imperfect tense. They are conjugated as follows:

	ser, to be	**ir**, to go	**ver**, to see
	I was I used to be	I used to go I was going (I went)	I was seeing I used to see (I saw)
Yo	era	iba	veía
tú	eras	ibas	veías
Ud., él, ella	era	iba	veía
nosotros (-a)	**éramos**	**íbamos**	veíamos
vosotros (-as)	erais	ibais	veíais
Uds., ellos, ellas	eran	iban	veían

4. Note the accent marks on the **e** of **éramos** and the **i** of **íbamos**.

5. Note that **ver** retains the **e** of the infinitive ending **-er**.

Practice B: Write the indicated forms of the imperfect tense for each of the three verbs.

1. mi primo: ser _____ ir _____ ver _____

2. María y yo: ir _____ ver _____ ser _____

3. las chicas: ver _____ ir _____ ser _____

4. tú: ir _____ ser _____ ver _____

6. It is important to note that in the imperfect tense the **first** and **third** person singular forms are identical.

Some Uses of the Imperfect Tense

1. En mi casa siempre cenábamos a las siete.

In my house we always had dinner at seven.

2. Cuando vivían en el campo, a menudo se levantaban temprano.

When they lived (used to live) in the country, they often got up early.

3. ¿Dónde estabas cuando tus padres entraron en la casa?

Where were you when your parents entered the house?

4. Iba al centro cuando encontró a Juan y a Lola.

He was going downtown when he met John and Lola.

7. The imperfect tense often denotes an action in the past that happened repeatedly (Sentence **1** above). It also may show actions that were going on at the same time (Sentence **2**). In Sentences **3** and **4** the actions (or states of being) in the imperfect are interrupted by the action in the preterit.

8. The following adverbial phrases often occur with verbs in the imperfect tense:

a menudo, often   **siempre**, always
generalmente, generally **todos los días**, every day

Practice C: Complete the English meaning of each sentence.

EXAMPLES: **Todas las mañanas jugábamos al fútbol.**
Every morning <u>we played (used to play)</u> soccer.

¿Qué hacías cuando empezó a llover?
What <u>were you doing</u> when it began to rain?

1. ¿Qué leían ellos mientras tú mirabas la televisión?

What _____ while you _____ television?

2. Todos los sábados íbamos al cine.

Every Saturday _____ to the movies.

3. Eran las tres cuando salimos de la escuela.

_____ three o'clock when we left the school.

4. ¿Qué hacías mientras yo escuchaba mis cintas?

What _____ while I _____ my tapes?

5. ¿No eran buenos amigos?

_____ they good friends?

▶ EXERCISES ◀

A.   Write the form of the indicated verb in the imperfect tense.

1. (ver)   Todas las noches nosotros _____ buenos programas en la televisión.

2. volver)   Mi madre siempre _____ del trabajo a la misma hora.

3. (divertirse)   Mis abuelos _____ todos los veranos en Europa.

4. (ir/llover)   ¿Adónde _____ tú mientras _____ anoche?

5. (ser/estar)   ¿Quién _____ ese hombre que _____ en tu casa?

6. (quedarse)   A menudo mi familia _____ en Méjico por tres semanas.

7. (escuchar)   ¿Qué discos compactos _____ Uds.?

8. (hacer)   ¿Qué _____ tú cuando sonó el teléfono?

9. (levantarse) Nosotros _____ a las seis todas las mañanas.

10. (ir)   Roberto y yo _____ al centro cuando encontramos a María.

B. Answer with a complete Spanish sentence.

1. ¿A qué escuela ibas tú cuando tenías once años? _____

2. Cuando estabas en el sexto grado, ¿cómo se llamaba tu profesor?

   _____

3. ¿Dónde querías pasar tus vacaciones el verano pasado?

   _____

4. ¿Qué hora era cuando tomaste el desayuno ayer? _____

5. ¿Siempre veían Uds. buenos programas de televisión en tu casa?

   _____

C. Your friend Martin always used to interrupt whatever people were doing. In the following exercise, you are supplied with the verb in the preterit which interrupts the action. You must supply the verb in the imperfect which indicates what someone was doing at the time of the interruption. Follow the example.

EXAMPLE: Mientras yo (hacer) _____hacía_____ mis tareas, Martín me llamó por teléfono.

1. Mientras mis padres (leer) _____ los periódicos, Martín entró en la sala.

2. Mientras el profesor (explicar) _____ la gramática, Martín interrumpió la lección.

3. Mientras nosotros (ir) _____ al cine, Martín se cayó en la calle.

4. Mientras mi hermana (ver) _____ la película, Martín empezó a gritar.

5. Mientras yo (bañarse) _____, Martín me llamó de la cocina.

D. Write the Spanish equivalent of each of the following sentences.

1. What were you (tú) writing to your grandparents?

   _____

2. We used to go to bed at ten o'clock when we were children.

   _____

3. We were going to school when we met (encontramos) our friends.

   _____

4. Where were you (Uds.) while it was snowing?

    _____

5. Who was that man who (que) was walking in (por) the street.

    _____

6. Were they watching television while you were studying?

    _____

7. It was raining all day (todo el día) yesterday.

    _____

8. I was listening to my CD's when the stereo (el estéreo) broke (se rompió).

    _____

9. They used to see good movies (películas) on television.

    _____

10. I couldn't (was not able to) arrive on time because the bus never came (nunca vino).

    _____

Part 8
Grouped Vocabulary

⋈⋈⋈⋈⋈⋈⋈⋈⋈⋈⋈⋈⋈⋈⋈⋈⋈⋈⋈⋈⋈⋈⋈

39
School

A. la **escuela**, school

1. el **director** ⎫
2. la **directora** ⎭ principal
3. la **escuela superior**, high school
4. **después de las clases**, after school
5. **no hay clases hoy**, there's no school today
6. **asistir a**, to attend
7. **llegar a**, to arrive at
8. **salir* de**, to leave

B. la **sala de clase**, classroom

9. el **asiento**, seat
10. el **borrador**, eraser
11. el **mapa**, map
12. la **mesa**, teacher's desk
13. la **pared**, the wall
14. la **pizarra**, blackboard
15. la **puerta**, door
16. el **pupitre**, pupil's desk
17. la **computadora**, computer
    (el **ordenador** in Spain)
18. la **impresora**, printer
19. la **calculadora**, calculator
20. el **reloj**, clock
21. la **silla**, chair
22. la **tiza**, (piece of) chalk
23. la **ventana**, window
24. **abrir**, to open
25. **cerrar**, to close
26. **borrar**, to erase
27. **entrar en**, to enter

28. **estar sentado(-a) a la mesa,**   to be seated at the desk
29.   **en la silla**   on the chair
30.   **en el pupitre**   in the pupil's desk
31. **sentarse,** to sit down
32. **tomar asiento**, to take a seat

---

*Some of the verbs listed in the Grouped-Vocabulary chapters are irregular or undergo stem-vowel changes. Such irregularities are not indicated in the Grouped-Vocabularies. The student who is uncertain of a verb form should consult the Verb Chart or the Spanish-English Vocabulary at the end of the book.

C. la **clase**, class

33. el **maestro** ⎫
34. la **maestra** ⎬ teacher (elementary school)
35. el **profesor** ⎫
36. la **profesora** ⎬ teacher
37. el **alumno** ⎫
38. la **alumna** ⎬ pupil
39. el (la) **estudiante**, student
40. el **lapicero**, automatic pencil*
41. el **bolígrafo**, ballpoint pen
42. el **cuaderno**, notebook
43. el **dictado**, dictation
44. el **ejercicio**, exercise
45. la **falta**, mistake
46. la **frase**, phrase, sentence
47. el **lápiz**, (pl. **lápices**), pencil
48. la **lección**, lesson
49. el **libro**, book
50. la **oración**, sentence
51. la **página**, page

52. la **palabra**, word
53. la **pluma**, pen
54. la **pregunta**, question
55. la **respuesta**, answer
56. la **tarea**, homework assignment
57. **aprender**, to learn
58. **comprender**, to understand
59. **empezar**, to begin
60. **enseñar**, to teach
61. **escribir**, to write
62. **escuchar**, to listen (to)
63. **estudiar**, to study
64. **explicar**, to explain
65. **leer**, to read
66. **preguntar**, to ask
67. **saber**, to know
68. **terminar**, to end
69. **hacer una pregunta**, to ask a question

70. **ser**   **aplicado, -a**, to be studious
71.   **estúpido, -a**,   stupid
72.   **inteligente**,   smart, intelligent
73.   **perezoso, -a**,   lazy
74. **estar ausente**,   to be absent
75.   **presente**,   present

D. el **examen**, test, examination (pl. **exámenes**)

76. **difícil**, difficult
77. **fácil**, easy

78. la **nota**, mark, grade

79. **recibir (sacar) una nota buena**, to receive a good grade
80.   **nota mala**,   bad grade
81. **tener que estudiar**, to have to study
82. **salir bien en el examen**, to pass the test
83. **salir mal**   to fail

E. la **cafetería**, cafeteria

84. el **almuerzo**, lunch
85. la **bebida**, drink, beverage
86. la **comida**, meal; food

87. **almorzar**, to have lunch
88. **beber**, to drink
89. **comer**, to eat

90. **escuchar música**, to listen to music
91. **hacer ruido**, to make noise
92. **tomar un sándwich**, to have a sandwich (in Spain, a "sandwich" is on white bread)
93.   **un bocadillo**,   a snack (in Spain, a bocadillo is a sandwich on a roll)

*__Lapicero__ is a ballpoint pen in some Latin-American countries.

EXERCISES

A. Complete each sentence with one of the following words:

almuerzo	director	nota	reloj
asiento	enseña	páginas	respuesta
bebida	examen	profesores	ruido
borrador	faltas	puerta	usa
cuadros	mapa	pupitres	ventana

1. En la cafetería de la escuela hay mucho _____.

2. El profesor tiene que corregir las _____ de sus alumnos.

3. En la pared hay _____ bonitos.

4. El libro contiene doscientas _____.

5. El profesor _____ y los alumnos aprenden.

6. Para saber la hora miramos el _____.

7. Para obtener una buena _____ tenemos que estudiar.

8. Tomamos el _____ en la cafetería.

9. En la escuela hay más alumnos que _____.

10. En cada escuela hay un _____.

11. Para saber dónde está España consultamos el _____.

12 & 13. Si hace calor en la sala de clase abrimos la _____ o la

_____.

14. El alumno hace una pregunta y el profesor le da la _____.

15. Tenemos que estudiar para un _____.

B. In each picture there is an error. Circle the errors and then complete the sentences with an appropriate item.

1.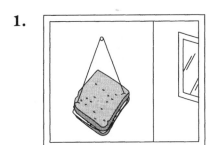

En la pared hay _____.

2.

El profesor está sentado a su _____.

3.

En la cafetería como _____.

4.

Escribimos con _____ en la pizarra.

5.

Trabajamos con _____.

C. Your teacher will aloud a question in Spanish. Circle the letter of the best answer.

1. a. Los libros asisten a la escuela.
   b. Los alumnos asisten a la escuela.
   c. Los mapas asisten a la escuela.

2. a. Toman el almuerzo.
   b. Enseñan el español a los profesores.
   c. Duermen porque hay silencio.

3. a. Estudio mucho.
   b. Borro la pizarra.
   c. Hago ruido en la cafetería.

4. a. Escribimos con lápiz.
   b. Escribimos en la silla.
   c. Escribimos en los cuadernos.

5. a. Debemos abrir las ventanas.
   b. Deseamos aprender mucho.
   c. Deseamos estar ausentes.

6. a. Cuando quiero comprar una bebida.
   b. Cuando quiero hablar con el profesor.
   c. Cuando quiero encontrar una ciudad.

7. a. Escuchamos al maestro.
   b. Escribimos en las paredes.
   c. Vamos al campo.

8. a. en el techo.
   b. en el pupitre.
   c. debajo de la mesa del profesor.

9. a. Lo como.
   b. Lo bebo.
   c. Lo leo.

10. a. a las ocho y media de la mañana.
    b. a las diez de la noche.
    c. a las tres de la tarde.

D. Underline the choice that does not apply.

1. Escribimos en (el papel, el cuaderno, la bebida).

2. No comprendo (la mesa, la palabra, la oración).

3. (La pregunta, La respuesta, El papel) es fácil.

4. El profesor da (exámenes, ventanas, notas).

5. Estoy sentado (a la mesa, en la silla, en la impresora).

6. Salimos de (la computadora, la sala de la clase, la escuela).

7. En la cafetería los alumnos (toman un bocadillo, comen sándwiches, escriben en la pizarra).

8. El profesor debe corregir (la pared, el dictado, la tarea).

9. (Teminamos, Bebemos, Aprendemos) la lección.

10. Juan no va a la escuela porque (hoy es sábado, recibe buenas notas, no hay clases hoy).

E. The author's word processor has gone haywire, producing the following scrambled sentences. See if you can unscramble each sentence so that it will make sense.

1. difícil enseña el una profesor lección

   _____

2. pared vemos mapa un la en grande

   _____

3. tres hoy ausentes alumnos están

_____

4. los todos buenas reciben alumnos notas

_____

5. con escribimos papel en el amarillo pluma

_____

F. Imagine that you are writing a letter in Spanish to a "pen pal" in Madrid. Among other things, you're going to tell your Spanish friend something about your life as a student. Write that part of your letter on the lines below. You can talk about the school you attend, your favorite classes, your after-school activities, etc. Use as many words and expressions from this chapter as you can.

EXAMPLE: Yo asisto a una escuela superior llamada John Adams High School. Las clases empiezan a las nueve menos cuarto. Todas las mañanas llego a la escuela a las ocho y media, y paso unos minutos charlando (chatting) con mis amigos. Mi primera clase es la historia, pero mi clase favorita es la ciencia. Las clases terminan a las tres, y entonces mis amigos y yo vamos a un parque para jugar a la pelota un rato, antes de volver a casa.

_____

_____

_____

_____

_____

_____

G. Many computer terms used throughout the world are in English. However there are some strictly in Spanish. See if you can guess the following terms.

1. correo electrónico

2. archivo

3. arrastrar el ratón

4. autopista de la información

5. directorio raíz

6. disco duro

7. fuente

8. placa madre

9. procesador de textos

10. salvar, guardar

11. multitarea

12. ciberespacio

13. escáner

14. baudios

15. los navegadores

40
The House

A. la **casa**, house

1. **estar en casa**, to be (at) home
2. **quedarse en casa**, to stay (at) home
3. **ir a casa**, to go home
4. **volver a casa**, to return home
5. la **llave**, the key
6. **abrir** la puerta **con llave**, to unlock the door
7. **cerrar** **con llave**, to lock

B. El **edificio** de apartamentos, apartment house

8. el **apartamento de cuatro piezas**, four-room apartment
9. el **piso**, floor, story
10. el **piso bajo** } ground floor
11. la **planta baja** }
12. el **primer piso**, second floor
13. el **sótano**, basement
14. el **techo** } roof
15. el **tejado** }
16. el **ascensor**, elevator (el elevador)
17. la **escalera**, stairs, staircase
18. **bajar**, to go downstairs
19. **subir**, to go uptairs
20. **subir la escalera**, (las escaleras), to go up the stairs
21. el **garaje**, garage
22. el **automóvil** }
23. el **carro** } automobile, car
24. el **coche** }
25. **conducir** } to drive
26. **manejar** }
27. **estacionar el coche**, to park the car

C. el **cuarto**, la **habitación**, room

28. la **puerta**, door
29. el **suelo**, floor, ground
30. el **techo**, ceiling
31. la **ventana**, window
32. **techo alto**, high ceiling
33. **bajo**, low
34. la **cocina**, kitchen
35. la **nevera** } refrigerador
36. el **refrigerador** }
37. **cocinar**, to cook
38. **preparar las comidas**, to prepare the meals
39. el **comedor**, dining room
40. **desayunar**, to have breakfast
41. **almorzar**, to have lunch
42. **cenar**, to have supper, dinner
43. **comer**, to eat.
44. **tomar el desayuno**, to have breakfast
45. **el almuerzo** lunch
46. **la cena** supper
47. el **(cuarto de) baño**, bathroom
48. **afeitarse**, to shave
49. **bañarse**, to bathe
50. **lavarse**, to wash up, to wash oneself
51. **limpiarse los dientes**, to brush one's teeth
52. **tomar una ducha**, to take a shower
53. el **dormitorio**, bedroom
54. **acostarse**, to lie down, to go to bed
55. **dormir**, to sleep
56. la **sala**, living room

D. los **muebles**, furniture

57. la **alfombra**, rug carpet
58. el **armario**, closet
59. **poner la ropa en el armario**, to put the clothes in the closet
60. la **cama**, bed
61. **acostarse en la cama** to go to sleep, to lie down in the bed
62. **cama ancha**, wide bed
63.   **estrecha**, narrow
64. la **cortina**, curtain
65. el **escritorio**, desk
66. **estar sentado(-a) al escritorio**, to be seated (seating) at the desk
67. la **mesa**, table
68. **poner la mesa**, to set the table
69. **sentarse a la mesa**, to sit down at the table
70. la **silla**, chair

71. la **butaca** } armchair
72. el **sillón** }
73. **cómodo, -a**, comfortable
74. el **sofá**, couch, sofa
75. la **lámpara**, lamp
76. **apagar la lámpara**, to turn off the lamp
77. **encender**   to turn on
78. el **teléfono**, telephone
79. **hablar por teléfono**, to speak (talk) on the phone
80. **llamar por teléfono**, to call up (on the phone)
81. la **televisión**, television
82. **mirar la televisión**, to watch television
83. el **canal**, (TV) channel
84. el **televisor**, TV set
85. la **computadora**, computer (el **ordenador** in Spain),
86. la **impresora**, the printer
87. el **video**, video

88. **televisor en blanco y negro**, black- and-white TV set
89.   **en colores**   color TV set
90. **apagar la televisión**,   to turn off the TV
91. **poner**   to turn on

La Paz.   La Paz, Bolivia, is the highest capital in the world, at an altitude of 12,000 feet above sea level. Sometimes, visitors to La Paz arrive at its airport, appropriately called El Alto, and a thousand feet above the level of La Paz, and suffer from severe headaches caused by the low atmospheric pressure. This condition is called *el soroche*, and visitors are urged to rest for a while before they resume their activities. An interesting aspect of La Paz is the fact that the poorer the people, the higher up they live. Besides the extreme altitude of the city, there are many hills within the city, and tourists must become accustomed to sightseeing in such an environment. The typical dress of the native women consists of a hoop skirt, called *la pollera*, a shawl, called *el chal*, and a bowler hat, called *el bombín*. One can buy just about anything from these women, who seem to be sitting in the same spot all day and night.

◤ EXERCISES ◥

A. Your teacher will read aloud a statement in Spanish about an activity that takes place at home. Indicate in which room the activity is most likely to occur. Choose your answers from the following list:

la cocina	el cuarto de baño	la sala
el comedor	el dormitorio	

1. _____   4. _____

2. _____   5. _____

3. _____

B. In the blank, write the letter of the expression in column B that completes the sentence in column A.

<table>
<tr><td colspan="2">Column A</td><td>Column B</td></tr>
<tr><td>_____</td><td>1. El coche está en . . .</td><td>a. la sala</td></tr>
<tr><td>_____</td><td>2. La ropa está en . . .</td><td>b. el dormitorio</td></tr>
<tr><td>_____</td><td>3. Los invitados (guests) están sentados en . . .</td><td>c. la lámpara
d. las ventanas</td></tr>
<tr><td>_____</td><td>4. El sótano está . . .</td><td>e. el garaje</td></tr>
<tr><td>_____</td><td>5. El techo está . . .</td><td>f. el suelo</td></tr>
<tr><td>_____</td><td>6. El ascensor nos lleva . . .</td><td>g. la puerta</td></tr>
<tr><td>_____</td><td>7. La alfombra cubre . . .</td><td>h. encima de nosotros
i. escritorio</td></tr>
<tr><td>_____</td><td>8. Para ver el programa, ponemos . . .</td><td>j. el teléfono</td></tr>
<tr><td>_____</td><td>9. La cama está en . . .</td><td>k. debajo de la casa</td></tr>
<tr><td>_____</td><td>10. Para escribir una carta, uno se sienta al . . .</td><td>l. el armario
m. de un piso a otro</td></tr>
<tr><td>_____</td><td>11. Para hablar con un amigo sin salir de la casa, se usa . . .</td><td>n. la televisión
o. la impresora</td></tr>
<tr><td>_____</td><td>12. Las cortinas cubren . . .</td><td></td></tr>
</table>

C. Find the error in each picture and circle it. Then complete each sentence with the equivalent of the words in parentheses.

1.

Yo duermo en _____. (the bedroom)

2.

Mi padre conduce _____ para ir al trabajo. (a car)

3.

Preparamos las comidas en _____. (the kitchen)

4.

Pongo la computadora en _____. (the table)

5.

Ponemos el coche en _____. (the garage)

D. Answer with a complete Spanish sentence.

1. ¿Qué usa Ud. para abrir o cerrar la puerta?

_____

2. ¿Por qué usamos la lámpara?

_____

3. ¿Qué ponemos en el garaje?

_____

4. Describa usted su cuarto.

_____

5. ¿Tienen ustedes una computadora en casa?

_____

6. ¿Viven ustedes en una casa o en un apartamento?

_____

7. ¿Dónde mira su familia la televisión?

_____

8. ¿Qué ponemos en el armario?

_____

9. Si su casa no tiene ascensor, ¿qué usa usted para bajar y subir?

_____

10. ¿Se queda usted en casa cuando llueve?

_____

E. Write an original dialogue in Spanish in which Luisa (or any name you choose) tells a friend about the new house or apartment that she and her family have just moved into. Use as many words and expressions from this chapter as you can.

EXAMPLE: CARLOS: ¿Te gusta tu casa nueva?
LUISA: Sí, es muy bonita pero pequeña.
CARLOS: ¿Cuántos pisos tiene?
LUISA: Tiene dos pisos y un sótano. En el piso bajo están la sala, la cocina y el comedor.
CARLOS: ¿Qué hay en el primer piso?
LUISA: En el primer piso hay dos dormitorios y un cuarto de baño. ¿Quieres ver la casa? No está lejos de aquí.
CARLOS: Con mucho gusto, pero después de la cena. En mi casa, cenamos a las siete.

_____
_____
_____
_____
_____
_____
_____

41
Family, Friends, and Neighbors; Occupations; Greetings, Good-Bye, and Expressions of Courtesy

A. la **familia**, family

1. el **esposo** ⎫ husband
2. el **marido** ⎭
3. la **esposa** ⎫ wife
4. la **mujer** ⎭
5. los **esposos**, husband and wife
6. el **padre** ⎫ father
7. el **papá** ⎭
8. la **madre** ⎫ mother
9. la **mamá** ⎭
10. los **padres**, parents
11. el **hijo**, son
12. la **hija**, daughter

13. los **hijos**, son(s) and daughter(s)
14. el **hermano**, brother
15. la **hermana**, sister
16. los **hermanos**, brother(s) and sister(s)
17. el **abuelo**, grandfather
18. la **abuela**, grandmother
19. los **abuelos**, grandparents
20. el **nieto**, grandson
21. la **nieta**, granddaughter
22. los **nietos**, grandchildren
23. el **perro**, dog
24. el **gato**, cat

B. los **parientes**, relatives; los **amigos**, friends

25. el **pariente** ⎫ relative
26. la **parienta** ⎭
27. el **primo** ⎫ cousin
28. la **prima** ⎭
29. el **sobrino**, nephew
30. la **sobrina**, niece
31. los **sobrinos**, nephew(s) and niece(s)
32. el **tío**, uncle
33. la **tía**, aunt
34. los **tíos**, uncle(s) and aunt(s)

36. el **amigo** ⎫ friend
37. la **amiga** ⎭
38. el **vecino** ⎫ neighbor
39. la **vecina** ⎭
40. el **chico** ⎫ boy
41. el **muchacho** ⎭
42. la **chica** ⎫ girl
43. la **muchacha** ⎭
44. los **chicos** ⎫ boy(s) and girl(s)
45. los **muchachos** ⎭

Observe:

1. **Mujer** means wife only when used possessively: **mi mujer**, my wife; **la mujer de Juan**, John's wife. Otherwise, **esposa** is used.

2. **Hijos**, sons, can also mean children (= sons and daughters) when used possessively: **los hijos del señor Castro**, Mr. Castro's children.

—Señora Méndez, ¿cuántos años tienen sus hijos?	"Mrs. Méndez, how old are your children?"
—Mi hijo tiene 18 años y mi hija tiene 24.	"My son is 18 years old and my daughter is 24."

3. The other masculine plural forms may also denote groups consisting of both sexes:
   los hermanos de Juan = John's brothers *or* John's brother(s) and sister(s)
   los amigos de María = Mary's male friends *or* Mary's male and female friends

46. **alto, -a**, tall
47. **bajo, -a**, short
48. **bonito, -a**, pretty
49. **feo, -a**, ugly
50. **guapo, -a**, handsome
51. **hermoso**, beautiful
52. **joven** (*pl.* **jóvenes**), young
53. **viejo, -a**, old
54. **mayor**, older, oldest
55. **menor**, younger, youngest
56. **simpático, -a**, likable, nice
57. **estar enfermo, -a**, to be ill
58. **estar contento, -a** ⎫
59. **ser feliz** (*pl.* **felices**) ⎬ to be happy
60. **ganar dinero**, to earn money

61. **gastar dinero**, to spend money
62. **pobre**, poor
63. **rico, -a**, rich
64. **jugar al tenis**, to play tennis
65. **jugar a las cartas** (los **naipes**), to play cards
66. **ir al cine**, to go to the movies
67. **ir al trabajo**, to go to work
68. **quedarse en casa**, to stay home
69. **saludar**, to greet
70. **trabajar**, to work
71. **visitar**, to visit
72. **vivir lejos de mí**, to live far from me; **lejos de Ud.**, far from you

C. oficios, occupations

73. el **abogado** ⎫ lawyer
74. la **abogada** ⎭
75. el* **ama de casa**, housewife
76. el (la) **comerciante**, merchant, businessman (-woman)
77. el (la) **dentista**, dentist
78. el **enfermero** ⎫ nurse
79. la **enfermera** ⎭
80. el (la) **estudiante**, student
81. el **maestro** ⎫ teacher (elementary school)
82. la **maestra** ⎭
83. el **médico** ⎫ physician, doctor
84. la **médica** ⎭

85. el **obrero** ⎫
86. la **obrera** ⎬ worker
87. el **trabajador** ⎪
88. la **trabajadora** ⎭
89. el **policía**, policeman
90. la **mujer policía**, policewoman
91. el **profesor** ⎫ teacher (high school
92. la **profesora** ⎭ and university)
93. el **cartero** (la **mujer cartero**), the mail deliverer
94. **ser abogado** (**médico**, etc.), to be a lawyer (doctor, etc.)

*The masculine article **el** is used with *ama* although the noun is feminine (See note 6, page 59.)

Patagonia. The southern third of Argentina is occupied by a region called Patagonia.

This area of Argentina has many cold dry plateaus and large sheep ranches. The soil is composed mainly of natural gravel. It was first visited by the Spanish explorer Ferdinand Magellan in 1520.

Charles Darwin, the famous English naturalist of the nineteenth century, visited Patagonia during his expedition to South America. It was there where he collected much data for his famous book "The Origin of the Species."

D. saludos, despedidas y expresiones de cortesía
Greetings, good-bye, and expressions of courtesy

1. **buenos días**, good morning, good day
2. **buenas tardes**, good afternoon
3. **buenas noches**, good evening, good night
4. **hasta la vista**, so long, good-bye
5. **hasta luego**, see you later
6. **hasta mañana**, see you tomorrow (until tomorrow)
7. **muchas gracias**, thanks a lot
8. **no hay de qué**, you're welcome, don't mention it
9. **con mucho gusto**, gladly, with pleasure
10. **está bien**, all right, okay

◣ EXERCISES ◢

A. Your teacher will read aloud some incomplete sentences in Spanish. Each sentence can be completed by adding a word from the list below. Choose the correct word and write it in the blank.

abuela	madre	padre
hermano	nietos	primo
hermana		

1. _____   4. _____

2. _____   5. _____

3. _____

B. Answer each question with a complete Spanish sentence.

1. ¿Dónde trabaja su padre (madre)?

_____

2. ¿Cuántos primos tiene usted?

_____

3. ¿Juega usted con los hijos de sus vecinos?

_____

4. ¿Ayuda usted a sus padres en la casa?

_____

5. ¿Tiene Ud. una hermana menor?

_____

C. Arrange the words in each group so that they form a sentence.

1. comerciante / mi / es / padre

_____

2. pobres / muy / vecinos / nuestros / son

_____

3. ¿ / su / feliz / es / familia / ?

_____

4. dinero / mi / mucho / padre / gana

_____

5. ¿ / primos / sus / viven / dónde / ?

_____

6. México / visitamos / amigos / a / en / nuestros

_____

7. muy / es / esposo / Susana / de / el / alto

_____

8. padres / mis / dinero / gastan / mucho

_____

9. son / sus / nietos / jóvenes

_____

10. ¿ / a / visita / parientes / menudo / usted / sus / a / ?

_____

D. Complete each sentence by using one of the following expressions:

el abogado	los enfermeros	la maestra	el dentista
el comerciante	los estudiantes	obreros	

1. _____ examina los dientes de Juanito.

2. Muchos _____ trabajan en la fábrica (factory).

3. _____ ayudan a los médicos en el hospital.

4. _____ va al tribunal (court) para defender a su cliente.

5. _____ enseña a los alumnos en una escuela primaria.

E. Describe this picture by answering the following questions. Use vocabulary from previous chapters if necessary. You may supply your own original sentences if you wish.

1. ¿Dónde está la familia?

2. ¿Quiénes miran la televisión?

3. ¿Qué hacen los abuelos?

4. ¿Qué hace la madre?

5. ¿Dónde están el gato y el perro?

6. ¿Quién entra en la casa?

7. ¿Qué hace el padre?

42
The City or Town

A. la **ciudad**, city; el **pueblo**, town

1. la **calle**, street
2. la **avenida**, avenue
3. la **acera**, sidewalk
4. la **cuadra** ⎫
5. la **manzana** ⎭ (city) block
6. la **plaza**, square
7. el **parque**, park
8. el **puente**, bridge
9. **es ancho, -a**, it is wide
10. **estrecho, -a**, narrow
11. **está limpio-a,** it is clean
12. **sucio, -a** dirty

13. **lleno, -a de gente** full of people
14. **tráfico** tráfico
15. **a tres cuadras**, three blocks down
16. **pasearse por el parque (por la calle)**, to stroll through the park (along the street)
17. la **gente**, people
18. **hay mucha gente**, there are many people
19. **poca gente** a few people
20. **tanta gente** so many people

B. el **tráfico**, (**tránsito**) traffic

21. el **autobús**, bus
22. el **metro**, subway
23. la **bicicleta**, bicycle
24. la **moto(cicleta)**, motorcycle
25. el **coche**, (el **carro**), car
26. la **estación**, station
27. la **parada**, (bus) stop

28. **conducir, manejar**, to drive
29. **parar**, to stop
30. **tomar el autobús**, to take the bus
31. **el metro** the subway
32. **ir en autobús**, to go by bus
33. **en bicicleta** by bicycle
34. **esperar el tren**, to wait for the train

C. de **compras**, shopping

35. el **centro**, downtown
36. **ir al centro**, to go downtown
37. **ir de compras**, to go shopping
38. el **mercado**, market (place)
39. la **tienda**, store
40. el **almacén**, department store
41. la **bodega** ⎫
42. la **tienda de comestibles** ⎭ grocery store
43. la **carnicería**, butcher shop
44. la **tienda de confección**, ready-made-clothes shop
45. la **farmacia**, drugstore
46. la **librería**, bookstore
47. la **panadería**, bakery

48. el **supermercado**, supermarket
49. la **tienda de ropa**, clothing store
50. la **tienda de electrodomésticos**, electrical appliance store
51. la **tienda de informática**, computer store
52. la **zapatería**, shoestore
53. el **dependiente** ⎫
54. la **dependienta** ⎭ sales clerk
55. el **dinero**, money
56. el **precio**, price
57. **comprar**, to buy
58. **pagar**, to pay (for)
59. **vender**, to sell

60. **¿Cuánto cuesta(n)?**
61. **¿Cuánto vale(n)?** } How much does it (do they) cost?

62. **Cuesta(n)**
63. **Vale(n)** } tres dólares, It costs (they cost) $3.

D. edificios públicos, public buildings

64. el **edificio**, building
65. la **escuela**, school
66. el **hospital**, hospital
67. el **hotel**, hotel
68. la **iglesia**, church
69. la **sinagoga**, synagogue

70. el **templo**, temple
71. la **mezquita**, mosque
72. el **museo**, museum
73. la **biblioteca**, library
74. **sacar libros**, to take out books

E. teatros y cines, theaters and movie houses

75. el **teatro**, theater
76. **ir al teatro**, to go to the theater
77. la **pieza (de teatro)**, (stage) play
78. la **comedia**, play, comedy
79. el **cine**, movie theater
80. **ir al cine**, to go to the movies

81. la **película**, film, movie
82. **sacar las entradas**, to buy (the) tickets
83. **entrada gratis**, admission free
84. **la cola**, the line (of people)
85. **formar cola**, to stand in line

► EXERCISES ◄

A. Complete each sentence with a word chosen from the column at the right.

1. En el _____ podemos ver obras de arte.

2. Hay muchos árboles en el _____.

3. La escuela, el hotel y el hospital son _____.

4. Podemos comprar pan en la _____.

5. Debemos esperar el _____ en la estación.

6. Para cruzar el río usamos el _____.

7. Hay mucha _____ en las calles.

8. Para ver una película vamos al _____.

9. Hay muchos enfermos en el _____.

10. Puedo comprar una computadora en _____.

hospital
parque
farmacia
biblioteca
cine
teatro
panadería
edificios
gente
puente
tiendas
museo
tren
tráfico
una tienda de
   informática

B. Underline the word that is not related to the others.

1. escuela, puente, iglesia, casa

2. plaza, avenida, calle, parque

CHAPTER 42   263

3. taxi, coche, tren, zapatería

4. teatro, bodega, supermercado, panadería

5. biblioteca, libro, autobús, revista

C. Your teacher will read aloud five statements in Spanish. Which of the following places does each statement refer to? Write your answer in the blanks.

la escuela   el museo   la plaza
el hospital   el parque   la tienda de ropa
el hotel

1. _____   4. _____

2. _____   5. _____

3. _____

D. In each blank, write an expression that can be substituted for the words in italics to make the sentence true.

1. Sacamos las entradas para entrar en *el hospital*.   _____

2. Para ir al centro tomamos *el árbol*.   _____

3. El *puente* circula por la ciudad.   _____

4. A las cinco de la tarde hay mucha *plaza* en la calle.   _____

5. No hay ni autobuses ni trenes; debemos buscar *una farmacia* para ir a casa.   _____

6. Nuestra escuela es *un hotel* grande.   _____

7. Puedo comprar libros en *la panadería*.   _____

8. Hay estatuas y pinturas en *la bodega*.   _____

9. Podemos ver películas en *la carnicería*.   _____

10. Cuando hace buen tiempo nos paseamos por *el teatro*.   _____

E. How much do you know about your city or town? Answer each question with a complete Spanish sentence.

1. ¿Adónde va usted para comprar medicinas?

_____

2. ¿Es grande o (pequeño el pueblo) pequeña la ciudad en que usted vive?

_____

3. ¿Dónde puede usted comprar zapatos?

_____

4. ¿Cuántos museos hay en su pueblo (ciudad)?

_____

5. Dé usted el nombre de un almacén grande.

   _____

6. ¿Cómo llega usted a la escuela?

   _____

7. ¿Dónde puede ir usted en bicicleta?

   _____

8. ¿Qué hay en el centro de su ciudad (pueblo)?

   _____

9. ¿Por dónde pasa mucho tráfico?

   _____

10. Cuando usted va al cine con una amiga (un amigo), ¿quién paga las entradas?

   _____

F. Imagine you are writing a letter to a "pen pal" in Mexico City. Tell your friend something about the city or town you live in. Use as many words and expressions from this chapter as you can.

   EXAMPLE: Mi ciudad es muy grande. En el centro hay muchas tiendas, y las calles siempre están llenas de gente. También hay un parque hermoso. Me gusta pasearme por el parque después de las clases. A unas cuadras del parque hay un mercado grande que mi madre visita muchas veces cuando va de compras.

   _____

   _____

   _____

   _____

   _____

   _____

G. Describe the picture below by answering the following questions or by supplying your own original sentences.

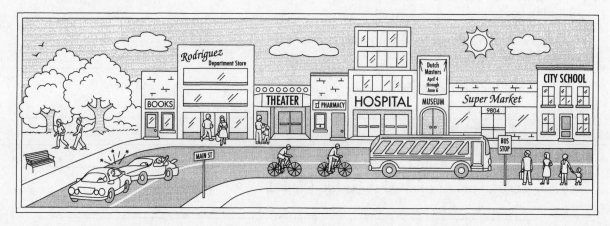

1. ¿En que parte de la ciudad (del pueblo) tiene lugar (take place) esta escena?

   _____

2. ¿Qué hace la gente en el parque?

   _____

3. ¿Qué pasa entre dos coches?

   _____

4. ¿Cuántas personas esperan el autobús?

   _____

5. ¿En qué calle está el museo?

   _____

6. ¿Dónde está la farmacia?

   _____

7. ¿Qué hace el hombre para entrar en el cine?

   _____

8. ¿Cómo se llama el almacén?

   _____

H. **Adivinanza** (riddle). En un autobús no pueden subir más de cuarenta personas. En la primera parada suben quince personas. En la segunda parada suben diez y bajan dos. En la tercera parada suben dieciocho personas y baja una. En la cuarta parada bajan doce personas y suben nueve. ¿En qué parada llega el autobús a su máxima capacidad (maximum load)?

   _____

   _____

   _____

   _____

43
Parts of the Body; Clothing

A. el **cuerpo**, body

1. la **cabeza**, head
2. el **pelo**, hair
3. **tiene el pelo largo**, he (she) has long hair
4.   **corto**   short
5.   **negro**   black
6.   **rubio**   blond
7.   **castaño**   brown
8.   **rojizo**   auburn ("red")
9. la **cara**, face
10. **tiene la cara hermosa**, he (she) has a handsome (beautiful) face
11.   **bonita**   pretty
12.   **fea**   ugly
13. la **nariz**, nose
14. el **ojo**, eye
15. **tiene los ojos azules**, he (she) has blue eyes
16.   **verdes**   green
17.   **castaños**   brown
18.   **negros**   dark brown

19. la **oreja**, (outer) ear
20. el **oído**, (inner) ear
21. la **boca**, mouth
22. el **diente**, tooth
23. **lavarse los dientes**, to brush one's teeth
24. el **labio**, lip
25. la **lengua**, tongue
26. el **cuello**, neck
27. el **pecho**, chest
28. el **hombro**, shoulder

29. la **espalda**, back
30. el **brazo**, arm
31. la **mano**, hand
32. la **mano derecha** right hand
33.   **izquierda** left
34. el **dedo**, finger
35. el **dedo del pie**, toe
36. la **pierna**, leg
37. el **pie**, foot

38. **lavarse**, to wash (oneself),* to "wash up"
39. **lavarse la cara** (las manos), to wash one's face (hands)
40. **bañarse**, to bathe (oneself)
41. **peinarse**, to comb oneself (one's hair)

B. la **ropa**, clothing

42. el **abrigo**, coat
43. la **blusa**, blouse
44. la **camisa**, shirt
45. la **camiseta**, T-shirt

46. el **calcetín**, sock
47. los **calcetines de lana**, woolen socks
48. la **media**, stocking

*See note 4, page 201.

266

49. las **medias de lana,**   woolen stockings
50.   **de algodón** cotton
51.   **de nilón**   nylon
52. la **corbata,** necktie
53. la **chaqueta,** jacket
54. el **chaleco,** vest
55. la **falda,** skirt
56. la **gorra,** cap
57. el **sombrero,** hat
58. el **guante,** glove

59. los **pantalones,** pants, slacks
60. el **pañuelo,** handkerchief
61. la **ropa interior,** underwear
62. el **traje,** suit
63. el **vestido,** dress
64. el **zapato,** shoe
65. el **bolsillo,** pocket
66. **llevar,** to wear
67. **ponerse,** to put on
68. **quitarse,** to take off

◢ EXERCISES ◣

A. Match the names of the garments and the parts of the body for which they are designed.

_____ **1.** las medias

_____ **2.** los zapatos

_____ **3.** la corbata

_____ **4.** el sombrero

_____ **5.** los guantes

a. la cabeza
b. las manos
c. el cuello
d. los pies
e. la cara
f. las piernas

B. Write the Spanish name for the part of the body that is most closely associated with each activity.

1. andar _____

2. oír _____

3. comer _____

4. escribir _____

5. ver _____

6. respirar y oler _____

7. pensar _____

8. hablar _____

9. besar (to kiss) _____

10. jugar al fútbol _____

C. Underline the expression that completes the sentence correctly.

1. En la cabeza llevamos (sombrero, zapatos, guantes).

2. Nos cepillamos (el pelo, el cuello, el brazo).

3. Caminamos con (los labios, las manos, los pies).

4. Tengo (ojos, pañuelos, un abrigo) de lana.

5. Llevamos (corbatas, piernas, pelo) de seda.

6. Sin (el pelo, la lengua, la nariz) no podemos hablar.

7. La blusa cubre (el pecho, el pie, la nariz).

8. Llevo (una falda, un pañuelo, un abrigo) en el bolsillo.

9. Cuando hace calor nos quitamos (el abrigo, los brazos, la nariz).

10. El padre lleva (*carries*) a su hijo en (la cara, el bolsillo, los hombros).

D. The following questions directed to you are rather silly, and most likely you would answer "no" to each. Answer each question so as to correct the information as shown in the example.

EXAMPLE: **¿Tiene usted dos cabezas?**   No, tengo una cabeza.

1. ¿Lleva Ud. pantalones en la cabeza?

_____

2. ¿Tiene usted seis dedos en cada mano?

_____

3. ¿Lleva usted guantes en el verano?

_____

San Fermín.   The city of Pamplona, in northern Spain, is a relatively quiet city most of the year. However, during the celebration of San Fermín the city awakens. People from all over the world come to participate in the celebration of the bulls, which takes place between July 7th and 14th. A little before midnight the bulls are set free and run to a corral where they spend the night. At 6 A.M. the next morning the bands begin to play, waking up the whole city. At 7 o'clock a rocket explodes, indicating that the gates of the corral have been opened. At that moment the bulls rush into the streets accompanied by adventurous people who risk their lives, even though they must follow certain rules. It takes the bulls no more than two minutes to get to the bull ring and their arrival is announced by another rocket. Then another exciting spectacle begins: another gate is opened and a young bull comes running full speed ahead knocking over the young people who have dared to remain in the ring to fight with it. The band plays, people shout and applaud, several young people are hurt and some are taken to the hospital. At about 8 A.M. the city begins to rest for a few hours, awaiting the bullfight that takes place at 5 P.M. All this is repeated for a full week. The city of Pamplona is in continuous excitement and animation. After the celebrations, the city returns to its normal routine.

4. ¿Se pone Ud. la ropa antes de acostarse?*

_____

5. ¿Son de algodón sus zapatos?

_____

6. ¿Usa Ud. los ojos para oler?

_____

7. ¿Se lava Ud. los pies antes de comer?

_____

8. ¿Se pone Ud. el sombrero en la nariz?

_____

9. ¿Lleva usted calcetines en la cabeza?

_____

10. ¿Tiene usted los ojos amarillos?

_____

E. Give a brief description of your best friend in Spanish.

Example: Mi amiga Kathy tiene los ojos negros y el pelo largo y castaño. Es una muchacha bonita. Hoy lleva una blusa roja, una larga falda amarilla, calcetines de algodón y zapatos verdes.

_____

_____

_____

_____

*A reflexive pronoun attached to an infinitive must agree with its subject: "quiero sentarme," "debes quedarte," "vamos a lavarnos," etc.

44
Foods and Utensils

A. los **alimentos**, foods

1. la **bebida**, drink, beverage
2. **frío, -a**, cold
3. **caliente**, hot
4. el **agua** (*f.*) water
5. la **leche**, milk
6. el **café**, coffee
7. **café con leche**, coffee with milk
8. **café solo**, black coffee
9. el **chocolate**, hot chocolate
10. el **té**, tea
11. **té con azúcar**, tea with sugar
12.   **con limón**   with lemon
13. la **gaseosa**, soda
14. la **cerveza**, beer
15. el **vino**, wine
16. la **comida**, food, meal, dinner
17. **toda clase de comidas**, all kinds of food
18. la **limonada**, lemonade
19. el **pan**, bread
20. **pan tostado**, toast
21. el **panecillo**, roll
22. la **mantequilla**, butter
23. el **queso**, cheese
24. el **huevo**, egg
25. **huevos fritos**   fried eggs
26.   **revueltos** scrambled

27. la **pimienta**, pepper
28. la **sal**, salt
29. la **legumbre**, vegetable
30. las **verduras** (*pl.* only), vegetables
31. le **lechuga**, lettuce
32. el **tomate**, tomato
33. las **patatas** } potatoes (Spain)
34. las **papas** } potatoes (Spanish America)
35. **papas fritas**, fried potatoes
36. la **ensalada**, salad
37. la **carne**, meat
38. el **pollo**, chicken
39. el **pescado**, fish (*ready to be eaten; when alive and free, fish* = **el pez**)
40. la **sopa**, soup
41. el **postre**, dessert
42. de **postre**, for dessert
43. el **helado**, ice cream
44. el **pastel**, pie, cake, pastry
45. las **frutas**, fruit
46. la **cereza**, cherry
47. la **naranja**, orange
48. la **pera**, pear
49. la **manzana**, apple
50. la **banana** } banana
51. el **plátano** } banana

52. **tomar café (leche)**, to drink (have) coffee (milk)
53. **tomar un panecillo**, to eat (have) a roll
54. **preparar la comida**, to prepare dinner (the meal)
55. **servir**, to serve
56. **ser delicioso, -a**, to be delicious
57. **me gusta más**, I like it better (best), I prefer it

B. utensilios y otras cosas, utensils and other things

58. el **plato**, plate, dish
59. **mi plato favorito**, my favorite dish
60. el **vaso**, glass
61. la **copa**, goblet
62. la **taza**, cup
63. la **botella**, bottle

64. la **servilleta**, napkin
65. el **tenedor**, fork
66. el **cuchillo**, knife
67. la **cuchara**, (table) spoon
68. la **cucharita**, teaspoon
69. **cortar**, to cut

C. **el restaurante**, restaurant

70. la **comida**, meal, dinner
71. el **desayuno**, breakfast
72. el **almuerzo**, lunch
73. la **cena**, supper
74. la **lista** ⎫ menu
75. el **menú** ⎭

76. el **mozo (camarero)**, waiter
77. la **camarera**, waitress
78. **tener hambre** (sed), to be hungry (thirsty)
79. **entrar en**, to enter
80. **salir de**, to leave
81. **llamar al mozo (camarero)**, to call the waiter

82. **pedir el menú** to ask for the menu
      la cuenta   the bill (check)
83. **tomar el desayuno (el almuerzo)**, to have (eat) breakfast (lunch)

► EXERCISES ◄

A.   Underline the word that does not belong to the group.

1. patatas, verduras, té, ensalada
2. cuchillo, servilleta, tenedor, cucharita
3. queso, pera, naranja, cereza
4. mozo, menú, cuenta, huevo
5. helado, pastel, fruta, sopa
6. agua, papa, té, café
7. pollo, pescado, carne, camarero
8. pimienta, vaso, taza, plato
9. alimento, bebida, cuchara, postre
10. cortar, comer, almorzar, beber

Las Cataratas de Iguazú.   In the middle of the jungle on the border between Brazil and Argentina are the famous Iguazú waterfalls. Each country has created a national park around these falls and you can get to them from both sides of the Iguazú River that separates the two countries. The most impressive part of the falls is "la garganta del diablo," (the devil's throat), a perpetual cloud of foam that gushes to a height of 500 feet. Above the main falls, the Iguazú River reaches an extension of two and a half miles while it launches forth towards a precipice of 200 feet. On the Brazilian side it is possible to take a helicopter ride to enjoy a panoramic view of the falls.

B. Complete each of the sentences.

1. Comemos carne con el _____ y el _____.

2. En el restaurante llamamos a la _____.

3. Para dar más sabor (taste) a la comida, usamos _____

   y_____.

4. Tomamos café con _____ y _____.

5. El camarero pone los _____ de agua en la mesa.

6. El helado es un _____.

7. Bebemos té en una _____.

8. La _____ consiste en lechuga y tomate.

9. En el verano me gusta beber _____ fría.

10. Mi postre favorito es _____ de manzana.

C. In each blank, write an expression that can be substituted for the words in italics to make the sentence true.

1. El mozo nos sirve en *la escuela*.   _____

2. *El pollo* es buen postre.   _____

3. *El pan* es una fruta.   _____

4. Cortamos la carne con *la cuchara*.   _____

5. Me gusta *comer* limonada.   _____

6. Tomamos la sopa con *el tenedor*.   _____

7. En el desayuno tomo dos *cerezas fritas*.   _____

8. Bebo agua en *un plato*.   _____

9. Me gusta poner *pimienta* en mi café.   _____

10. Quiero *una servilleta* de té.   _____

D. Your teacher will read aloud a question in Spanish. Circle the letter of the most appropriate response.

1. a. cuando tengo sed   2. a. las papas y las naranjas
   b. cuando duermo   b. las cerezas y el pan
   c. cuando tengo sueño   c. las peras y las manzanas

3. a. la pimienta
   b. la cuenta
   c. el menú

4. a. un cuchillo
   b. una cuchara
   c. un tenedor

5. a. una servilleta
   b. un panecillo
   c. un pollo

6. a. mozo
   b. gaseosa
   c. taza

7. a. pollo
   b. ensalada
   c. helado

8. a. un alimento
   b. una bebida
   c. un utensilio

9. a. por la mañana
   b. por la tarde
   c. por la noche

10. a. Como.
    b. Bebo.
    c. Escribo.

E. Describe in Spanish what you had (or wish you had) for dinner last night. Use as many words and expressions from this chapter as you can. Note: if your class has not studied the preterit tense, you may use the present tense, changing "anoche" to "esta noche."

EXAMPLE: Anoche comimos a las siete. Primero tomamos sopa de pollo y una ensalada de lechuga y tomates. Después, comimos pescado frito con patatas. Yo tomé también un vaso de gaseosa y pan tostado con mantequilla, pero mi hermana menor tomó un vaso de agua y un panecillo. De postre, tomamos pastel con helado. La comida fue deliciosa.

_____

_____

_____

_____

_____

F. Below is a picture of a table from which you can choose food and utensils. How many foods, drinks, and utensils can you identify in Spanish?

G. Here is a sample recipe for a vanilla yogurt shake. See if you can make out the instructions. Your teacher should help with any words you can't make out.

En un recipiente alto pongan un poco de yogur y una porción de helado de vainilla. Con la batidora eléctrica bátanlo uno o dos minutos y sírvanlo en seguida. Si quieren, pueden añadir un poco de azúcar para endulzarlo.

45
Amusements and Pastimes

A. los **pasatiempos**, pastimes, hobbies

1. el **cine**, movies, movie theater
2. **ir al cine**, to go the movies
3.   **una vez por semana**, once a week
4.   **todos los viernes**, every Friday
5. la **película**, film, movie, picture
6. **ver una película buena (mala)**, to see a good (bad) movie
7. —**¿Te gustó la película?** "Did you enjoy the film?
8. —**Sí, me gustó.**   "Yes, I enjoyed it."
      (For the use of **gustar**, see Chapter 31)
9. **¿Qué clase de película es?** What kind of movie is it?
10. **un cuento de amores**, love story
11.   **cuento policíaco**, detective story, police drama
12. **una película de cowboys**, a "western," cowboy drama
13. **una película de ciencia-ficción**, a science fiction movie
14.   **película de dibujos animados**, cartoon
15. la **radio**, radio
16. **escuchar el programa**, to listen to the program
17.   **las noticias**   the news
18.   **la música**   the music
19. la **televisión**, television
20. **ver programas interesantes**, to watch interesting programs
21.   **a mis actores favoritos**   my favorite actors
22.   **a mi actriz favorita**   my favorite actress
23. el **video**, video
24. el **magnetoscopio, la cámara de video**, video cassette recorder
25. el **videojuego**, video game
26. el **paseo**, walk, stroll, ride
27. **pasearse**   } to take a walk (ride)
28. **dar un paseo**
29. **dar un paseo en coche**, to take a ride in a car
30. **dar un paseo (pasearse) en bicicleta**, to go bicycle-riding
31.   **a caballo**   horseback-riding
32. la **playa**, beach
33. la **piscina**, pool
34. **ir a nadar**, to go swimming
35. **jugar en la arena**, to play in the sand
36. **tomar el sol**, to take a sunbath, "to get some sun"

B. los **deportes** y los **juegos de casa**, sports and home games

37. el **básquetbol**, basketball
38. el **béisbol**, baseball
39. el **fútbol**, soccer
40. la **pelota**, ball (for baseball or tennis)
41. el **balón**, ball (for soccer or basketball)
42. el **tenis**, tennis
43. **tenis de mesa**, ping-pong
44. el **ajedrez**, chess
45. las **damas**, checkers
46. el **juego**, game

47. **mis juegos favoritos**, my favorite games
50. el **partido**, game (= match)
51. **tres partidos de béisbol**, three games of baseball
52. **jugar a (la pelota)**, to play (ball)
53. **tomar parte en el partido**, to take part in the game
54. **me gustan los deportes**, I like sports
55. **una partida**, game, match (indoors)

C. la **música**, music

56. la **canción**, song
57. **canciones populares**, popular songs
58. el(la) **cantante folklorista**, folk singer
59. **cantar**, to sing

60. **oír**, to hear
61. **escuchar**, to listen (to)
62. **tocar la guitarra (el piano)**, to play the guitar (piano)

63. la **música popular**		popular music
64.	**clásica**	classical
65.	**sinfónica**	symphonic
66.	**de campo**	country
67.	**jazz**	jazz
68.	**de guitarra**	guitar
69.	**rock**	rock

70. la **orquesta**, orchestra
71. el **concierto**, concert
72. **asistir a un concierto**, to attend a concert
73. el **tocadiscos**, phonograph, record player; **el estéreo**, stereo
74. el **disco compacto**, compact disc (CD)
75. **tocar un disco, poner un disco**, to play a record
76. **bailar a la música de discos**, to dance to recorded music
77. la **cinta**, tape
78. el **casete**, cassette
79. la **grabadora**, tape recorder
80. **grabar**, to tape, record

D. cosas que leer, things to read

81. el **libro**, book
82. el **libro** de cuentos, book of short stories
83. la **revista**, magazine

84. **revista de deportes**, sports magazine
85. **de modas** fashion
86. **de informática** computer related

87. la **novela**, novel
88. **novela de amor**, love story
89. **novela policíaca**, detective story
90. **novela de ciencia-ficción**, science-fiction story

91. **me gusta la ciencia-ficción**, I like science fiction
92. el **periódico**, newspaper
93. **leer las noticias**   to read the news
94.   **la sección de deportes**   the sports pages
95.   **artículos interesantes**   interesting articles

E. las **vacaciones**, vacation.

96. las **vacaciones de verano**, summer
    vacation
97. **vacaciones de Navidades**, Christmas
    holiday
98. **estar de vacaciones**, to be on vacation

99. **ir de vacaciones**, to go on vacation
100. **ir al campo**, to go to the country
101.   **a la playa**   to the beach
102. **hacer un viaje**, to take a trip
103. **quedarse en casa**, to stay (at) home

◄ EXERCISES ►

A.   In the blank at the left, write the letter of the expressions that complete the sentence.

_____ 1. En la playa jugamos en la arena y . . .

_____ 2. Tocamos discos y . . .

_____ 3. Leemos revistas y . . .

_____ 4. Puedo ver una película en . . .

_____ 5. Vemos a los actores buenos . . .

_____ 6. Hay programas de noticias . . .

_____ 7. Por las calles . . .

_____ 8. Quiero hacer un viaje . . .

_____ 9. Prefiero jugar a . . .

_____ 10. Me gusta . . .

a. el cine
b. periódicos
c. vamos en bicicleta
d. durante las vacaciones
e. el fútbol
f. tomamos el sol
g. la pelota
h. en la radio
i. a pie
j. bailamos a la música
k. viajar
l. en la televisión

B.   Your teacher will read aloud ten statements in Spanish. In each case, write **Sí** if the statement is true, **No** if it is false.

1. _____   3. _____   5. _____   7. _____   9. _____

2. _____   4. _____   6. _____   8. _____   10. _____

C.   Answer the following questions about how you and your family spend your leisure time.

1. ¿Qué hace Ud. en la playa?

_____

2. ¿Le gusta a usted pasearse* en bicicleta?

*See footnote, page 269.

3. ¿Qué tipo de revista prefiere usted?

_____

4. ¿Va su familia a hacer un viaje a Sudamérica el verano próximo?

_____

5. ¿Cuántas veces por mes va Ud. al cine?

_____

6. ¿Cuáles son sus deportes favoritos?

_____

7. ¿Qué tipo de canciones escucha Ud.?

_____

8. ¿Cuál es su programa favorito de televisión?

_____

9. ¿Qué clase de música prefiere su padre (madre)?

_____

10. ¿Cuál es su videojuego favorito?

_____

La Península de Yucatán. The Yucatán Península of southeastern Mexico, between the Caribbean Sea and the gulf of Mexico, is a famous site for archeologists all over the world. This was the center of the Mayan civilization. About eighty miles to the east of Mérida, the capital, are the ruins of Chichén-Itzá, where we find pyramids and temples constructed by the Mayas and the Toltecs and which were occupied between the sixth and twelfth centuries A.D. Here we find the great ball court, erected by the Toltec conquerors in 1000 A.D. Stone rings in the walls were the targets for the ball. Another interesting archeological site is Uxmal, a Mayan ceremonial center that flourished between the seventh and tenth centuries, A.D., but was abandoned toward the middle of the fifteenth century. One of Uxmal's achievements was the Nunnery, a group of four rectangular buildings which represented a late architectural style of the Mayas.

11. ¿Qué programas de televisión le gusta a usted grabar en la cámara video (el magnetoscopio).

_____

12. ¿Asiste usted muchas veces a conciertos?

_____

13. ¿Con quién (quiénes) puede dar Ud. paseos en coche?

_____

14. ¿Le gusta a usted jugar al ajedrez?

_____

15. ¿Qué sección del periódico prefiere Ud. leer?

_____

D. Describe your hobbies or pastimes in Spanish. Use as many words and expressions from this chapter as you can.

EXAMPLE: Por la noche, cuando termino mi trabajo escolar* me gusta mirar la televisión. Mis programas favoritos son cuentos policíacos, pero me gustan también los programas de deportes. En la primavera, después de las clases, mis amigos y yo vamos a un parque para jugar al béisbol. Los sábados voy al cine. En el verano estamos de vacaciones, y mi familia y yo vamos al campo. Allí me gusta ir a pescar y dar paseos en bicicleta.

_____

_____

_____

_____

_____

_____

* Since a *tarea* can be any kind of task or chore, it is sometimes better to use *trabajo escolar* as a translation for "homework"—especially when speaking to someone who is neither a student nor a teacher.

Part 9
Additional Practice in Reading and Listening

⋈⋈⋈⋈⋈⋈⋈⋈⋈⋈⋈⋈⋈⋈⋈⋈⋈⋈⋈⋈⋈⋈⋈⋈⋈⋈

46
Reading Practice

Read each passage and answer the questions that follow. Base your answers on the information given in the passage.

I

Manuel Pérez y María Santos son dos jóvenes colombianos que estudian inglés en la escuela. Manuel le dice a su amiga que el inglés es su asignatura favorita porque es muy interesante y él va a hacer un viaje con su familia a los Estados Unidos el año próximo.

A. Circle the letter of the correct answer.

1. El apellido de la amiga de Manuel es
   a. Santos
   b. Pérez
   c. Colombiano

2. _____ es interesante.
   a. Manuel
   b. El inglés
   c. María

3. ¿Quiénes van a los Estados Unidos?
   a. Manuel y su familia
   b. Manuel y María.
   c. María y la familia de Manuel.

B. Many Spanish words resemble English words because of a common ancestry—usually Latin or Greek. For example, **médico** and "medical" are obviously related in this way. Such word-pairs are called **cognates**. Some cognates are easily recognizable as such because they are spelled almost alike and have the same meaning: **accidente** and "accident," for example. Others are not so easy to recognize or have related but different meanings: **parientes** and "parents" are cognates, but the Spanish word means "relatives." Note that a Spanish word beginning with *es* + a consonant usually has an English cognate that begins with *s* + a consonant: **estudiar**—*st*udy, **especial**—*sp*ecial, etc.

279

The underlined words in paragraph **I** are listed below. In each blank write an English cognate. If the cognate has a different meaning, write the English translation of the Spanish word.

		English cognate	Translation (if needed)
EXAMPLE:	**favorita**	*favorite*	
	próximo	*approximate*	*near, next*
1.	colombianos		
2.	estudian		
3.	inglés		
4.	escuela		
5.	asignatura		
6.	interesante		
7.	viaje		
8.	familia		
9.	estados		
10.	unidos		
11.	año		

II

Mi _familia_ _vive_ en una casa _particular_. Tenemos siete _habitaciones_: la sala, el comedor, la cocina y cuatro _dormitorios_. También hay dos _cuartos_ de baño. Hay un _garaje_ para nuestro _coche_. Después de la comida toda la familia _pasa_ a la sala donde _mira_ la _televisión_. Después de mirar la _televisión_ yo voy a mi cuarto para _preparar_ mis _lecciones_ y estudiar.

A.   Complete each statement with the proper words. (Each blank represents one word.)

1. La casa tiene _____ habitaciones y dos _____ de

   _____.

2. Ponemos el _____ en el garaje.

3. La familia _____ _____ _____ en la sala.

4. Yo estudio en _____ _____.

B. The underlined words in paragraph **II** are listed below. Write an English cognate for each word. If the cognate has a different meaning, write the English translation of the Spanish word.

		English cognate	Translation (if needed)
EXAMPLE:	**familia**	*family*	
	vive	*vivid*	*lives*
1.	particular		
2.	habitaciones		
3.	dormitorios		
4.	cuartos		
5.	garaje		
6.	coche		
7.	pasa		
8.	mira		
9.	televisión		
10.	preparar		
11.	lecciones		

III

En la clase de español todos los alumnos son muy aplicados menos Carlos. Él es muy perezoso y no le gusta estudiar en casa. Casi nunca hace su tarea porque mira la televisión toda la noche. Un día, el profesor nota que Carlos tiene su tarea y le dice:

—Carlos, veo que has hecho (*you've done*) la tarea. ¡Esto es muy raro!

—Sí, señor, es verdad—contesta Carlos.—Es que (*It's because*) mi televisor está roto (*broken*).

A. If the statement is true, write *Sí*. If it is false, write *No*.

_____ **1.** Carlos es aplicado.

_____ **2.** Carlos estudia poco en casa.

_____ **3.** Los alumnos miran la televisión en casa toda la noche.

_____ **4.** El profesor da tareas a la clase.

_____ **5.** Una noche el televisor de Carlos no funciona.

B. In the passage, find an antonym for:

1. perezosos _____   **4.** al aire libre _____

2. siempre _____   **5.** todo el día _____

3. común _____

C. Write an English cognate for:

1. menos _____   4. estudiar _____

2. alumno _____   5. todo _____

3. raro _____

IV

Nuestra ciudad no es <u>grande</u>, pero es muy <u>moderna</u> y tiene algunos <u>edificios altos</u>. En el <u>centro</u> de la ciudad hay un <u>parque</u> pequeño con muchos árboles bonitos. Cuando hace buen <u>tiempo</u> la gente da paseos por el parque. No hay metro y tenemos que <u>usar</u> el autobús para ir de un lugar a otro.

A. If the statement is true, write *Sí*. If it is false, write *No*.

_____ 1. Hay pocos árboles en la ciudad.

_____ 2. Hay árboles en los edificios.

_____ 3. La ciudad es pequeña.

_____ 4. La gente usa el tren para viajar.

B. In the passage, find antonyms for the following words:

1. campo _____   5. grande _____

2. pequeña _____   6. pocos _____

3. antigua _____   7. mal _____

4. bajos _____   8. venir _____

C. The words underlined in paragraph **IV** are listed below. In each blank, write an English cognate. If the cognate has a different meaning, write the English translation of the Spanish word.

	English cognate	Translation (if needed)
1. grande	_____	_____
2. moderna	_____	_____
3. edificios	_____	_____
4. altos	_____	_____
5. centro	_____	_____
6. parque	_____	_____
7. tiempo	_____	_____
8. usar	_____	_____

V

Fernando Herrera es un joven dominicano que visita a la familia de Johnny Thompson, su amigo en Nueva York. Una noche, después de la cena, todos los miembros de la familia de Johnny están sentados en la sala y le hacen preguntas a Fernando acerca de su país.

—¿Dónde está la República Dominicana?—le pregunta el padre de Johnny.

—Está situada en el Mar Caribe y ocupa parte de la isla llamada La Española.

—Y, ¿qué país ocupa la otra parte de la isla?—le pregunta Sara, la hermana de Johnny.

—Haití ocupa la otra parte.

—¿De qué ciudad eres tú?—le pregunta la madre de Johnny.

—Soy de Santo Domingo, la capital. Es una ciudad bonita y tiene una universidad muy antigua.

A.   **1.**   De dónde es Fernando?
       a. de Santo Domingo   **b.** de Nueva York   **c.** de Haití

       2.   ¿Quién visita a la familia de Johnny?
       a. el señor Thompson   **b.** la hermana de Johnny   **c.** Fernando Herrera

       3.   ¿Dónde vive la familia Thompson?
       a. en Santo Domingo   **b.** en Nueva York   **c.** en el Mar Caribe

       4.   ¿Qué es Haití?
       a. una isla cerca de Santo Domingo   **b.** un país de La Española   **c.** una universidad antigua

B.   Find Spanish cognates in the reading passage for the following words.

    1. juvenile _____   **3.** antique _____   **5.** paternal _____

    2. insulate _____   **4.** salon _____   **6.** amicable _____

VI

Los niños de los países hispanos asisten a una escuela primaria por seis años. Después van a una escuela secundaria por cinco o seis años, y al graduarse, reciben su *bachillerato*. Luego, si quieren, van a la universidad para prepararse para una profesión.

A.   Complete the statement. Each blank represents one word.

    1. Los niños hispanos pasan _____ _____ en una escuela primaria.

    2. Los niños reciben el bachillerato después de pasar _____ años en una

        _____ _____ .

    3. Pueden prepararse para una profesión en la _____ .

B.   Although *asistir* is a cognate of "assist," it does not have that meaning. What does the Spanish verb mean? _____ Similarly, *bachillerato* is a cognate of "baccalaureate"—the "bachelor's degree" earned at American colleges. Is a *bachillerato* the equivalent of an American bachelor's degree? _____

VII

La pampa es una región muy fértil de la Argentina. Aquí viven los gauchos, los cowboys de la Argentina. Al gaucho le gusta tocar la guitarra e (*and*) improvisar canciones.* Hoy día los gauchos viven en ranchos.

A. Complete the sentences. (A blank may represent more than one word.)

1. Los _____ viven _____ en _____ .

2. Con su guitarra el gaucho puede _____ .

3. La pampa es una parte de _____ .

B. **1.** What English word is both the cognate and the meaning of

improvisar? _____   *guitarra?* _____

rancho? _____

2. Which Spanish word in the passage is spelled exactly like its English equivalent (except

for an accent mark)? _____

VIII

Margarita asiste a una escuela secundaria en una ciudad grande. La clase de español comienza a las ocho de la mañana. Ella llega tarde todos los días. Su profesora le pregunta:

—Margarita, ¿por qué llegas tan tarde todos los días?

Margarita contesta:—No puedo llegar temprano porque tengo tres hermanas.

—¿Qué importa eso (*What does that matter*)?

—Pues—contesta Margarita—, todas nos levantamos a la misma hora, y en mi casa tenemos un solo (*single*) cuarto de baño.

A. Circle the letter of the correct answer.

1. ¿Dónde vive Margarita?
    a. en su escuela
    b. en la ciudad
    c. en la clase

2. ¿Cuándo empieza la clase de español?
    a. muy temprano
    b. por la tarde
    c. por la noche

3. ¿Quién llega tarde a la escuela?
    a. la profesora
    b. la hermana de Margarita
    c. Margarita

4. ¿Quiénes se levantan a la misma hora?
    a. Margarita y su madre
    b. Margarita y sus hermanas
    c. las amigas de Margarita

5. ¿Dónde hay un solo cuarto de baño?
    a. en la casa de Margarita
    b. en la escuela
    c. en la casa de la profesora

*The word for "and" is "e" in Spanish when it precedes a word that begins with "i" or "hi."

B. In the passage, find an antonym for:

1. pequeña _____   5. temprano _____

2. termina _____   6. pregunta _____

3. noche _____   7. nos acostamos _____

4. sales _____

IX

Francisco Rivera y Juana Muñoz son dos chicos de San Juan, la capital de Puerto Rico. Viven en Santurce, un sector de la ciudad. Un domingo, los dos deciden ir a la playa muy bonita de Luquillo. Esta playa no está lejos de San Juan. Van allí porque les gusta nadar en las aguas azules y descansar debajo de las hermosas palmeras (*palm* trees).

A. Complete the sentences.

1. Los dos muchachos se llaman _____ y _____.

2. Ellos viven en la ciudad de _____.

3. Los dos desean ir a _____ para _____.

4. Hay palmeras en la _____ de _____.

B. In the passage, find an antonym for each of the following:

1. aquí _____   4. trabajar _____

2. fea _____   5. encima de _____

3. cerca de _____

C. In the passage, find a synonym for:

1. muchachos _____   4. bañarse _____

2. residen _____   5. bellas _____

3. linda _____

X

El señor Gómez trabaja en una biblioteca. Él es muy distraído (*absentminded*). Un día está pre-ocupado (*worried*) porque no puede encontrar sus gafas (*eyeglasses*). Busca por todas partes (*everywhere*) pero no puede encontrarlas. Por fin le pregunta a otro empleado (*employee*) de la biblioteca:

—¿Ha visto usted (*Have you seen*) mis gafas? No puedo encontrarlas en ninguna parte (*anywhere*).

—Sí—contesta su amigo—, usted las lleva en la nariz.

A. If the statement is true, write *Sí*. If it is false, write *No*.

_____ **1.** Sólo el Sr. Gómez trabaja en la biblioteca.

_____ **2.** (lo que = *what*) El Sr. Gómez muchas veces no sabe lo que hace.

_____ **3.** El Sr. Gómez lleva gafas.

_____ **4.** Con gafas podemos oler mejor.

_____ **5.** El amigo de Gómez sabe dónde están las gafas.

B. In the passage, find an antonym for:

1. descansa _____   **4.** mismo _____

2. perder _____   **5.** pregunta _____

3. en ninguna parte _____

XI

Bárbara y Juanito hablan de sus pasatiempos favoritos. Bárbara dice que le gusta jugar al tenis, trabajar con la computadora y escuchar música clásica en sus discos. Juanito dice que prefiere jugar al fútbol, dar paseos en coche y mirar programas de televisión. Los dos dicen que quieren hacer un viaje durante el verano y no quieren quedarse en casa.

A. If the statement is true, write *Sí*. If it is false, write *No*.

_____ **1.** Juanito prefiere el tenis.

_____ **2.** Bárbara da paseos en coche.

_____ **3.** Bárbara prefiere la música rock.

_____ **4.** A Juanito le gusta jugar al fútbol.

_____ **5.** Los dos prefieren quedarse en casa en el verano.

B. In the passage, find a synonym for:

1. automóvil _____   **5.** diversiones _____

2. pasearse _____   **6.** oír _____

3. desean _____   **7.** ver _____

4. viajar _____

C. In the passage, find a Spanish cognate for:

1. computer _____   **4.** classical _____

2. voyage _____   **5.** coach _____

3. mirror _____   **6.** disk _____

XII

Read the following advertisement and answer the questions that follow in English.

Useful vocabulary:

alquilar, to rent   **el barrio**, neighborhood   **los medios**, means

> Apartamentos para alquilar de 1,2,3 dormitorios, uno o dos baños, en un barrio nuevo, cerca de un centro comercial grande y buenos medios de transporte.
>
> Llame al 239-0172 de las nueve de la mañana hasta las cinco de la tarde.

1. What is this ad for? _____

2. What are two benefits? _____

3. How does one get information about the ad? _____

XIII

La península de Yucatán, en México, es el centro de la civilización maya. La capital de Yucatán es Mérida, una ciudad muy pintoresca que tiene un mercado donde la gente puede comprar cosas de henequén (*hemp*), el producto principal de Yucatán. A una distancia de 128 kilómetros (80 millas) de Mérida están las ruinas de Chichén-Itzá, donde hay pirámides y templos muy antiguos.

A. Complete the sentences by writing an appropriate word in each blank.

    1. El centro de la civilización maya es _____.

    2. Hay un mercado en _____.

    3. _____ es un producto de _____.

    4. En Chichén-Itzá podemos ver _____ y _____.

    5. Mérida es la _____ de _____.

B. In the passage, find a cognate for:

    1. antique _____   **4.** ruin _____

    2. mile _____   **5.** temple _____

    3. picturesque _____

XIV

El Ecuador es un país de Sudamérica. Se llama así porque el ecuador (*equator*) pasa por allí a 26 kilómetros (16 millas) de Quito, la capital. En el Ecuador hay muchos volcanes activos. Cerca de Quito está el volcán llamado Cotopaxi, que tiene casi 6,000 metros (20.000 pies) de altura (*height*). Quito es una ciudad moderna en cierto modo (*in some respects*) pero todavía tiene la apariencia de una ciudad colonial española.

A. Each sentence can be changed to a true statement by changing the word(s) in italics. In the blank provided, write the word(s) that should be substituted for italicized word(s).

1. La capital del Ecuador es *Cotopaxi*. _____

2. El ecuador pasa a una distancia de *26 millas* de Quito. _____

3. Cotopaxi es *un país*. _____

4. El Ecuador está en *la América Central*. _____

5. Quito es una ciudad *de España*. _____

B. In the passage, find a cognate for:

1. appearance _____   4. altitude _____

2. meter _____   5. colonial _____

3. volcano _____

XV

El Perú es la tierra de los incas. Lima, la capital, fue fundada por Pizarro, el conquistador de estos indios. Los descendientes de los incas viven todavía en el Perú. Ellos cultivan la *papa*, una palabra derivada del quechua, la lengua de los indios peruanos.

A. If the statement is true, write *Sí*. If it is false, write *No*.

_____ 1. La capital del Perú es Pizarro.

_____ 2. Los incas vivieron en el Perú.

_____ 3. Los indios del Perú comen «quechua».

_____ 4. La papa es una bebida.

B. In the passage, find a cognate for:

1. derive _____   4. founded _____

2. territory _____   5. language _____

3. conquest _____

XVI

El español es la lengua de veinte países. Hablan español en España, México, seis países de Centroamérica, nueve países de Sudamérica y tres países del Caribe. Todas las personas que hablan español se llaman *hispanos*. En cada país el español es un poco diferente aunque (*although*) todos hablan la misma lengua. Por ejemplo, casi todos los hispanos dicen «autobús» pero los mexicanos dicen «camión» y los cubanos y puertorriqueños usan la palabra «guagua».

A. Complete the sentences.

1. Hablan español en _____.

2. Todos los _____ hablan español.

3. En inglés «autobús» quiere decir _____.

4. En Cuba _____ es un autobús.

B. In the passage, find a cognate for:

1. linguistic _____   3. Caribbean _____

2. use   _____   4. different _____

XVII

La familia Smith vive en San Diego, California. La familia García vive en la Ciudad de México. La familia García invitó a la familia Smith a su casa por una semana. Durante la visita fueron a ver algunos lugares de interés. Los miembros de la familia Smith notaron que la Ciudad de México era (*was*) muy moderna y que tenía (*it had*) muchos edificios nuevos. Vieron el metro (*subway*) nuevo. Vieron también calles y avenidas muy anchas y muchos monumentos.

A. Circle the letter of the correct answer.

1. La familia Smith   3. ¿Quiénes viven en San Diego?
    a. visita México   **a.** la familia García
    b. vive en México   **b.** las dos familias
    c. vive en una casa grande   **c.** la familia Smith

2. Hay un metro nuevo en   4. La Ciudad de México tiene
    a. San Diego   **a.** edificios modernos
    b. la Ciudad de México   **b.** pocos monumentos
    c. un edificio nuevo   **c.** un metro muy viejo

B. Which word in passage XVII is associated with each of the following?

1. período de siete días   _____

2. personas de la familia   _____

3. tren subterráneo   _____

4. estatuas de personas famosas   _____

C. In the passage find an antonym for:

1. estrechas _____   3. antigua _____

2. pocos   _____   4. viejos _____

D. List ten words in the passage that have English cognates and write the cognates below.

	Spanish word	English cognate			Spanish word	English cognate
1.	_____	_____	**6.**		_____	_____
2.	_____	_____	**7.**		_____	_____
3.	_____	_____	**8.**		_____	_____
4.	_____	_____	**9.**		_____	_____
5.	_____	_____	**10.**		_____	_____

XVIII

Read the following advertisement and answer in English the questions that follow. Here is some vocabulary to serve as a guide.

cuidar, to take care of   **las aptitudes,** qualifications

Se busca un/una joven entre 15 y 17 años de edad para cuidar a un niño de 7 años, dos noches por semana, entre las 7 y las 10 de la noche.

Escriba una carta incluyendo sus aptitudes, con 2 referencias a:

los señores González
Calle Neptuno, 175

o, si quiere, puede llamar al 597-8021 los sábados y domingos entre la 1 y las 6 de la tarde.

---

1. What is this position for? _____

2. What are the age requirements? _____

3. What must the applicant include in his or her application? _____

4. What two possible ways does the applicant have to get in touch with the prospective employer? _____

XIX

Por la mañana los españoles y los hispanoamericanos toman un desayuno muy ligero (*light*). Un desayuno típico consiste en una taza de café o chocolate y un panecillo o pan tostado con mantequilla. La comida principal del día es el almuerzo (o «comida» en algunos países), que consiste en varios platos y se sirve (*is served*) entre la una y las dos de la tarde. La gente hispana toma la cena entre las nueve y las diez de la noche. La cena generalmente es una comida ligera.

Each of the following sentences can be changed to a true statement by changing the word(s) in italics. In the blank provided, write the word(s) that should be substituted for the italicized word(s).

1. El desayuno español consiste en *muchas cosas.*   _____

2. El almuerzo se sirve por la *noche.*   _____

3. Los españoles cenan a las *cinco* de la *tarde*. _____

4. *El almuerzo* es una comida ligera. _____

XX

La familia Rodríguez vive en Madrid en un piso (apartamento) muy grande. En esta familia hay ocho personas: el padre, la madre, tres hijos y tres hijas. El domingo el padre dice que toda la familia va al parque zoológico (el zoo), que está en la parte de Madrid llamada «Casa del campo». El zoo es nuevo y muy moderno, y tiene animales de todas partes del mundo. Si una familia es grande, no tiene que pagar mucho para entrar. Por eso toda la familia va al zoo.

Circle the letter of the correct answer.

1. ¿Por qué necesita la familia un piso grande?
   a. la familia es grande
   b. hay poca gente
   c. no hay pisos pequeños

2. ¿Cuántas personas van a visitar el zoo?
   a. 2
   b. 6
   c. 8

3. El zoo
   a. es viejo
   b. está cerca de la casa
   c. está en Madrid

4. En el zoo viven
   a. animales
   b. alumnos
   c. los Sres. Rodríguez

5. ¿Quiénes pagan poco dinero para entrar en el zoo?
   a. las familias pequeñas
   b. las familias grandes
   c. los animales pobres

XXI

Study the following vocabulary before reading the selection:

los grandes almacenes, department store
el dependiente, clerk
el requisito, requirement

el aspecto, appearance
el puesto, position, job
a mano, by hand

¡Estudiantes de español de la escuela secundaria!

Ustedes tienen la oportunidad de ganar dinero durante las vacaciones de Navidad. Los grandes Almacenes López buscan estudiantes para trabajar como dependientes en varios departamentos de la tienda.

—Buen trabajo
—Buen salario

Requisitos:
- saber hablar inglés
- ser agradable y simpático
- tener buen aspecto
- tener entre 16 y 18 años de edad

Si Ud. se interesa en un puesto, escriba una carta a mano a:

Almacenes López
Sección del Personal
Avenida López Garrido, 25 San José

Answer the following questions in English based on the above advertisement.

1. To whom is this ad directed? _____

2. Who is offering the jobs? _____

3. During what period of the year is the work for? _____

4. What are the requirements? _____

5. How and to whom should *candidates* apply? _____

XXII

En España hay muchas ciudades interesantes. Muchos turistas visitan Segovia porque esta ciudad tiene un acueducto construido por los romanos hace 2000 años. Burgos, en el norte de España, es famoso por tener la tumba del Cid, el héroe legendario de España. Madrid, la capital, está en el centro de España. En esta ciudad el turista puede ver muchos lugares interesantes como el Museo del Prado y la Puerta del Sol, una plaza famosa donde hay siempre mucha gente. En Madrid hay un zoo muy moderno y un parque de atracciones que es popular entre los niños de esta ciudad.

A. Circle the letter of the correct answer.

1. Segovia está en
    a. Madrid
    b. un acueducto
    c. España

2. ¿Cúal es la capital de España?
    a. Segovia
    b. Burgos
    c. Madrid

3. En Madrid hay
    a. un museo y un zoo
    b. una tumba y una plaza
    c. un acueducto y un parque de atracciones.

4. ¿Dónde hay mucha gente?
    a. en la tumba del Cid
    b. en la Puerta del Sol
    c. en la Luna

5. ¿Quiénes prefieren ir al zoo?
    a. los niños
    b. los héroes
    c. las atracciones

B. In the passage, find a cognate for:

1. tourist _____

2. aqueduct _____

3. legendary _____

4. construct _____

5. much _____

XXIII

Es una noche oscura (*dark*). Un policía anda por las calles. En una esquina, ve a un borracho (*drunkard*) que está de rodillas (*on his knees*) debajo del farol (*street lamp*). Él busca algo en el suelo.

—¿Qué busca usted?—pregunta el policía.

—Busco mi reloj. Lo perdí.

—¿Dónde lo perdió usted?

—Allí en la otra esquina.

—Si lo perdió en la otra esquina—dice el policía—, ¿por qué lo busca usted aquí?

—Hay más luz aquí—contesta el borracho.

A. If the statement is true, write *Sí*. If it is false, write *No*.

_____ 1. El policía conoce al borracho.

_____ 2. Un farol es una clase de lámpara.

_____ 3. El policía busca algo en el suelo.

_____ 4. El policía encuentra al borracho en una esquina.

_____ 5. El borracho perdió su reloj debajo del farol.

B. Find an antonym for:

1. un día _____   4. encontré _____

2. corre _____   5. aquí _____

3. contesta _____   6. menos _____

XXIV

Ayer fue el cumpleaños de Javier, el hermano de Lola. Él tiene ahora diez años y su hermana tiene quince años. Su papá le dio una computadora, su mamá le dio un reloj y su hermana le dio una tarjeta (*card*) bonita. Su mamá invitó a seis de sus compañeros a una fiesta en su honor. Después de la fiesta su padre lo llevó al cine a ver una buena película. Fue un día muy alegre para Javier.

A. Circle the letter of the correct answer.

1. ¿Quién tiene diez años?
   a. Lola
   b. Javier
   c. el padre

2. ¿ De quién recibió Javier el reloj?
   a. de su madre
   b. de su hermana
   c. de su hermano

3. ¿Qué le dio Lola?
   a. una tarjeta
   b. un reloj
   c. dinero

4. ¿Cuántos amigos vinieron a la fiesta?
   a. 10
   b. 15
   c. 6

5. ¿Adónde fue Javier con su papá?
   a. al cine
   b. a la escuela
   c. a la fiesta

B. In the passage, find an antonym for:

1. triste _____

2. antes de _____

3. hoy _____

4. recibió _____

5. mala _____

XXV

Study the following vocabulary before reading the selection.

sigue igual, continues to be the same

próximo, -a, next

corregir, to correct

lo mismo, the same thing

por ahora, for now

los recuerdos, regards

los abrazos, hugs

las asignaturas, school subjects

The following is a letter written by a Spanish-American youngster to her pen-pal in the United States.

Querida Jane:

¿Cómo estás? Aquí todos estamos muy bien. Mi vida sigue igual. Los días de escuela me levanto a las siete y me preparo para ir a la escuela. Voy a la escuela en autobús con algunos amigos. Llegamos a las ocho y las clases empiezan a las ocho y cuarto. Estudio español, matemáticas, historia, ciencia y, naturalmente inglés. Francamente encuentro el inglés un poco difícil, como tú encuentras el español. En mi próxima carta te voy a escribir en inglés y tú puedes corregir mis faltas. Si quieres, tú puedes contestarme en español y yo puedo hacer lo mismo. Por ahora, eso es todo. Recuerdos a la familia.

Abrazos de tu amiga Isabel.

Indicate whether each of the following statements is true or false, according to the above letter. Write *T* or *F*.

_____ **1.** Isabel le escribe una carta a Jane.

_____ **2.** Isabel sale de la casa a las siete de la mañana.

_____ **3.** Isabel llega a la escuela en coche.

_____ **4.** Isabel empieza sus estudios a las ocho y cuarto.

_____ **5.** Jane estudia cinco asignaturas.

_____ **6.** Para Jane el inglés es difícil.

_____ **7.** La familia de Isabel manda recuerdos a Jane.

47
Listening Practice

Group I

The teacher will read aloud a statement in Spanish.* Write *T* if the statement is true or makes sense, write *F* if the statement is false or does not make sense.

1. ____	8. ____	15. ____	22. ____	29. ____
2. ____	9. ____	16. ____	23. ____	30. ____
3. ____	10. ____	17. ____	24. ____	31. ____
4. ____	11. ____	18. ____	25. ____	32. ____
5. ____	12. ____	19. ____	26. ____	33. ____
6. ____	13. ____	20. ____	27. ____	34. ____
7. ____	14. ____	21. ____	28. ____	35. ____

Group II

Sentence Completion: The teacher will read aloud the first few words of a Spanish sentence. Choose the word or expression that completes the sentence correctly. Circle the letter of your choice.

1. a. el señor Brown
   b. la señorita López
   c. un hospital
   d. el cuaderno

2. a. bebidas
   b. hablar
   c. azules
   d. perezosos

3. a. roja
   b. cerrada
   c. en la página
   d. fácil

4. a. difícil
   b. ausente
   c. la profesora
   d. amarilla

5. a. las ventanas
   b. los cuadernos
   c. la carne
   d. el padre

6. a. cenamos
   b. compramos zapatos
   c. nos bañamos
   d. comemos y bebemos

7. a. la puerta
   b. el ruido
   c. la lección
   d. el pelo

8. a. con la televisión
   b. en el hotel
   c. por la mañana
   d. en casa

9. a. Elena
   b. Pedro
   c. Elena y Pedro
   d. teléfono

10. a. es grande
    b. en la ciudad
    c. muy viejo
    d. es médico

11. a. mi abuelo
    b. mi sobrino
    c. mi madre
    d. mi primo

12. a. en California
    b. de Nueva York
    c. a Nevada
    d. cuatrocientos años

*To the teacher: For these aural-comprehension drills, the statements or questions that are to be read to the class will be found in the Answer Key.

295

13. a. mi bolsillo
b. el garaje
c. la sala
d. el techo

14. a. flores
b. frutas
c. muebles
d. edificios

15. a. en el armario
b. por teléfono
c. al vino
d. muy populares

16. a. la puerta
b. la alfombra
c. el dinero
d. la llave

17. a. está en la biblioteca
b. es grande
c. va al centro
d. compra pan

18. a. la zapatería
b. la farmacia
c. la bodega
d. la tienda de ropa

19. a. duermo en mi cama
b. escribo en la pizarra
c. cruzo el agua
d. espero el tren

20. a. pasatiempos
b. paseos
c. libros
d. canciones

21. a. jugamos en la nieve
b. vamos al campo
c. asistimos a la escuela
d. hace frío

22. a. revistas
b. conciertos
c. comidas
d. playas

23. a. paseo
b. libro
c. tenis
d. pelo

24. a. en el deporte
b. en la radio
c. en los guantes
d. en la televisión

25. a. deportes
b. frutas
c. verduras
d. periódicos

26. a. los ojos
b. los oídos
c. la nariz
d. la falda

27. a. izquierdo
b. pobre
c. largo
d. alegre

28. a. los pies
b. las manos
c. la leche
d. la lengua

29. a. verduras
b. oro
c. madera
d. nilón

30. a. pies
b. cabezas
c. dedos
d. hijos

31. a. helado de chocolate
b. mantequilla
c. pan tostado
d. tenedor

32. a. sol
b. café
c. ensalada
d. pelo

33. a. servir al mozo
b. nadar
c. acostarnos
d. comer y beber

34. a. una fruta
b. una bebida
c. un hombre
d. un mueble

35. a. a la comida
b. en casa
c. a Sudamérica
d. al sol

Group III

Logical Responses: The teacher will read a statement. Choose the logical response.

1. a. Entonces vamos a dar un paseo.
b. Mañana es sábado.
c. Pues no podemos ir a la playa.
d. Vamos a comer.

2. a. Está en casa ahora.
b. Es mi hermano.
c. Tengo sed.
d. Quiero ir a Puerto Rico.

3. a. Debes trabajar.
   b. Y yo voy a la escuela.
   c. Me gustan los deportes.
   d. Hay mucho tráfico.

4. a. Sí, él enseña muy bien y es simpático.
   b. Sí, me lavo las manos.
   c. Sí, es una buena película.
   d. Sí, es un buen programa.

5. a. Mi tío es rico.
   b. Vendo mi casa.
   c. Quiero ir contigo.
   d. No me gusta la música.

6. a. Vamos a la bodega.
   b. Tú lo necesitas para la fiesta.
   c. Mi coche es nuevo.
   d. Estoy en casa ahora.

7. a. La música es buena.
   b. Esta novela es interesante.
   c. Jugamos al fútbol.
   d. Tenemos que estudiar.

8. a. Podemos comer ahora.
   b. Escuchan la radio.
   c. Necesito tres libros.
   d. Lea Ud. el periódico.

9. a. Y mis amigos son ricos.
   b. Y tiene unos artículos muy buenos.
   c. Y mañana es jueves.
   d. Y el profesor baila muy bien.

10. a. Tenemos que ir a la escuela.
    b. Mis abuelos son simpáticos.
    c. Me gusta ese programa.
    d. Podemos ir al cine.

11. a. Vamos a dar un paseo por la ciudad.
    b. Podemos usarlo en la casa.
    c. Los actores son malos.
    d. La comida es muy buena.

12. a. Mi vestido es nuevo.
    b. Yo escribo una carta.
    c. Almorzamos a las doce.
    d. Debes estudiar más.

13. a. Yo prefiero las manzanas.
    b. Quiero ir a España.
    c. Pero es muy temprano.
    d. Ellos esperan el tren.

14. a. Tengo muchos amigos.
    b. El traje cuesta mucho.
    c. La escuela es muy grande.
    d. El agua está fría.

15. a. La farmacia no está lejos de aquí.
    b. Podemos ir al cine hoy.
    c. Es una canción bonita.
    d. Voy a tomar vino.

16. a. Tenemos que levantarnos.
    b. Es un buen postre.
    c. Tu blusa es muy bonita.
    d. Hay mucha gente en la plaza.

17. a. Sí, quiero comprar pantalones.
    b. Sí, tiene el pelo negro.
    c. Sí, mi hermana está muy enferma.
    d. Sí, estoy sentado al escritorio.

18. a. Es nueva.
    b. Es deliciosa.
    c. Está en México.
    d. Trabaja en el centro.

19. a. De nada.
    b. En voz alta.
    c. Por la mañana.
    d. Con mucho gusto.

20. a. No hay de qué.
    b. Hasta luego, amigo.
    c. Mucho tiempo, señorita.
    d. Muchas veces, señora.

21. a. Doy un paseo ahora.
    b. Aprendo a leer.
    c. Es muy bonito también.
    d. Tengo calor aquí.

22. a. No me gusta ese deporte.
    b. Me gusta comerlo.
    c. Asistimos a la universidad.
    d. Le doy las gracias.

23. a. Toco la guitarra.
    b. Voy a comer pronto.
    c. Yo quiero ir también.
    d. Hay libros en la mesa.

24. a. El parque es muy bonito.
    b. Mi padre gana mucho dinero.
    c. Está en la escuela ahora.
    d. No hay buenos programas esta noche.

25. a. Buenos días.
    b. Pero no puedo oírte.
    c. Todo el mundo.
    d. Y hace calor.

Appendixes

Verb Chart

Regular Verbs

Infinitive Present Participle	Present	Preterit	Imperfect	Future	Command
tomar, *to take* **tomando,** *taking*	*I take* *I am taking*	*I took*	*I used to take,* *I was taking*	*I will take*	*Take!*
	tomo	tomé	tomaba	tomaré	Tome Ud.
	tomas	tomaste	tomabas	tomarás	Tomen Uds.
	toma	tomó	tomaba	tomará	
	tomamos	tomamos	tomábamos	tomaremos	
	tomáis	tomasteis	tomabais	tomaréis	
	toman	tomaron	tomaban	tomarán	
vender, *to sell* **vendiendo,** *selling*	*I sell* *I am selling*	*I sold*	*I used to sell,* *I was selling*	*I will sell*	*Sell!*
	vendo	vendí	vendía	venderé	Venda Ud.
	vendes	vendiste	vendías	venderás	Vendan Uds.
	vende	vendió	vendía	venderá	
	vendemos	vendimos	vendíamos	venderemos	
	vendéis	vendisteis	vendíais	venderéis	
	venden	vendieron	vendían	venderán	
vivir, *to live* **viviendo,** *living*	*I live* *I am living*	*I lived*	*I used to live,* *I was living*	*I will live*	*Live!*
	vivo	viví	vivía	viviré	Viva Ud.
	vives	viviste	vivías	vivirás	Vivan Uds.
	vive	vivió	vivía	vivirá	
	vivimos	vivimos	vivíamos	viviremos	
	vivís	vivisteis	vivíais	viviréis	
	viven	vivieron	vivían	vivirán	

Irregular Verbs

Note: 1. Only conjugations that contain irregular forms are listed here.

2. The preterit forms of certain -IR verbs are included in this chart although the type of irregularity they display—a stem change in the 3rd-person forms—is not taught in this book. (See sentir—s*i*ntió, s*i*ntieron; dormir—d*u*rmió, d*u*rmieron, etc.)

3. Verbs that are conjugated in the same ways as the verbs in the chart are listed alphabetically at the end of the chart.

Infinitive Present Participle	Present	Preterit	Imperfect	Future	Command
andar, *to walk* andando, *walking*		**anduve** **anduviste** **anduvo** **anduvimos** **anduvisteis** **anduvieron**			
caer, *to fall* **cayendo**	**caigo** caes cae caemos caéis caen	caí **caíste** **cayó** **caímos** **caísteis** **cayeron**			**Caiga** Ud. **Caigan** Uds.
conocer, *to know* conociendo	**conozco** conoces conoce conocemos conocéis conocen				**Conozca** Ud. **Conozcan** Uds.
dar, *to give* dando	**doy** das da damos dais dan	**di** **diste** **dio** **dimos** **disteis** **dieron**			**Dé** Ud. **Den** Uds.
decir, *to say, tell* **diciendo**	**digo** **dices** **dice** decimos decís **dicen**	**dije** **dijiste** **dijo** **dijimos** **dijisteis** **dijeron**		**diré** **dirás** **dirá** **diremos** **diréis** **dirán**	**Diga** Ud. **Digan** Uds.
dormir, *to sleep* **durmiendo**	**duermo** **duermes** **duerme** dormimos dormís **duermen**	dormí dormiste **durmió** dormimos dormisteis **durmieron**			**Duerma** Ud. **Duerman** Uds.
entender, *to understand* entendiendo	**entiendo** **entiendes** **entiende** entendemos entendéis **entienden**				**Entienda** Ud. **Entiendan** Uds.

Infinitive Present Participle	Present	Preterit	Imperfect	Future	Command
estar, *to be* estando	**estoy** **estás** **está** estamos estáis **están**	**estuve** **estuviste** **estuvo** **estuvimos** **estuvisteis** **estuvieron**			**Esté** Ud. **Estén** Uds.
hacer, *to do, make* haciendo	**hago** haces hace hacemos hacéis hacen	**hice** **hiciste** **hizo** **hicimos** **hicisteis** **hicieron**		**haré** **harás** **hará** **haremos** **haréis** **harán**	**Haga** Ud. **Hagan** Uds.
ir, *to go* **yendo**	**voy** **vas** **va** **vamos** **vais** **van**	**fui** **fuiste** **fue** **fuimos** **fuisteis** **fueron**	iba ibas iba íbamos ibais iban		**Vaya** Ud. **Vayan** Uds.
jugar *to play* jugando	**juego** **juegas** **juega** jugamos jugáis **juegan**	**jugué** jugaste jugó jugamos jugasteis jugaron			**Juegue** Ud. **Jueguen** Uds.
leer, *to read* **leyendo**		leí **leíste** **leyó** **leímos** **leísteis** **leyeron**			
llover, *to rain* lloviendo	— — **llueve** — — —	llovió		lloverá	—
nevar, *to snow* nevando	— — **nieva** — — —	nevó		nevará	—
oír, *to hear* **oyendo**	**oigo** **oyes** **oye** **oímos** oís **oyen**	oí **oíste** **oyó** **oímos** **oísteis** **oyeron**			**Oiga** Ud. **Oigan** Uds.
pensar, *to think* pensando	**pienso** **piensas** **piensa** pensamos pensáis **piensan**				**Piense** Ud. **Piensen** Uds.

Infinitive Present Participle	Present	Preterit	Imperfect	Future	Command
poder, *to be able* **pudiendo**	**puedo** **puedes** **puede** podemos podéis **pueden**	**pude** pudiste pudo pudimos pudisteis pudieron		podré podrás podrá podremos podréis podrán	—
poner, *to put* poniendo	**pongo** pones pone ponemos ponéis ponen	puse pusiste puso pusimos pusisteis pusieron		pondré pondrás pondrá pondremos pondréis pondrán	**Ponga** Ud. **Pongan** Uds.
querer, *to want, wish* queriendo	**quiero** **quieres** **quiere** queremos queréis **quieren**	**quise** quisiste quiso quisimos quisisteis quisieron		querré querrás querrá querremos querréis querrán	—
recordar, *to remember* recordando	**recuerdo** **recuerdas** **recuerda** recordamos recordáis **recuerdan**				**Recuerde** Ud. **Recuerden** Uds.
repetir, *to repeat* **repitiendo**	**repito** **repites** **repite** repetimos repetís **repiten**	repetí repetiste **repitió** repetimos repetisteis **repitieron**			**Repita** Ud. **Repitan** Uds.
saber, *to know* sabiendo	**sé** sabes sabe sabemos sabéis saben	supe supiste supo supimos supisteis supieron		sabré sabrás sabrá sabremos sabréis sabrán	**Sepa** Ud. **Sepan** Uds.
salir, *to leave, go out* saliendo	**salgo** sales sale salimos salís salen			saldré saldrás saldrá saldremos saldréis saldrán	**Salga** Ud. **Salgan** Uds.
sentir, *to be sorry* **sintiendo**	**siento** **sientes** **siente** sentimos sentís **sienten**	**sentí** **sentise** **sintió** sentimos sentisteis **sintieron**			**Sienta** Ud. **Sientan** Uds.
ser, *to be* **siendo**	**soy** eres es **somos** **sois** **son**	fui fuiste fue fuimos fuisteis fueron	era eras era éramos erais eran		**Sea** Ud. **Sean** Uds.
tener, *to have* teniendo	**tengo** **tienes** **tiene** tenemos tenéis **tienen**	tuve tuviste tuvo tuvimos tuvisteis tuvieron		tendré tendrás tendrá tendremos tendréis tendrán	**Tenga** Ud. **Tengan** Uds.

Infinitive Present Participle	Present	Preterit	Imperfect	Future	Command
traducir, *to translate* traduciendo	**traduzco** traduces traduce traducimos traducís traducen	**traduje** **tradujiste** **tradujo** **tradujimos** **tradujisteis** **tradujeron**			**Traduzca** Ud. **Traduzcan** Uds.
traer, *to bring* **trayendo**	**traigo** traes trae traemos traéis traen	**traje** **trajiste** **trajo** **trajimos** **trajisteis** **trajeron**			**Traiga** Ud. **Traigan** Uds.
venir, *to come* **viniendo**	**vengo** **vienes** **viene** venimos venís **vienen**	**vine** viniste vino vinimos vinisteis vinieron		vendré vendrás vendrá vendremos vendréis vendrán	**Venga** Ud. **Vengan** Uds.
ver, *to see* **viendo**	**veo** ves ve vemos veis ven		veía veías veía veíamos veíais veían		**Vea** Ud. **Vean** Uds.
volver, *to return* volviendo	**vuelvo** **vuelves** **vuelve** volvemos volvéis **vuelven**				**Vuelva** Ud. **Vuelvan** Uds.

 ## Other Verbs With Irregular Forms

Each verb in the following list is similar to the verb in parentheses, which is included in the Verb Chart. For example, to conjugate *pedir* in any tense, refer to the forms of *repetir* that are displayed in the Chart. If the form desired is the present participle of *pedir*, note that the stem vowel of *repetir* changes to *i* in that form: repitiendo. Hence, the corresponding form is pidiendo.

acostarse (recordar)
almorzar (recordar)
   command: almuerce, almuercen
cerrar (pensar)
comenzar (pensar)
   command: comience, comiencen
conducir (traducir)
contar (recordar)
costar (recordar)
   (3rd-person forms only)

creer (leer)
despertarse (pensar)
devolver (volver)
divertirse (sentir)
empezar (pensar)
   command: empiece, empiecen
encontrar (recordar)
morir (dormir)

mostrar (recordar)
pedir (repetir)
perder (entender)
preferir (sentir)
sentarse (pensar)
sentirse (sentir)
servir (repetir)
vestirse (repetir)

The Present Progressive Tense

The present progressive tense = the present tense of *estar* + a present participle: (*yo*) *estoy hablando*, I am speaking. (For the forms of the present participle and the conjugation of *estar* in the present tense, see the Verb Chart.)

English-Spanish Vocabulary

Note: Verbs marked with an asterisk (*) have irregular forms. Consult the Verb Chart. Stem-changing verbs are indicated by the letters in parentheses, e.g., **dormir(ue).**

a, an, un, una
able: to be able, poder*
after, después (de)
afternoon, la tarde; **in the afternoon,** por la tarde; (*with clock time*) de la tarde
Albert, Alberto
all, todo, -a, todos, -as
all right, está bien
aloud, en voz alta
A.M., de la mañana
answer, la respuesta; contestar, responder
apple, la manzana
April, abril
architect, el arquitecto
arm, el brazo
armchair, el sillón
arrive, llegar
as, tan, como
ask, preguntar; **to ask for** (= *to request*), pedir*
at, a, en
attend, asistir a
August, agosto
aunt, la tía

back: in back of, detrás de
bad, malo, -a (mal)
bakery, la panadería
banana, la banana, el plátano
be, estar,* ser*; **to be cold (warm):** (*things*) estar frío, -a (caliente); (*persons*) tener frío (calor); (*weather*) hacer frío (calor)
bed, la cama
bedroom, el dormitorio
beer, la cerveza
before, antes (de)
begin, empezar (ie), comenzar (ie)
behind (= *in back of*), detrás de
believe, creer*
best: the best, el (la) mejor, los (las) mejores
better, mejor
black, negro, -a
blue, azul
board (= **chalkboard**), la pizarra
book, el libro
boy, el muchacho, el chico
bread, el pan
breakfast, el desayuno
bring, traer*

brother, el hermano
building, el edificio
bus, el autobús, (*in Cuba & Puerto Rico*) la guagua, (*in Mexico*) el camión
buy, comprar

calculator, la calculadora
can (= be able), poder*
candy, los dulces; (*piece of*) el dulce
car, el coche, el carro
chair, la silla
cherry, la cereza
chest (of drawers), la cómoda
church, la iglesia; **to go to church,** ir a la iglesia
city, la ciudad
class, la clase; **classroom,** la sala de clase
close, cerrar (ie)
clothes, clothing, la ropa
coat, el abrigo
cold, frío, -a; (*noun*) el frío; **to be cold,** (*persons*) tener frío, (*weather*) hacer frío, (*things*) estar frío, -a; **I am (very) cold,** tengo (mucho) frío; **it is (very) cold (weather),** hace (mucho) frío; **the soup is (very) cold,** la sopa está (muy) fría
color, el color; **what color is the house?** ¿de qué color es la casa?
comb: to comb one's hair, peinarse
come, venir*
compact disk, el disco compacto
computer, la computadora (el ordenador in Spain)
cool: it is cool (weather), hace fresco
cost, costar (ue)
cotton, el algodón
country, (*nation*) el país; (*opposite of city*) el campo
cover, cubrir
cup, la taza

dance, bailar
daughter, la hija
day, el día
December, diciembre
describe, describir
desk, la mesa, el escritorio
dessert, el postre

difficult, difícil
dining room, el comedor
dish, el plato
divide, dividir
do, hacer*
dress: to get dressed, vestirse (i)
drink, la bebida, beber
drive, conducir*
drugstore, la farmacia

ear, (*inner*) el oído, (*outer*) la oreja
early, temprano
eat, comer
egg, el huevo
eight, ocho
eighteen, dieciocho (diez y ocho)
eight hundred, ochocientos, -as
eighty, ochenta
eleven, once
English, inglés, inglesa; (*language*) el inglés
enough, bastante
evening, la noche; **in the evening,** por la noche, (*with clock time*) de la noche; **at nine o'clock in the evening,** a las nueve de la noche; **good evening,** buenas noches
every, cada, todos los, todas las
everybody, everyone, todo el mundo
example, el ejemplo; **for example,** por ejemplo
exercise, el ejercicio
eye, el ojo

fall, caer (se);* (*autumn*) el otoño
family, la familia
far (from), lejos (de)
father, el padre
favorite, favorito, -a
February, febrero
feel, sentir(se) (ie)
few, pocos, -as
fifteen, quince
fifty, cincuenta
finger, el dedo
finish, terminar
first, primero, -a (primer)
five, cinco
five hundred, quinientos, -as
flower, la flor
food, el alimento, la comida
foot, el pie
for, para, por

fork, el tenedor
forty, cuarenta
four, cuatro
four hundred, cuatrocientos, -as
fourteen, catorce
France, Francia
French, francés, francesa; (*language*) el francés
Friday, el viernes
friend, amigo, -a
from, de

game, el juego; (= *match*) el partido; **a game of tennis,** un partido de tenis
garden, el jardín
gentleman, el caballero, el señor
get up, levantarse
gift, el regalo
girl, la muchacha, la chica
give, dar*
glass, el vaso; **a glass of water,** un vaso de agua; **wineglass,** la copa
go, ir;* **to go away,** irse
good, bueno, -a (buen)
government, el gobierno
grandfather, el abuelo
grandmother, la abuela
great, gran, grandes; **a great man,** un gran hombre; **the great city,** la gran ciudad (*pl*, las grandes ciudades)
green, verde
greet, saludar
group, el grupo

half past, y media; **at half past ten,** a las diez y media
hand, la mano
happy: to be happy, estar contento, -a, ser feliz (*pl*, felices)
hat, el sombrero
have, tener;* **to have a good time,** divertirse (ie), pasar un buen rato; **to have to (= must),** tener que + *inf*; **I have to study,** tengo que estudiar
he, él
head, la cabeza
hear, oír*
help, ayudar
Henry, Enrique
her, la, (*after a prep.*) ella; (= *to her*) le; **I see her,** la veo; **I give her the book,** le doy el libro; **for her,** para ella; (*possessive*) su, sus
here, aquí
him, lo, le, (*after a prep.*) él; (= *to him*) le; **I see him,** lo (le) veo; **I give him the book,** le doy el libro; **for him,** para él
his, su, sus

home: at home, en casa; **to go (to return) home,** ir (regresar) a casa; **to leave home,** salir de casa
homework, (= *a single assignment*) la tarea; (= *two or more assignments*) las tareas
hot = "*very warm*" (*see* **warm**)
hour, la hora
house, la casa
how? ¿cómo?
hundred, cien, ciento
hungry: to be (very) hungry, tener (mucha) hambre

I, yo
idiom, el modismo
immediately, en seguida
in, en
intelligent, inteligente
intend, pensar (ie) + *inf*
interesting, interesante
it, (*as object*) lo, la; *as subject pronoun, not expressed:* **it is a good day,** es un buen día

jacket, la chaqueta
January, enero
July, julio
June, junio

key, la llave
knife, el cuchillo
know, (*facts*) saber*: (*persons and places*) conocer*

language, la lengua
large, grande
last, último, -a; **last week,** la semana pasada; **last night,** anoche
late, tarde
later, más tarde; **see you later,** hasta luego
lazy, perezoso, -a
learn, aprender
leave, salir* (de), partir, irse*
lesson, la lección (*pl*, lecciones); **the English lesson,** la lección de inglés
letter, la carta
lettuce, la lechuga
light, la luz (*pl*, luces)
like (be pleasing), gustar; **I like,** me gusta(n)
likeable, simpático, -a
live, vivir
living room, la sala
long, largo, -a; (*time*) **how long?** ¿cuánto tiempo?
look (at), mirar
lose, perder (ie)
lot: a lot (of), mucho, -a
loudly, en voz alta

lunch, el almuerzo; **to eat (have) lunch,** almorzar (ue), tomar el almuerzo

magazine, la revista
make, hacer*
map, el mapa
March, marzo
market, el mercado
Mary, María
May, mayo
me, me; **to me,** me; (*after prep.*) mí; **for me,** para mí; **with me,** conmigo
meat, la carne
mention: don't mention it, de nada, no hay de qué
menu, el menú
midnight, (la) medianoche
milk, la leche
mirror, el espejo
Monday, el lunes
money, el dinero
month, el mes
more, más
morning, la mañana; **in the morning,** por la mañana; (*with clock time*) de la mañana; **at ten o'clock in the morning,** a las diez de la mañana; **good morning,** buenos días
most, más
mother, la madre
mouth, la boca
movie, la película
movies: to go to the movies, ir al cine
museum, el museo
music, la música
must, deber + *inf*, tener que + *inf*; **I must study,** debo (tengo que) estudiar; **one must,** hay que + *inf*; **one must work,** hay que trabajar
my, mi, mis

name, el nombre; **to be named,** llamarse; **what is your name?** ¿cómo se llama Ud.? **my name is Peter,** me llamo Pedro
narrow, estrecho, -a
near, cerca (de)
necessary, necesario, -a
need, necesitar
neighbor, vecino, -a
new, nuevo, -a
news, las noticias; (*news item or piece of news*) la noticia
newspaper, el periódico
nice (= likeable), simpático, -a
night, la noche; **at night,** por la noche; **last night,** anoche; **tonight,** esta noche

nine, nueve
nine hundred, novecientos, -as
nineteen, diecinueve (diez y nueve)
ninety, noventa
no, no, ninguno, -a (ningún); **I have no money,** no tengo ningún dinero
noise, el ruido
noon, (el) mediodía; **at noon,** a mediodía
nose, la nariz
notebook, el cuaderno
novel, la novela
November, noviembre
now, ahora
nylon, el nilón

o'clock: at nine o'clock, a las nueve; **it is one o'clock,** es la una
October, octubre
often, a menudo, muchas veces
old, viejo, -a; (= *ancient*) antiguo, -a; **he is 14 years old,** tiene 14 años; **the oldest,** el (la) mayor, los (las) mayores
on, en; **on Tuesday,** el martes; **on Wednesdays,** los miércoles; **on December 7,** el 7 de diciembre
once, una vez; **at once,** en seguida
one, uno, un, una
open, abrir
orange, la naranja
order: in order to, para + *inf*
our, nuestro, -a

package, el paquete
pants, los pantalones
parents, los padres
party, la fiesta
pay, pagar; **to pay attention,** prestar atención
pear, la pera
pen, la pluma; **ball point pen,** el bolígrafo
pencil, el lápiz (*pl*, lápices)
pepper, la pimienta
Philip, Felipe
picture, el cuadro
pie, el pastel
platform (*of a train station*), el andén
play, (*theater*) la pieza, la comedia; jugar (ue)
pleasant, agradable, simpático, -a
please, *command* + por favor, haga Ud. el favor de + *inf;* **please read,** lea Ud., por favor; haga Ud. el favor de leer
P.M., de la tarde, de la noche; **at 3 P.M.,** a las tres de la tarde; **it is 10 P.M.,** son las diez de la noche

popular, popular
potato, (*Spain*) la patata, (*Spanish America*) la papa
prefer, preferir (ie)
pretty, bonito, -a
price, el precio
printer, la impresora
program, el programa
put, poner;* **to put on** (*the radio, etc.*), poner; (*clothes*) ponerse

quarter, el cuarto; **at a quarter to seven,** a las siete menos cuarto; **it is a quarter after five,** son las cinco y cuarto
question, la pregunta; **to ask a question,** hacer una pregunta

rain, la lluvia; llover (ue)
raincoat, el impermeable
Raymond, Ramón
read, leer*
receive, recibir
record (*phonograph*), el disco
red, rojo, -a
regret, sentir (ie)
remember, recordar (ue)
repeat, repetir (i)
restaurant, el restaurante
return (go back), volver (ue), regresar
rich, rico, -a
right: to be right, tener razón
room, el cuarto
rug, la alfombra
ruler (*straightedge*), la regla

salad, la ensalada
salt, la sal
Saturday, el sábado
say, decir*
school, la escuela; **to school,** a la escuela; **in (at) school,** en la escuela
see, ver*
sell, vender
send, mandar, enviar (yo envío)
sentence, la frase, la oración
September, septiembre
serve, servir (i)
seven, siete
seven hundred, setecientos, -as
seventeen, diecisiete (diez y siete)
seventy, setenta
sharp: at nine o'clock sharp, a las nueve en punto
shirt, la camisa
shoe, el zapato
short, (*opposite of "tall"*) bajo, -a; (*opposite of "long"*) corto, -a
show, mostrar (ue)
sick, enfermo, -a

sing, cantar
sit down, sentarse (ie)
sitting, sentado, -a
six, seis
six hundred, seiscientos, -as
sixteen, dieciséis (diez y seis)
sixty, sesenta
sleep, dormir (ue)
sleepy: to be (very) sleepy, tener (mucho) sueño
slow(ly), despacio
small, pequeño, -a
snow, la nieve; nevar (ie)
soap, el jabón
some, alguno, -a (algún); (= *a few*) unos, -as, algunos, -as
sometimes, algunas veces
son, el hijo
sorry: to be sorry, sentir (ie)
Spain, España
Spanish, español, -la; (*language*) el español
speak, hablar
spoon, (*teaspoon*) la cucharita; (*tablespoon*) la cuchara
spring(time), la primavera
stairs, la escalera
standing, de pie; **they are standing,** están de pie
stay, quedarse
store, la tienda
story, el cuento
street, la calle
study, estudiar
stupid, estúpido, -a
sugar, el azúcar
summer, el verano
sun, el sol
sunny: it is sunny, hace sol
Sunday, el domingo
swim, nadar

table, la mesa
take, tomar; **to take off** (*a garment*), quitarse; **he takes off his coat,** se quita el abrigo
tall, alto, -a
tape, la cinta; **tape recorder,** la grabadora
teach, enseñar
teacher, el profesor, la profesora; **Spanish teacher** (= *teacher of Spanish*), profesor(-ra) de español
television, la televisión; **television set,** el televisor
tell, decir*
ten, diez
than, que
thank, dar las gracias
that, ese, esa; (*at a distance*) aquel, aquella
the, el, la, los, las

theater, el teatro

their, su, sus

them, los, las; (= *to them*) les; (*after a prep.*) ellos, -as; **I see them,** los veo, las veo; **I give them the book,** les doy el libro; **for them,** para ellos(-as)

there, allí

these, estos, estas

they, ellos, ellas

third, tercero, -a (tercer)

thirsty: to be (very) thirsty, tener (mucha) sed

thirteen, trece

thirty, treinta

this, este, esta

those, esos, esas; (*at a distance*) aquellos, aquellas

thousand, mil

three, tres

three hundred, trescientos, -as

Thursday, el jueves

ticket, el billete

time, el tiempo, la hora, la vez; **on time,** a tiempo; **a long time,** mucho tiempo; **what time is it?** ¿qué hora es? **three times,** tres veces

to, a; (= *in order to*) para + *inf*

today, hoy

tomato, el tomate

tomorrow, mañana

tonight, esta noche

train, el tren

translate, traducir*

travel, viajar

tree, el árbol

trip, el viaje; **to take a trip,** hacer un viaje

truth, la verdad

Tuesday, el martes

twelve, doce

twenty, veinte

twice, dos veces

two, dos

two hundred, doscientos, -as

umbrella, el paraguas (*pl,* los paraguas)

under, debajo de

understand, comprender, entender (ie)

university, la universidad

until, hasta

us, nos; **to us,** nos; (*after prep.*) nosotros, -as

use, usar

vegetables, las verduras

verb, el verbo

very, muy; (*in idioms with* tener *and* hacer) mucho, -a

video, el video (vídeo)

visit, visitar

wait (for), esperar

waiter, el camarero, el mozo

wake up, despertar(se) (ie)

walk, andar,* ir* a pie

wall, la pared

wallet, la cartera

want, querer,* desear

warm: to be warm, (*weather*) hacer calor, (*persons*) tener calor, (*things*) estar caliente; **it is very warm today,** hoy hace mucho calor; **I am very warm,** tengo mucho calor; **the soup is very warm,** la sopa está muy caliente

wash: to wash oneself, "get washed," lavarse

watch, (= *wristwatch*) el reloj; **to watch a film (baseball game, etc.),** ver una película (un partido de béisbol, etc.)

water, el agua, *f*

we, nosotros, -as

weather, el tiempo; **how is the weather?** ¿qué tiempo hace?; **the weather is good (bad),** hace buen (mal) tiempo

Wednesday, el miércoles

week, la semana

welcome: you're welcome, de nada, no hay de qué

well, bien

what? ¿qué?

when? ¿cuándo?

where? ¿dónde?

white, blanco, -a

who? ¿quién, -es?

whom? ¿a quién, -es?

window, la ventana

windy: it is windy, hace viento

winter, el invierno

with, con

without, sin

woman, la mujer

wool, la lana

word, la palabra

work, trabajar

write, escribir

wrong: to be wrong, no tener razón

year, el año

yesterday, ayer

you, usted (Ud.), ustedes (Uds.), tú, vosotros, -as; (*direct object*) te, lo (le), la, los, las, os; (*indirect object*) te, le, les, os; (*after a prep.*) Ud., Uds., ti, vosotros, -as; **with you** (*fam.*) contigo

young, joven (*pl,* jóvenes); **younger,** menor; **the youngest,** el (la) menor, los (las) menores

your, su, sus, tu, tus, vuestro, -a, vuestros, -as

Spanish-English Vocabulary

Note: Verbs marked with an asterisk (*) have irregular forms. Consult the Verb Chart. Stem-changing verbs are indicated by the letters in parentheses, e.g., **dormir(ue)**.

a, to, at
abierto, -a, open
abogado, *m,* lawyer
abrigo, *m,* coat
abril, April
abrir, to open
abuelo, *m,* grandfather; **abuela,** *f,* grandmother; **abuelos,** *m pl,* grandparents
acerca de, about, concerning
acompañar, to accompany
acostarse (ue), to go to bed, to lie down
activo, -a, active
acueducto, *m,* aqueduct
además (de), besides
adiós, good-bye
¿adónde? (to) where?
agosto, August
agradable, pleasant
agua (el), *f,* water
ahora, now
aire, *m,* air; **al aire libre,** outdoors, in the open air
al, to the, at the; **al** + *inf,* on (upon) . . . -ing: **al entrar,** on entering
Alberto, Albert
alcalde, *m,* mayor
alegre, happy
alemán, alemana, German
alfombra, *f,* rug, carpet
algo, something
algodón, *m,* cotton
alguien, someone, somebody
alguno, -a (algún), some
alimento, *m,* food
almorzar (ue), to eat lunch
almuerzo, *m,* lunch
alto, a, high, tall; **en voz alta,** aloud
alumno, -a, pupil, student
allá, allí, there
amable, kind, nice
amarillo, -a, yellow
americano, -a, American
amigo, -a, friend
Ana, Anna, Ann
ancho, -a, wide
***andar,** to walk, to go, to travel
Andes, *m pl,* Andes Mountains
aniversario, *m,* anniversary
anoche, last night
antiguo, -a, old, ancient
Antonio, Anthony
anuncio, *m,* announcement, advertisement

añadir, to add
año, *m,* year; **el Día de Año Nuevo,** New Year's Day
apariencia, *f,* appearance
apartamento, *m,* apartment
apellido, *m,* family name
aplicado, -a, studious
aprender, to learn
aquel, aquella, that (over there); **aquellos, as,** those (over there)
aquí, here
árbol, *m,* tree
arena, *f,* sand
armario, *m,* closet
arquitecto, *m,* architect
arquitectura, *f,* architecture
arte, *m,* art
artículo, *m,* article
ascensor, *m,* elevator
así, so, thus
asiento, *m,* seat
asignatura, *f,* (school) subject
asistir a, to attend
atención, *f,* attention
atento, -a, attentive
atracción, *f,* attraction; **parque de atracciones,** amusement park
aunque, although
ausente, absent
autobús, *m,* bus
automóvil, *m,* automobile
avenida, *f,* avenue
aviador, *m,* aviator
ayer, yesterday
ayudar, to help
azúcar, *m,* sugar
azul, blue

bachillerato, *m,* degree received upon graduation from a secondary school
bailar, to dance
baile, *m,* dance
bajar, to get off *or* out of (a vehicle)
bajo, -a, low, short
banco, *m,* bank
bandera, *f,* flag
bañar(se), to bathe (oneself), to go swimming
barato, -a, cheap
barrio, *m,* neighborhood
básquetbol, *m,* basketball
beber, to drink
bebida, *f,* drink
béisbol, *m,* baseball

bello, -a, beautiful, handsome
besar, to kiss
beso, *m,* kiss
biblioteca, *f,* library
bicicleta, *f,* bicycle
bien, well
blanco, -a, white
blusa, *f,* blouse
boca, *f,* mouth
bodega, *f,* grocery store (*Spanish America*)
bolígrafo, *m,* ballpoint pen
bolsillo, *m,* pocket
bondad, *f,* kindness
bonito, -a, , pretty
borrador, *m,* eraser
brazo, *m,* arm
brillar, to shine
bueno, -a (buen), good
buscar, to look for

caballero, *m,* gentleman
caballo, *m,* horse; **a caballo,** on horseback
cabeza, *f,* head
cada, each, every
***caer(se),** to fall (down)
café, *m,* coffee; café
calcetín, *m,* sock
caliente, warm, hot
calle, *f,* street
calor, *m,* heat; **hace calor,** it is warm; **tener calor,** to be (= *to feel*) warm
cama, *f,* bed
camarero, *m,* waiter
caminar, to walk
camión, *m,* truck; bus (*in Mexico*)
camisa, shirt
campesino, *m,* farmer
campo, *m,* country, field
canción, *f,* song
cansado, -a, tired
cantar, to sing
cara, *f,* face
Caribe, *m,* Caribbean Sea
Carlos, Charles
Carlota, Charlotte
carnaval, *m,* carnival
carne, *f,* meat
carnicero, *m,* butcher
carta, *f,* letter
cartera, *f,* wallet
casa, *f,* house; **en casa,** at home; **a casa,** home (*with verb of motion*)

casarse, to get married
casi, almost, nearly
casino, *m*, clubhouse
castaño, -a, brown (chestnut)
catedral, *f*, cathedral
catorce, fourteen
celebrar, to celebrate
cena, *f*, supper
cenar, to have supper
centavo, *m*, cent
centro, *m*, center; downtown; **en el centro,** downtown; **ir al centro,** to go downtown
Centroamérica, Central America
cepillar(se), to brush (oneself)
cerca (de), near
cereza, *f*, cherry
cero, zero
cerrado, -a, closed, shut
cerrar (ie), to close
cerveza, *f*, beer
chaqueta, *f*, jacket
charlar, to chat
cheque, *m*, check
chica, *f*, child, girl
chicano, -a, Mexican-American
chico, *m*, child, boy
chocolate, *m*, chocolate (flavor or drink); hot chocolate
cielo, *m*, sky
cien, ciento, one hundred
cierto, -a, certain
cigarrillo, *m*, cigarette
cinco, five
cincuenta, fifty
cine, *m*, movies, moviehouse
cinta, *f*, tape
circular, to circulate, to move
ciudad, *f*, city
civilización, *f*, civilization
clase, *f*, class; kind *or* type
clásico, -a, classical
clavel, *m*, carnation
coche, *m*, car, automobile
cocina, *f*, kitchen
cocinero, -a, cook
colección, *f*, collection
colombiano, -a, Colombian
colonia, *f*, colony
comedor, *m*, dining room
comenzar (ie), to begin
comer, to eat
comerciante, *m*, merchant
comida, *f*, food; meal; dinner (*midday meal in some countries*)
comienzo: al comienzo, at the beginning
como, as, like; ¿cómo? how?
cómodo, -a, comfortable
compañero, -a, companion, friend
comprar, to buy
comprender, to understand
computadora, *f*, computer
común, common

con, with
concierto, *m*, concert
*conducir, to drive; to lead
confianza, *f*, confidence
*conocer, to know, to be acquainted with (*persons or places*)
conquistador, *m*, conqueror
consistir en, to consist of
construido, -a, constructed, built
consultar, to consult
contacto, *m*, contact
contar (ue), to count; to tell
contener (*conj. like* tener), to contain
contento, -a, happy
contestar, to answer
conversación, *f*, conversation
corbata, *f*, tie
correctamente, correctly
correcto, -a, correct
corregir (yo corrijo), to correct
correr, to run
corresponder, to correspond
cortar, to cut
cortina, *f*, curtain
corto, -a, short
cosa, *f*, thing
costar (ue), to cost
costumbre, *f*, custom
*creer, to believe
Cristo, Christ
Cristóbal Colón, Christopher Columbus
cruzar, to cross
cuaderno, *m*, notebook
cuadro, *m*, picture
¿cuál(-es)? which? what?
cuando, when; ¿cuándo? when?
¿cuánto(-a)? how much? ¿cuántos(-as)? how many?
cuarenta, forty
cuarto, *m*, room; quarter; **cuarto de baño,** bathroom; **es la una y cuarto,** it's a quarter after one
cuatro, four
cuatrocientos, -as, four hundred
cubano, -a, Cuban
cubrir, to cover
cuchara, *f*, tablespoon
cucharita, *f*, teaspoon
cuchillo, *m*, knife
cuello, *m*, neck
cuenta, *f*, bill, check
cuento, *m*, story
cuerpo, *m*, body
cuidado, *m*, care; **con cuidado,** carefully
cultivar, to cultivate, to grow
cumpleaños, *m*, birthday
curandero, -a, folk healer (*person who treats illnesses with herbs and special foods*)
curar, to cure

*dar, to give; **dar un paseo,** to take a walk (ride)
de, of, from, in
debajo (de), under, underneath
deber (+ *inf*), to have to, must
decidir, to decide
*decir, to say, to tell
dedo, *m*, finger
del, of the, from the
delante (de), in front (of)
delgado, -a, thin
delicioso, -a, delicious
demasiado, -a, too much; **demasiados, -as,** too many
deporte, *m*, sport
derivar, to derive
desayuno, *m*, breakfast
descansar, to rest
descendencia, *f*, descent
describir, to describe
descripción, *f*, description
descubrir, to discover
desear, to want, to wish
despacio, slowly
despertarse (ie), to wake up
después (de), after
destruir, to destroy
detrás (de), behind, in back (of)
día, *m*, day; **todos los días,** every day; **al día,** a day, per day
diario, *m*, diary; **diario, -a,** daily
diccionario, *m*, dictionary
diciembre, December
dictado, *m*, dictation
diente, *m*, tooth
diez, ten
diferente, different
difícil, difficult, hard
dinero, *m*, money
dirección, *f*, address
director, *m*, (school) principal
disco, *m*, record
discurso, *m*, speech
distancia, *f*, distance
diversión, *f*, pastime, hobby
divertirse (ie), to enjoy oneself, to have a good time
dividir, to divide
doce, twelve
docena, *f*, dozen
dólar, *m*, dollar
domingo, *m*, Sunday
donde, where; ¿dónde? where? ¿a dónde? (to) where?
dormir (ue), to sleep
dormitorio, *m*, bedroom
dos, two
doscientos, -as, two hundred
dulce, *m*, piece of candy; *pl*, candy
durante, during

e, and (*before words beginning with* i- *or* hi-)

ecuador, *m*, equator; **el Ecuador,** Ecuador
edificio, *m*, building
ejemplo, *m*, example; **por ejemplo,** for example
ejercicio, *m*, exercise
él, he
eléctrico, -a, electric
Elena, Ellen, Helen, Elaine
ella, she; **ellas,** they (*f*)
ellos, they (*m*)
embargo: sin embargo, however, nevertheless
empezar (ie), to begin
empleo, *m*, job
en, in, on
encender (ie), to light, to turn on
encima (de), above, on top (of)
encontrar (ue), to find; to meet
enero, January
enfermedad, *f*, sickness, illness
enfermo, -a, sick, ill
Enrique, Henry
ensalada, *f*, salad
enseñar, to teach
entender (ie), to understand
entonces, then
entrada, *f*, entrance; ticket of admission
cntrar (cn), to enter, to go into
entre, between, among
equipo, *m*, team
escalera, *f*, staircase, stairs
escribir, to write
escritorio, *m*, desk
escuchar, to listen (to)
escuela, *f*, school
ese, -a, that; **esos, -as,** those
eso, that; **por eso,** therefore
espacio, *m*, space
España, *f*, Spain
español, -la, Spanish; **el español,** Spanish (language)
especial, special
especialmente, especially
esperar, to wait (for); to hope, to expect
esposa, *f*, wife
esposo, *m*, husband
esquina, *f*, street corner
estación, *f*, season; station
estado, *m*, state
Estados Unidos, *m pl*, United States
*estar, to be
estatua, *f*, statue
este, -a, this; **estos, -as,** these
Esteban, Stephen
estrecho, -a, narrow
estrella, *f*, star
estudiante, *m & f*, student
estudiar, to study
estúpido, -a, stupid
Eugenio, Eugene

Europa, *f*, Europe
examen, *m* (*pl*, **exámenes**), examination
excelente, excellent
exclamar, to exclaim
explicar, to explain
exportar, to export

fácil, easy
falda, *f*, skirt
falso, -a, false
falta, *f*, mistake, error
familia, *f*, family
famoso, -a, famous
farmacéutico, *m*, pharmacist, druggist
farmacia, *f*, pharmacy, drugstore
favor, *m*, favor; **haga Ud. el favor de** + *inf*, please; **por favor,** please
favorito, -a, favorite
febrero, February
fecha, *f*, date
Federico, Frederick
Felipe, Philip
feliz (*pl*, **felices**), happy
feo, -a, ugly
Fernando, Ferdinand
fértil, fertile
ficsta, *f*, party; holiday
fin: por fin, finally
finalmente, finally
físico, -a, physical
flor, *f*, flower
francés, francesa, French
Francia, *f*, France
Francisca, Frances
Francisco, Frank
frase, *f*, phrase, sentence
frecuencia: con frecuencia, frequently
fresco, -a, cool; **hace fresco,** it is cool
frío, -a, cold; **hace frío,** it is cold; **tener frío,** to be (= *to feel*) cold
frito, -a, fried
frontera, *f*, border
fruta, *f*, fruit
fuerte, strong
fui (**fuiste,** etc.), *forms of preterite of* **ser** *and* **ir**
funcionar, to function, to "work"; **el radio no funciona,** the radio doesn't work
fundar, to found, to establish
fútbol, *m*, soccer

ganar, to win; to earn
garaje, *m*, garage
gastar, to spend (money)
gato, -a, cat
gaucho, *m*, Argentine cowboy
generalmente, generally
gente, *f*, people

geografía, *f*, geography
Gerardo, Gerald
Gilberto, Gilbert
gimnasio, *m*, gymnasium
gobernador, *m*, governor
gobierno, *m*, government
gordo, -a, fat
gorra, *f*, cap
grabadora, *f*, tape recorder
gracias, thanks, thank you; **muchas gracias,** thanks very much
graduarse, to be graduated
gramática, *f*, grammar
gran, great
grande, large, big
gripe, *f*, grippe, flu
gris, grey
gritar, to shout
grupo, *m*, group
guagua, *f*, bus (*in Cuba and Puerto Rico*)
guante, *m*, glove
guapo, -a, handsome, good-looking
guardar, to keep
guitarra, *f*, guitar
gustar, to please; **me gusta(n),** I like
gusto, *m*, pleasure; **con mucho gusto,** gladly

habitación, *f*, room
habitante, *m*, inhabitant
habla (el), *f*, speech; **de habla española,** Spanish-speaking
hablar, to speak, to talk
*hacer, to do, to make; **hacer un viaje,** to take a trip; **hace un año,** a year ago
hacia, towards
hambre (el), *f*, hunger; **tener (mucha) hambre,** to be (very) hungry
hasta, until, up to
hay, there is, there are; **¿hay?** is there, are there? **no hay de qué,** you're welcome
helado, *m*, ice cream
hermano, *m*, brother; **hermana,** *f*, sister
hermoso, -a, beautiful, handsome
héroe, *m*, hero
hierba, *f*, herb; grass
hijo, *m*, son; **hija,** *f*, daughter; *m pl*, children (= *offspring*)
hispano, -a, Hispanic (*see page 1*); a person whose native language is Spanish
hispanoamericano, -a, Spanish American
historia, *f*, story, history
hola, hello
hombre, *m*, man
hombro, *m*, shoulder

hora, *f,* hour, time; **¿a qué hora?** at what time?
hoy, today; **hoy día,** nowadays
huevo, *m,* egg

iglesia, *f,* church
importante, important
imposible, impossible
impresora, *f,* printer
improvisar, to improvise
inca, *m & f,* Inca
incendio, *m,* fire
independencia, *f,* independence
indio, -a, Indian
influencia, *f,* influence
información, *f,* information
inglés, inglesa, English; **el inglés,** English (language)
inmediatamente, immediately, at once
inteligente, intelligent
interés, *m,* interest
interesado, -a, interested
interesante, interesting
invención, *f,* invention
invierno, *m,* winter
invitar, to invite
*ir, to go; **ir a** + *inf,* to be going to: **voy a leer,** I'm going to read; **irse,** to go away, to leave
isla, *f,* island
italiano, -a, Italian
izquierdo, -a, left

jardín, *m,* garden
jirafa, *f,* giraffe
Jorge, George
José, Joseph
joven (*pl,* **jóvenes**), young
Juan, John; **Juanito,** Johnny
Juana, Joan, Jane, Jeanne
jueves, *m,* Thursday
jugador, *m,* player
jugar (ue), to play; **jugar al tenis (a las damas** etc.), to play tennis (checkers, etc.)
jugo, *m,* juice
juguete, *m,* toy
julio, July; **Julio,** Julius
junio, June
juntos, -as, together

kilómetro, kilometer (*about 5/8 of a mile*)

la, the, it, her, you
labio, *m,* lip
lado, *m,* side; **al lado de,** next to
lámpara, *f,* lamp
lana, *f,* wool
lápiz, *m* (*pl,* **lápices**), pencil
largo, -a, long
las, the, them, you
lavar(se), to wash (oneself)

le, him, to him, to her, to it, to you
lección, *f* (*pl,* **lecciones**), lesson
lectura, *f,* reading
leche, *f,* milk
lechuga, *f,* lettuce
*leer, to read
legendario, -a, legendary
lejos (de), far (from)
lengua, *f,* language, tongue
les, to them, to you
levantarse, to get up, to rise
librería, *f,* bookstore
libro, *m,* book
ligero, -a, light (*in weight*)
limón, *m,* lemon
limpiar, to clean
limpio, -a, clean
lindo, -a, pretty
lista, *f,* list
llamado, -a, called, named
llamar, to call; **llamarse,** to be called, to be named
llave, *f,* key
llegar, to arrive
llevar, to wear; to carry; to take
llover (ue), to rain
lo, it, him, you
los, the, them, you
luchar, to fight
luego, then; **hasta luego,** so long
lugar, *m,* place
Luis, Louis
luna, *f,* moon
luz, *f* (*pl,* **luces**), light

madre, *f,* mother
maestro, -a, teacher (*elementary school*)
magnífico, -a, magnificent
mal, badly
malo, -a (mal), bad
mamá, *f,* mother, mama
mandar, to send
mano, *f,* hand
mantequilla, *f,* butter
manzana, *f,* apple
mañana, tomorrow; *f,* morning; **por la mañana,** in the morning; **de la mañana,** in the morning, A.M.
mapa, *m,* map
Margarita, Margaret
María, Mary
Mariana, Marianne
martes, *m,* Tuesday
marzo, March
más, more, most
matar, to kill
matemáticas, *f pl,* mathematics
maya, Mayan
mayo, May
mayor, older, oldest
me, me, to me, myself
mecánico, *m,* mechanic, repairman

media, *f,* stocking
medianoche, *f,* midnight
medicina, *f,* medicine
médico, -a, *m & f,* doctor
medio, -a, half; **es la una y media,** it is 1:30
mediodía, *m,* noon
mejor, better, best
menor, younger, youngest
menos, less, fewer; except
mentira, *f,* lie
menú, *m,* menu
menudo: a menudo, often
mercado, *m,* market
mes, *m,* month
mesa, *f,* table, desk; **a la mesa,** at the table
metro, *m,* subway; meter
mexicano, -a, Mexican
México, *m,* Mexico
mi, mis, my
mí, me; **para mí,** for me; **sin mí,** without me; **conmigo,** with me
miembro, *m,* member
mil, one (a) thousand
milla, *f,* mile
millón, *m,* million
millonario, -a, millionaire
minifalda, *f,* miniskirt
minuto, *m,* minute
mirar, to look (at)
mismo, -a, same
moderno, -a, modern
momento, *m,* moment; **en este momento,** at this moment
montaña, *f,* mountain
monumento, *m,* monument
morir (ue), to die
mostrar (ue), to show
mozo, *m,* waiter
muchacho, *m,* boy; **muchacha,** *f,* girl; **muchachos,** *m pl,* boys and girls
mucho, *adv,* much, a great deal, a lot; **mucho, -a,** *adj,* much, a lot of; **muchos, -as,** many
mueble, *m,* piece of furniture; **muebles,** *m pl,* furniture
mujer, *f,* woman, wife
mundo, *m,* world; **todo el mundo,** everyone, everybody
museo, *m,* museum
música, *f,* music
músico, *m,* musician
muy, very

nacer (nazco), to be born
nación, *f,* nation, country
nada, nothing, anything; **de nada,** you're welcome
nadar, to swim
nadie, nobody, no one, anyone
naranja, *f,* orange
nariz, *f,* nose

Navidad, *f,* Christmas
necesario, -a, necessary
necesitar, to need
negro, -a, black
nevar (ie), to snow
ni . . . ni, neither . . . nor
nieto, -a, grandchild; *m,* grandson;
  f, granddaughter; **nietos,** *m pl,*
  grandchildren
nieve, *f,* snow
nilón, *m,* nylon
ninguno, -a (ningún), none, no,
  any
niño, -a, child; *m,* boy; *f,* girl;
  niños, *m pl,* children
no, no, not
noche, *f,* evening, night; **buenas**
  noches, good evening, good
  night; **esta noche,** tonight; **por la**
  noche, in the evening, at night;
  de la noche, in the evening, P.M.
nombre, *m,* name; **nombre y**
  apellidos, full name
norte, *m,* north
norteamericano, -a, American
  (*from the U.S.*)
nos, us, to us, ourselves
nosotros, -as, we; (*after a prep.*) us
nota, *f,* note; grade, mark (*in school*)
notar, to note, to notice
noticia, *f,* news item; **noticias,** *f pl,*
  news
novecientos, -as, nine hundred
novela, *f,* novel
noventa, ninety
noviembre, November
nuestro, -a, our
Nueva York, New York
nueve, nine
nuevo, -a, new
numeroso, -a, numerous, large
nunca, never, ever

obra, *f,* work
obtener (*conj. like* **tener**), to obtain,
  to get
ocasión, *f,* occasion
octubre, October
ocupar, to occupy
ochenta, eighty
ocho, eight
oficio, *m,* trade, profession
***ofrecer,** to offer
***oír,** to hear
ojo, *m,* eye
oler (huelo), to smell
once, eleven
oración, *f,* sentence
oreja, *f,* (outer) ear
origen, *m,* origin
orquesta, *f,* orchestra
os, you, to you, yourselves
otoño, *m,* fall, autumn
otra vez, again

otro, -a, other, another

Pablo, Paul
Paca, *nickname for* **Francisca** (*a*
  girl's name)
Paco, Frankie
padre, *m,* father; **padres,** *m pl,*
  parents
pagar, to pay
página, *f,* page
país, *m,* country, nation
pájaro, *m,* bird
palabra, *f,* word
pan, *m,* bread; **pan tostado,** toast
panadería, *f,* bakery
panecillo, *m,* roll
pantalones, *m pl,* pants
pañuelo, *m,* handkerchief
papa, *f,* potato (*in Spanish America*)
papá, *m,* father, papa, daddy
papel, *m,* paper
paquete, *m,* package
par, *m,* pair
para, for; in order to
pared, *f,* wall
pariente, *m & f,* relative
parque, *m,* park; **parque**
  zoológico, zoo
parte, *f,* part
particular, private
partido, *m,* game, match
partir, to leave, to depart
pasado, -a, past, last; **la semana**
  pasada, last week
pasar, to pass, to go; to spend
  (*time*); to happen
pasatiempo, *m,* pastime, hobby
pasear(se), to take a walk (ride)
paseo, *m,* walk, ride; **dar un**
  paseo, to take a walk (ride)
pastel, *m,* pie, pastry
patata, *f,* potato (*in Spain*)
patio, *m,* patio, courtyard
paz, *f,* peace
pecho, *m,* chest
pedir (i), to ask (for)
peinarse, to comb one's hair
película, *f,* film, movie
pelo, *m,* hair
pelota, *f,* ball
pensar (ie), to think; + *inf,* to
  intend to
peor, worse, worst
Pepe, Joe
pequeño, -a, little, small
pera, *f,* pear
perder (ie), to lose; to miss
perezoso, -a, lazy
perfectamente, perfectly
periódico, *m,* newspaper
período, *m,* period
permiso, *m,* permission; **permiso**
  de conducir, driver's license
pero, but

perro, *m,* dog
persona, *f,* person
Perú, *m,* Peru
pescado, *m,* fish (*ready to be cooked*
  and eaten)
pie, *m,* foot; **de pie,** standing; **a**
  pie, on foot; **ir a pie,** to go on
  foot, to walk
pierna, *f,* leg
pimienta, *f,* pepper
pintoresco, -a, picturesque
pintura, *f,* picture, painting
pirámide, *f,* pyramid
piso, *m,* floor, apartment
pizarra, *f,* chalkboard
planta, *f,* plant
plata, *f,* silver
plato, *f,* dish, plate
playa, *f,* beach
plaza, *f,* square (*of a city or town*)
pluma, *f,* pen
pobre, poor
poco, *adv,* little; **poco, -a,** *adj,* little
  (*in quantity*); **pocos, -as,** few
***poder,** to be able, can, could
policía, *f,* police; *m,* policeman
pollo, *m,* chicken
***poner,** to put; to turn on (*the radio,*
  TV, etc.); **poner la mesa,** to set
  the table; **ponerse,** to put on (*a*
  garment)
por, through, by, for, in; multiplied
  by ("times"); **por fin,** finally
¿por qué? why?
porque, because
portugués, portuguesa,
  Portuguese
postre, *m,* dessert
practica, *f,* practice
practicar, to practice
precio, *m,* price
preferir (ie), to prefer
pregunta, *f,* question; **hacer una**
  pregunta, to ask a question
preguntar, to ask
preparar, to prepare
presentar, to present; to introduce
  (*persons*)
presidente, *m,* president
prestar, to lend; **prestar atención,**
  to pay attention
primario, -a, primary; **escuela**
  primaria, elementary school
primavera, *f,* spring (time)
primero, -a (primer), first
primo, -a, cousin
principal, main, principal
producto, *m,* product
profesión, *f,* profession
profesor, -ra, teacher
programa, *m,* program
pronto, soon
próximo, -a, next; **el año**
  próximo, next year

pueblo, *m,* town
puente, *m,* bridge
puertorriqueño, -a, Puerto Rican
pues, well, then, well then
punto, *m,* point, period; **a las dos en punto,** at 2 o'clock sharp
pupitre, *m,* (pupil's) desk

que, who, which, that; than
¿qué? what?
quechua, *m,* Quechua (*the language of the Incas of Peru*)
quedarse, to stay, to remain
*****querer,** to want, to wish; **querer decir,** to mean: **¿Qué quiere decir la palabra?** What does the word mean?
queso, *m,* cheese
¿quién(-es)? who? **¿a quién(-es)?** (to) whom? **¿de quién(-es)?,** whose?
quince, fifteen
quinientos, -as, five hundred
quitarse, to remove, to take off (*clothes*)

Rafael, Ralph
Ramón, Raymond
rancho, *m,* ranch
rápidamente, rapidly, fast
Raquel, Rachel
raro, -a, rare
rato, *m,* while
raza, *f,* race (*biology*)
razón, *f,* reason; **tener razón,** to be right
recibir, to receive
recientemente, recently
recordar (ue), to remember
refresco, *m,* refreshment
regalo, *m,* gift, present
región, *f,* region
regla, *f,* rule; ruler (= *straight-edge*)
regresar, to return, to go (come) back
reloj, *m,* watch, clock
remedio, *m,* remedy
repetir (i), to repeat
república, *f,* republic; **la República Dominicana,** the Dominican Republic
resfriado, *m,* cold (*illness*)
residir, to live, to reside
respirar, to breathe
responder, to answer
respuesta, *f,* answer, response
restaurante, *m,* restaurant
revista, *f,* magazine
Ricardo, Richard
rico, -a, rich
rojo, -a, red
romano, -a, Roman
ropa, *f,* clothes, clothing
rosa, *f,* rose; **Rosa,** Rose

rubio, -a, blond
ruido, *m,* noise
ruina, *f,* ruin

sábado, *m,* Saturday
*****saber,** to know; + *inf,* to know how: **¿sabes conducir?** do you know how to drive?
sacar, to take out; **sacar las entradas,** to buy the (theater) tickets
sal, *f,* salt
sala, *f,* living room; **sala de clase,** classroom
*****salir (de),** to leave, to go out
saludar, to greet
Santiago, James, St. James
santo, *m,* saint
se, yourself, himself, herself, yourselves, themselves
sección, *f,* section
secretario, -a, secretary
secundario, -a, secondary
sed, *f,* thirst; **tener sed,** to be thirsty
sed.., *f,* silk
seguida: en seguida, at once, immediately
segundo, -a, second; *m,* second
seis, six
semana, *f,* week; **por semana,** a week; **una vez por semana,** once a week
semestre, *m,* (school) term, semester
sentado, -a, seated, sitting
sentarse (ie), to sit down
sentir (ie), to be sorry; **sentirse,** to feel (sick, etc.)
señor, *m,* sir, Mr., gentleman
señora, *f,* lady, madame, Mrs., wife
septiembre, September
*****ser,** to be
servilleta, *f,* napkin
servir (i), to serve
sesenta, sixty
setecientos, -as, seven hundred
setenta, seventy
si, if
sí, yes
siempre, always
siesta, *f,* siesta, mid-afternoon nap
siete, seven
siglo, *m,* century
significar, to mean
silencio, *m,* silence
silla, *f,* chair
sillón, *m,* armchair
símbolo, *m,* symbol
simpático, -a, nice, likeable
sin, without
sinagoga, *f,* synagogue
sistema, *m,* system
situado, -a, situated, located

sobre, on, on top of, over; about (= concerning)
sobrino, *m,* nephew; **sobrina,** *f,* niece
sofá, *m,* sofa, couch
sol, *m,* sun; **hace (hay) sol,** it is sunny; **al sol,** in the sun
solamente, only
soldado, *m,* soldier
solo, -a, alone
sólo, only
sombrero, *m,* hat
sonar (ue), to ring
sopa, *f,* soup
sótano, *m,* basement, cellar
soy, I am (*from* **ser**)
su, sus, his, her, your, their, its
subir, to go up; to get into (*a vehicle*)
subterráneo, -a, subterranean, underground; *m,* subway
Sudamérica, *f,* South America
suelo, *m,* ground; floor
sueño, *m,* sleep; **tener sueño,** to be sleepy
sufrir, to suffer
supermercado, *m,* supermarket
superstición, *f,* superstition

también, also, too
tan, so, as
tango, *m,* tango (dance)
tanto, -a, so much, as much; **tantos, -as,** so many, as many
tarde, late; **más tarde,** later; *f,* afternoon; **por la tarde,** in the afternoon; **de la tarde,** in the afternoon, P.M.
tarea, *f,* task, homework; *pl,* homework assignments
taza, *f,* cup
té, *m,* tea
te, you, to you, yourself
teatro, *m,* theater
techo, *m,* ceiling
telefonear, to telephone
teléfono, *m,* telephone; **por teléfono,** on the telephone
televisor, *m,* television set
templo, *m,* temple
temprano, early
tenedor, *m,* fork
*****tener,** to have; **tener que** + *inf,* to have to, must; **tener . . . años,** to be . . . years old
tenis, *m,* tennis
tercero, -a (tercer), third
terminar, to finish, to end
tiempo, *m,* time, weather; **a tiempo,** on time; **mucho tiempo,** a long time; **¿cuánto tiempo?** how long? **hace buen (mal) tiempo,** the weather is good (bad)

tienda, *f,* store
tierra, *f,* land
tigre, *m,* tiger
tío, *m,* uncle; **tía,** *f,* aunt
típico, -a, typical; **típicamente,** typically
tiza, *f,* chalk
tocadiscos, *m,* record player, phonograph
tocar, to play (*an instrument*)
todavía, still, yet
todo, -a, all, every; **todo el día,** all day; **todos los días,** every day; **todos,** everybody
tomar, to take; to have (*food or drink*)
Tomás, Thomas
tomate, *m,* tomato
toro, *m,* bull
trabajador, -ra, industrious, hardworking
trabajar, to work
trabajo, *m,* work
***traducir,** to translate
***traer,** to bring
tráfico, *m,* traffic
traje, *m,* suit
tranvía, *m,* streetcar
tratar de + *inf,* to try to
trece, thirteen
treinta, thirty
tren, *m,* train
tres, three
trescientos, -as, three hundred
triste, sad
tu, tus, your (*fam sing*)

tú, you (*fam sing*)
tumba, *f,* tomb
turista, *m & f,* tourist

último, -a, last
un, una, a, an, one
universidad, *f,* university
uno, una, one
unos, -as, some
usar, to use
usted, ustedes, you

va (vas, vamos, vais, van), *forms of pres. tense of* **ir**
vacaciones, *f pl,* vacation
vapor, *m,* steam; steamship
varios, -as, several
vaso, *m,* (drinking) glass
vecino, -a, neighbor
vegetal, *m,* vegetable
veinte, twenty
vender, to sell
***venir,** to come
ventana, *f,* window
***ver,** to see
verano, *m,* summer
verbo, *m,* verb
verdad, *f,* truth; **es verdad,** it is true, that's right; **¿verdad? (¿no es verdad?)** right? isn't it so? isn't he? don't they? etc.
verde, green
verduras, *f pl,* vegetables
vestido, *m,* dress
vestir(se) (i), to dress (= get dressed)

vez, *f* (*pl,* **veces**), time; **otra vez,** again; **una vez,** once; **dos veces,** twice; **muchas veces,** often
viajar, to travel
viaje, *m,* trip; **hacer un viaje,** to take a trip
Vicente, Vincent
viejo, -a, old
viento, *m,* wind; **hace viento,** it is windy
viernes, *m,* Friday
vino, *m,* wine
violeta, *f,* violet
violín, *m,* violin
visita, *f,* visit
visitar, to visit
vista, *f,* view, sight; **hasta la vista,** see you again
vivir, to live
volcán, *m,* volcano
volver (ue), to return, to go (come) back
vosotros, -as, you (*fam pl*)
voy, I go (am going) (*see* **ir**)
voz, *f,* voice; **en voz alta,** aloud; **en voz baja,** in a low voice
vuestro, -a, your (*fam pl*)

y, and
ya, already
yo, I

zapatería, *f,* shoe store
zapato, *m,* shoe